Colonel Michael Edward Masters
"The Host of Kentucky"

Presents

Hospitality –
Kentucky Style

Kentucky Heritage Grand Tour

Kentucky Fine Foods and Spirits

D1249237

The Colonel's Cottage Inn

114 South Fourth Street, Bardstown, KY 40004
1-800-704-4917
www.kystyle.com

The Colonel's Cottage Inn is for couples on a romantic getaway. It is a private, unhosted bed and breakfast across the street from Pioneer Park, in Bardstown's downtown historic district. The Colonel's Cottage is reserved by a couple, who have the entire inn to themselves throughout their stay.

The residence was built in 1850 and is in the Federalist style of cottage architecture. The high ceilings and their broad crown moldings are spectacular. The cottage is furnished in Kentucky antiques and furniture that reflects the period prior to the War Between the States.

The Colonel's Cottage Inn has a beautiful living room with a fireplace, a stunning dining room, two bedrooms and two baths, one a spa with wonderful cherry woodwork, and a double whirlpool bath for all-season relaxation.

Colonel Michael Masters, "The Host of Kentucky"℠ and the author of *Hospitality – Kentucky Style* is the proprietor of The Colonel's Cottage Inn. Call the Colonel when you would like to schedule your honeymoon, a romantic get away from the children or a small wedding. The Colonel's Cottage Inn is very elegant and very private.

Hospitality– Kentucky Style Toast

I raise a toast to my family and friends,
To the women and children in my life –
beauties one and all;
To America that bore me,
To the South that nurtured me,
And to Kentucky!

—Col. Michael Edward Masters

Hospitality–
Kentucky Style

Library of Congress Catalog Number: 2002090374

Edited by Christine Clough
Page Layout and Design by Kim Paul
Sketches by Natalie Cox, John Neal, Katy Parrish
Cover by John Bramel
at:
Elmwood, home of Masters family
Col. Michael Masters, sitting
Carolyn Masters, violin
Margaret Sue Masters, standing

1st printing	March 2000	5,000
2nd printing	October 2001	10,000
3rd printing	February 2003	10,000

Equine Writer's Press
P.O. Box 1101
Bardstown, Ky 40004

Printed in the United States of America

ISBN 09709343-2-7

Table of Contents

Acknowledgments

It gives me great pleasure to thank all of the wonderful people who purchased my first book, *Hospitality – Kentucky Style*. The patrons of my first effort to capture the essence of the Kentucky tradition of hospitality made that book very successful from the first day. I am humbled by all of my family and friends and the strangers that I have encountered along the way who have taken *Hospitality--Kentucky Style* into their hearts.

In the section of *Hospitality – Kentucky Style* entitled "Kentucky Heritage Grand Tour," I have asked every Kentuckian to explore and to search for their identity amongst the art, artifacts and architecture of Kentucky. In a very public sense, history defines our commonwealth by the architecture and monuments that we as Kentuckians have chosen to preserve. I have endeavored to find those architectural sites that have meaning to Kentuckians and that we as a people present to the world as representative of our Kentucky past. To the Kentucky Historical Society, The Filson Club, The University of Louisville, The University of Kentucky and Eastern Kentucky University, thank you for your assistance.

I have admired the Kentucky writings of George Morgan Chinn, Dr. Thomas A. Clark's *A Kentucky History* and Thomas Crittenden's *Kentucky*. My knowledge of Kentucky history is based upon my reading of these historians. My reference for chronology of Kentucky history has been the landmark reference work *The Kentucky Encyclopedia*. The Kentucky poetry in *Hospitality – Kentucky Style* has been taken from *All That's Kentucky* by Jesiah Combs, 1911.

I would like to pay homage to Clay Lancaster, author of *Antebellum Houses of the Bluegrass* and *Antebellum Architecture of Kentucky*. I never knew him, but he has been my teacher and a point of inspiration in the writing of my book, *Hospitality – Kentucky Style*. Natalie Cox, a student of Clay Lancaster at the University of Kentucky, is the very talented artist for most of the sketches in *Hospitality – Kentucky Style*. As far as I am concerned, Clay Lancaster lives in my book, through Natalie Cox, and I am very grateful to both of them. The very talented Natalie Cox received her B.F.A. at the Cleveland Institute of Art and she was an admirer and friend of Clay Lancaster and she currently is on the Board of Trustees of his "Warwick Foundation." She lives in Salvisa, Kentucky. Contact Information: Natalie M. Cox, P.O. Box 135, Salvisa, Kentucky 40372

I have a good-looking book because Kim Paul, my talented and tireless friend, dedicated herself to the page layout and design of *Hospitality – Kentucky Style*.

I am grateful to Eddie Zweydorff and John Shelburne for their assistance.

I have endeavored in every instance to obtain copyright permission to use the images in this book. If I have failed to discover a copyright holder, it has been unintentional. The purpose of using the images in this book is to honor and preserve the historical memory of our

1

Kentucky past. I have worked diligently to ascertain the correct information about our commonwealth's history, a daunting task, as so much of Kentucky's early history is shrouded in romance and mythology.

In the section of *Hospitality – Kentucky Style* entitled "Kentucky Fine Foods and Spirits" I have endeavored to present the foods and libations that we use and that I feel represent the best in Kentucky cooking. My references in cooking Kentucky fare really do not change over time. I rely upon Marion Flexner's book, *Out of Kentucky Kitchens*, Cissy Gregg's *Courier Journal* writings; Camille Glenn's *Heritage Southern Cookbook*; and the work of James Beard and Mrs. Dull. These references have been standards in several generations of my family. My ancestor, Daniel Boone, once declared that he had never been lost in the woods but had been confused several times. I have experienced that feeling on more than one occasion. When my cooking has lost its way by becoming too routine, I have never hesitated to consult the teachers and literature of my younger days.

I owe my life and my early appreciation for simply elegant entertaining to my father, Dr. V. Edward Masters and my mother, Barbara Gallagher Masters, known to all as Mimi. My parents practiced a form of Southern hospitality in their home Elmwood that was so very graceful. Etiquette at Elmwood, though at times formal, was based in daily casual courtesy and thoughtfulness. I have embraced so many of Mimi's Kentucky cooking practices; she intuitively passed her Kentucky and Southern ways onto me.

To my friends, thank you for a lifetime of companionship.

To my children, Colin Masters and Carolyn Masters, thank you for your kind and understanding support of my work. To my sisters, Carolyn Clark and Martha Masters, you are my angels. My intent in publishing has been to record and illustrate the practice of Kentucky hospitality culture for the benefit of our children and the next generation of Kentuckians.

To Margaret Sue, my dear wife and friend, I could never have accomplished any of this without you. To Margaret Sue's mother, Sue Carol, I am endeared to you. To Margaret Sue's grandmother, Mama Sudie, a truly charming and graceful, Kentucky woman, I cherish my memory of you.

To the Honorable Order of Kentucky Colonels.

And to Kentucky.

Col. Michael E. Masters
"The Host of Kentucky"
McManus House
Bardstown, Kentucky

Hospitality – Bardstown Style

Bardstown, my town, is absolutely and utterly beautiful. It is the second oldest city in Kentucky, and its historic district has a hundred homes and commercial buildings that were built before the Civil War. We invite couples to visit Bardstown for a romantic retreat, a honeymoon or a weekend getaway. Visitors to Bardstown fall in love with the town again and again.

Bardstown, Kentucky, is a romantic place. Grand old homes, history, fine aged Kentucky bourbon whisky, good food, beautiful women and chivalrous men are all here in abundance. Bardstown is a small town that routinely entertains guests from all over the world.

Our visitors come to see My Old Kentucky Home, the Kentucky mansion owned by the people of the commonwealth, who have made it their state shrine. And believe me, it is a Kentucky plantation house so majestic that it takes your breath away. They come to hear the story and the music of Stephen Foster, who wrote the song "My Old Kentucky Home, Goodnight," the state song of the Commonwealth of Kentucky.

Travelers to Bardstown come to visit the grave and memorial dedicated to John Fitch, the inventor of the steamboat. By way of that invention, John Fitch arguably initiated the first step of the Industrial Revolution. The travelers to Bardstown come to discover and commune with the many talented artists, writers and musicians that reside in and around our town, some of whom have achieved national and international reputations. The bookstores, art galleries and music festivals in Bardstown are regionally acclaimed as the best of their kind.

The visitors come to visit our world-renowned museums, notably the Civil War Museum, the Getz Museum of Whisky History, the Pioneer Village and the Train Museum. They come for the thirty events scheduled each year to celebrate our Kentucky life in Bardstown. And they come to view our outdoor dramas and musicals.

The inns of Bardstown, located within the historic district, are opportunities to experience the elegance of the past while enjoying the ambience of these historic houses. Stay in one of the inns, dine in one of Bardstown's exquisite restaurants, sample the premium brands of fine aged Kentucky bourbon whisky, drink and eat until you are content. Then, walk back to your inn. I say again, Bardstown is absolutely and utterly unique.

Thousands of the faithful make a religious pilgrimage each year to the Bardstown Roman Catholic holy sites. We believe the Bardstown holy trinity of religious sites to be blessed with the healing power of serenity. Here, in 1809, Bishop Benedict Joseph Flaget founded St. Thomas Plantation and Church, the first Roman Catholic Church west of the Allegheny Mountains. The other two sites in the holy trinity, the Basilica of St. Joseph Proto-Cathedral and the Church at Nazareth were conceived at St. Thomas Plantation.

One is humbled in realizing that the Basilica of St. Joseph Proto-Cathedral, the second archdiocese in the United States, was hewn out of the forest and rock of the Kentucky wilderness in 1812.

The Church at Nazareth, the motherhouse of the Sisters of Charity, was built near Bardstown in 1814. The Sisters of Charity have founded and currently administer many schools and hospitals. I tell you most honestly that to attend the Sunday worship service at Nazareth and to hear the choir of the sisterhood is to visit with angels personified by the Sisters of Charity.

The Trappist Order, founded in France in 1050, established the Abbey of Gethsemani near Bardstown in 1822. It is the monastery where Brother Thomas Merton authored many of his philosophical and theological works. It is also within the cloistered walls of Gethsemani that the monks make their world-renowned fruitcakes, cheeses and bourbon chocolates for shipment around the globe. The monks offer a special kind of Kentucky hospitality by offering overnight retreats and granting laypersons the opportunity to experience the meditative peace of Gethsemani.

The motherhouse of the Dominican Sisterhood is in Springfield on the grounds of St. Catherine College. St. Rose Priory, famous as one of the early Catholic parishes, is also known for the early education of President Jefferson Davis.

An Inn for a Couple
on a Romantic Retreat:
The Colonel's Cottage Inn
114 S. Fourth St.
Bardstown, KY 40004
1-800-704-4917
www.kystyle.com

Bardstown Visitor
Information:
Bardstown Tourism
107 E. Stephen Foster Ave.
Bardstown, KY 40004
1-800-638-4877
www.bardstowntourism.com

My Kentucky

The social season in Kentucky extends throughout the year. It is in keeping with our hospitable nature to perceive each season as an opportunity to entertain our family and friends. In our house, no distinction is made between the friends we grew up with and the friends we spend time with now. Of course, we celebrate all of the usual passages throughout the year. But we also regard the passing seasons in Kentucky as a time for entertainment.

The Spring Thoroughbred Meet

The spring horse-racing season is a magical time in Kentucky, a time when those "near and dear" to our home enjoy a two-centuries-old unspoken invitation to bring their out-of-town guests. It is a time when the sons and daughters of Kentucky who live in foreign states and lands feel nostalgic for the home they have left behind. The Stephen Foster song "My Old Kentucky Home" evokes memories of the times in their past, of the family and friends that remain and of those that have departed this life. It is also a time of joyous reunion with our extended families and the friends we hold dear.

Keeneland Race Course in Lexington is the most beautiful racetrack in America. It is here that Kentucky-bred Thoroughbred racehorses find their shrine. The Keeneland sales in the summer and fall draw the great wealth of the world to this legendary racing establishment to bid on the bloodstock that is sired on the historic horse farms of central Kentucky. The Keeneland sale barns house 200 years of winning bloodlines. In the spirited auctions, millions of dollars are spent on the hope that a single horse, from the champion bloodstock of its ancestors, standing alone in the sales ring, will outrun the great Thoroughbred horses of the world and capture fortunes.

We make our pilgrimage to Keeneland Race Course for the spring meet in April with the anticipation that we will spend the afternoon with the most celebrated horse-racing stock upon the globe. Many of the horses will be running their maiden races as two-year-olds, fresh from the training stables of their central Kentucky farms.

Keeneland Race Course is a small racing plant and was built for the showcasing of Kentucky Thoroughbreds. The barns and the hot walking arena are in front of the clubhouse, and a Keeneland green rail is all that separates the Keeneland patrons from the horses. The owners and trainers walk their prized horseflesh in front of you, preparing them for the race. The jockeys, many of them the most famous names in horse racing, mount within your view. Whether we elect to watch the race from the elegant clubhouse or at the rail is almost unimportant. It is the horses we are there to see. Racing fans, groomsmen, trainers and owners all stand shoulder to shoulder, equal in their appreciation of the horse, feeling proud to be at Keeneland Race Course watching the Thoroughbreds run.

Then it is to Churchill Downs we go for the week of racing that precedes the Kentucky Derby, held on the first Saturday in May in Louisville. It is the time that McManus House sets to work in earnest on the Kentucky breakfast and on the Derby party that we will host on the lawn.

Every year, as I prepare for our Derby party, I hear from friends about the Derby parties they are hosting at their homes in New York, San Francisco, London and other ports of call. The Kentucky Derby will last two minutes, but the feelings that the race engenders last all year in the Kentucky heart, whether the participants reside comfortably in their Kentucky homes or find themselves "far, far away."

A Kentucky woman, in this man's opinion, never looks better than she does on Derby Day. There is an excitement in the air that fills the senses — whether one is going to the track, going to someone's house for a Derby party, going to the club or the tavern, or staying at home where this year, "we're just having some of the neighbors over to watch the race." The women find resplendent hats for the Derby: if in a box seat at the track — elegant, broad-brimmed and generously decorated with feathers and flowers; if standing in the infield — broad-brimmed but more on the sun-protection, survival side; if going to or having a party — spanning the spectrum.

The Kentucky Derby is an international sporting event. The entire commonwealth is caught up in the high spirit, and the women know that the colorful and fashionable presentation of their dress is part and parcel of the human and equine pageantry that is the Derby. Men have a role too — to serve the women, to provide the transportation and to enjoy the charm and romance of Derby week.

For as it is written, so it is indeed:

> *"If you haven't been to the Derby,*
> *you ain't been nowhere*
> *and you ain't done nothin."*
>
> **— Irvin Cobb**

Kentucky Breakfast

When a breakfast is declared and invitations are received in the mail, you are alerted to the fact that you are invited to an elegant party. Casual dress is implied, but to meet the breakfast head-on, one must remember that casual dress in Kentucky means sporting attire: blazer and ties for the gentlemen and colorful sun-dresses and broad-brimmed hats for the gentlewomen. The breakfast gains a special prominence during the spring horse-racing season that begins with visits to Keeneland Race Course in Lexington during the last two weeks of April and concludes at McManus House with the running of the Kentucky Derby, held in Louisville on the first Saturday in May.

The breakfast on Derby day is a meal that is an event. Weather permitting, we serve the breakfast on the lawn, with seating for all of the guests in attendance at tables draped in white linen, with vases of fresh flowers as centerpieces.

Our bar is stocked with orange, tomato and cranberry juices and the liquors that complement them. Two coffees are offered: usually French roast, for those bracing it with a fine aged Kentucky bourbon whisky, and a more tepid blend. A good violin, cello or harp is heard playing off to the side.

The buffet table is a sight to behold.

For the entrées, we serve turkey hash or creamed chicken Louisville on wild rice in chafing dishes, rows of rare beef tenderloin on silver platters and mounds of country ham on beaten biscuits and angel biscuits. Hellmann's mayonnaise, Durkee's dressing and Masters Steak Sauce are in view.

Scrambled eggs garnished with chopped parsley and paprika in chafing dishes complement the entrées.

Marinated asparagus and peeled tomatoes with a side dressing of smearcase layered on silver platters set upon ice are the cold vegetables; green beans and baked cheese grits, steaming hot in chafing dishes, are the warm vegetables.

Chilled cantaloupe, pineapple and honeydew mixed with strawberries, blackberries and blueberries served in an oversized bowl are the fruit.

Bourbon balls, lemon squares and Kentucky pecan pie are the desserts.

The breakfast is served at ten in the morning and is completed by eleven-thirty, when those going to the track depart. Those remaining will make themselves comfortable, drinking their preference. The signal that the breakfast is at a proper conclusion is when the bar is packed up and the bartender leaves the property, about two o'clock. A close contingent of guests will find their best seats in the McManus House living room, to watch the race at five-thirty. We will dine on Beef Masters at seven in the evening, feeding the elated, weary, sun-baked gang who have returned from the track exhausted but full of testimony about their experiences at Churchill Downs and the Kentucky Derby.

Summer Weddings

I would not like to miss a wedding. If I am graced with an invitation, it is my pleasure to be in attendance. I cannot imagine a party that is more fun than a wedding. Have I ever been to a bad one? Never.

Certainly, there is a considerable range in the opulence. And to be sure, the length of the guest list is determined by the money in the purse. But, regardless of the size of the venture, the reason for the gathering is the same—to bless and to record a marriage of two people in love. The feeling of hope for the future and the promise of lifelong companionship is in full evidence. The more seasoned married couples find their partners' hands, remembering their time before the altar; the younger adults are apprehensive, knowing that their time is near. After the nuptial rite has concluded, the revelry begins.

My friends know how to provide for their guests. They engage their club, reserve the ballroom of a great hotel or employ a brand-name catering concern to erect tents on their lawn, having the buffet repast transported to them. In all three cases, they have given the proper instructions to the management. There is a bountiful table or two of the traditional foods known and respected in Kentucky, along with great silver bowls of shrimp, oysters on the half shell and salmon filet, all beautifully arranged on beds of ice.

When Margaret Sue and I married, I wanted to throw a party at our reception that was so hot it sizzled. And it did, until three in the morning. Because we had invited 400 guests and were nervous about the weather, we decided to relieve at least some of the stress and anxiety of the day and let my club stage the event. The club was in fine form, resplendent with flowers and garlands of ivy throughout the ballroom. There was a band with five horns, three bars and a table overflowing with food. Glad I did it, had the time of my life, and have no desire to do it again.

There are other ways to traverse the reception ground. Margaret Sue maintains that my joy in entertaining comes from my doing it, not having it done for me. As always, she is right, even when I protest with all my vigor to soften my feeling that once again, she has called the shot. A month after we had spent a small fortune on our wedding reception, we summoned together our close family and our best friends and held a second reception on the lawn at McManus House. We had a well-stocked bar, our favorite bartender and a loaded buffet table, accompanied by a good quartet. Saints preserve me—this is just the way I like it.

Margaret Sue's grandmother, Mama Sudie, lived more than sixty years at Holloway House, her 1840s farmhouse of 10,000 square feet in central Kentucky. Mama Sudie was so beautiful and so elegant in her unassuming style. She hosted over a hundred weddings in that house.

She taught school for forty years, and the girls who had enjoyed school outings to Holloway House dreamed of descending her three-story spiral staircase on their wedding days. It was her pleasure to oblige.

The reception for her girls on these occasions was simple. Mama Sudie baked pies and cakes and served coffee and a fruit punch. Mama Sudie did not indulge in the drinking of spirit beverages, though she always kept bourbon in the pantry for cooking. That was her story, and she stuck with it. Gentlemen mixed their drinks on a table reserved for that purpose on the brick walk at the side of the house. Those were grand times. I wish I could have been at every one of those receptions.

There is a tradition in Kentucky of hosting a party for your friends who are soon to be wed. In the time in which we live, there does not appear to be a standard age for this blessed event; the age of the betrothed covers a good bit of the human lifespan, and some have had several cracks at it. At McManus House, we are nonjudgmental; we present a well-turned-out table for all the generations and try to stay out of the politics of the matter.

When a large contingent of guests is to be entertained at McManus House, we use the pick-up foods strategy. However, a small wedding party of fifteen guests or fewer at McManus House calls for rare beef tenderloin. We complement the tenderloin with country ham slices on angel biscuits, baked cheese grits, asparagus with cheese sauce, a Bibb lettuce salad with vinaigrette, yeast rolls and any dessert that is topped with chocolate or bourbon sauce.

Margaret Sue can be counted on to find just the right gift for the bride, leaning heavily toward ceramic bowls that have multiple everyday uses. A dinner of rare beef tenderloin is my contribution.

Funerals and the Visitation Thereto

I do not like attending funerals. It makes me reflect too closely on life's only inevitability, namely, my eventual demise. My more enlightened friends have become comfortable with the passing stages of their lives, and they articulate a soothing message of life everlasting and hope eternal as they anchor themselves firmly to the rock of their spiritual salvation. I know that these fortunate friends of mine have achieved a higher level of understanding than I. All I can tell you is that the inner peace that comforts them has eluded me. I intend to go out in full battle gear.

Having dispensed with the dark side of the thing, let me tell you that in Kentucky, we know how to send the dear departed to their rewards. We throw a party. As a matter of fact, we throw a number of parties, all designed to comfort the more grief-stricken and to celebrate the life taken from those of us still standing.

Nothing brings Kentucky clans together like the prospect of a visitation. Three days before the service, close family become paragons of industry. The more meticulous housekeepers move directly to food preparation. Those who have scarcely hit a lick on their houses throughout the year spring into concerted action to make their homes presentable, for family and friends are coming to town.

No other singular life experience has the power of a visitation to heal broken and estranged family relationships, to bring back the long-lost cousins and to rekindle old friendships that fell out decades before over an issue now forgotten. And so the word goes out by telephone to a dozen key people that the clan is gatherin', and these in turn contact other key people. This continues until almost everyone who might care has been contacted, all within the space of an hour. The miracle of a Kentucky homecoming is about to unfold.

Knowing that certain houses within the bereaved family will be hit hardest by out-of-town friends and relations, the food deliveries begin. Platters of sliced country ham, roast beef and turkey and baskets of rolls and condiments are the first victuals to arrive. Second on the scene are the pimiento cheese, Benedictine and pecan chicken salad. Last, come the cakes and pies, as their preparation requires lead time. The host house provides the bar and any help that may be required.

Mama Sudie felt the weight of her duty and made every attempt to get to everyplace the family groups in her life congregated over the three-day visitation period. She came to several of my family's visitations, never missing a house. She knew very few of the out-of-town people but was not deterred. She came prepared, wearing her best silk dress, her treasured ivory brooches and silver jewelry. Never one to shirk a task at hand, she always donated a car full of cakes, pies and vegetable casseroles. Mama Sudie liked to get to the place of visitation early so she could get a good seat to hold court with the family in question. Mama Sudie did not want to miss an opportunity for folks to meet her.

I have borne witness to many touching reunions of relations and the mending of friendship fences at these visitations. The power of showing up to salute the passing of one of our own allows us to appreciate our own lives.

I promise you, if I catch you grieving for my passing, I will call a Kentucky hant upon you. Give me a swell party, host a homecoming, recount the fine times we have shared and give me a good toast. I assure you, I have enjoyed every moment of my time with you.

Standardbred Harness Racing

There are certain immutable truths that I have discovered. One is that to have a friend, you must be a friend. Another truth, closely related, is that you must accept friends as they are, bad eyes and all.

It is this way with the Kentucky summer. The other three seasons we extol in rhyme and verse, but I tell you straight, our summers are hot, humid and devoid of wind and rain. And let there be no doubt about it, this is just the way we like it.

The Kentucky sweltering summer having been noted, allow me to pronounce that Margaret Sue and I embrace our long, hot summer. For it is when we enjoy Standardbred racing. The Thoroughbred, sleek, high strung, with a long, lengthy stride, is all about galloping speed. The Standardbred, on the other hand, is steady of nerve and physically compact with well-developed shoulders for front-end propulsion. The Standardbred is an outstanding breed of horse for the quick diagonal-trotting and lateral-pacing gaits.

Margaret Sue and I start our summer with several visits to the Red Mile in Lexington. The Red Mile features world-class harness racing in the trotting style. We watch the harness races throughout May and June in the comfortable confine of the glass-enclosed clubhouse. We often return to the Red Mile in September to watch the running of the Kentucky Futurity, the oldest harness race in the country, first run in 1893 and one of the three legs of the trotting Triple Crown. The fact that Margaret Sue and I tend to have good luck at the Red Mile parimutuel betting window is an additional delight.

The cuisine in the dining room at the Red Mile is regionally renowned. The dinner is served buffet-style and sports rare prime rib of beef, shrimp and crab legs on ice, beautifully steamed vegetables and a dessert selection second to none. Watching harness racing at the Red Mile, dining on its sumptuous repast, drinking a fine aged Kentucky bourbon whisky or a gin Alexander is a wonderful way to commune with the Standardbred horse.

American Saddlebred Horse Shows

Then, throughout the summer, Margaret Sue and I enter the non-betting, highly competitive world of the Kentucky county fair championship horse shows. The American Saddlebred, with a high-stepping leg movement characteristic of the breed, dominates these events. The horses, trained to compete in five-gaited, three-gaited or pleasure class, will be on review and will be judged by the omnipotent show officials standing solemnly in the middle of the arena.

The riders of these truly-American horses range in age from eight to eighty, seek a commanding presence and are dressed to a stylized perfection. The American Saddlebred show horses are trained to a competitive razor's edge and are impeccably groomed. There is bloom in the bearing of the riders and the horses that reflects their intense desire to win. The warrior partnership of rider and horse enters the show ring to join the other combatants. A first-place ribbon is the prize.

The county fair show ring can be as simple as a four-board white fence encircling the arena, with a rural crowd of fairgoers pressed against it. Alternately, the arena can be a great show pavilion, with a cantilevered roof to shade the grandstand and the box seats. If you will look beyond the show ring architecture and pay attention to the contest in the arena, you will share in a centuries-old experience. The rider, horse and trainer have worked together for years to prepare for this moment in the show ring. Keep your eyes on the horses as they perform the commanded gaits, each one straining to be the best of class. It is riveting and never fails to send chills of competitive excitement down the back of my neck.

Margaret Sue and I pack two ice chests, one for libation and general thirst abatement, the other for our supper and midnight snack. The idea is to be self-sufficient. Most of the rural counties in the commonwealth are dry, which means that spirit beverages are not sold. I do not offer advice on the question of the appropriateness of packing a well-stocked bar for the horse show, but as in all things that are either important, profitable or fun, discretion has value.

When traveling to a Kentucky county-fair horse show, you never know with whom you will spend the evening. We play it loose, choosing to see how the afternoon and evening will unfold. At times, we tailgate with other couples we encounter at the show. And at times, we find friends and acquaintances, locate under an oak tree on the edge of the fairground and make trips to the show ring. Everyone shares the contents of their respective ice chests, which lean heavily toward country ham and rolls, cut fresh vegetables and dips, crackers and cheese. The lie is that we keep our supper light in deference to the heat. The truth is that fair food is close by. In Kentucky, that means grilled center-cut pork chop and grilled rib-eye steak on a bun.

Only if pressed by the offer of a free box seat do I settle in one spot. The action is not in the seat, it is in the arena. At a county-fair horse show, I am a railbird by inclination, that is for certain. I want to be close to the American Saddlebred horses in the show ring, looking them in the eye, feeling with them their need to excel and win.

The Fall Thoroughbred Meet

The fall racing season at Keeneland Race Course in October and Churchill Downs in November is a fabulous time for Margaret Sue and me. The hardwood trees turn golden, red and orange with the changing season. The bushes and shrubbery yield every color of crimson, yellow and brown. The migrating birds take to flight in great waves, responding to ancient instincts to find warmer climates and more abundant feeding grounds. The chill is in the air, as arctic air forces itself down into the rolling hills of central Kentucky.

Margaret Sue and I are creatures of the same autumn impulses, except that our destination and change of venue are Keeneland and Churchill Downs for the fall race meet. We will go with a small group or hook up with our Lexington and Louisville friends at the track. Several trips will be to dine in the tracks' respective dining rooms, watching the racing panorama from the balcony of the clubhouse, eating rare roast beef and sampling their stock of liqueurs. And several trips will be to join the crowd in the grandstand, bundled against the cold, supping on homemade burgoo purchased at the track and drinking hot coffee laced with Kentucky bourbon whisky, poured from a flask, sequestered discreetly in the side vent of my coat. Perfect.

Kentucky Women

Kentucky is known the world over for "fast horses, fine aged bourbon whisky and beautiful women." In my travels throughout America and to the foreign capitols I have visited this phase invariably greets me when I proclaim that I am a Kentucky man.

Visitors to our commonwealth are charmed by our horses, our largest agricultural industry. Guests to our state are fascinated by our tradition of distilling fine aged bourbon whisky. But let me tell you there is nary a man who travels the length and breath of Kentucky that fails to note the plethora of absolutely gorgeous women that seem to be everywhere. A Kentucky boy, be they fifteen or ninety-five, lives in a continual state of having been struck by lightning. Beautiful Kentucky women are everywhere.

We anticipate finding charming, elegant and sophisticated ladies at Churchill Downs and Keeneland, especially at the spring race meetings. A visit to a Kentucky college campus is an experience like no other– smart, good-looking women by the thousands. It is this way in every public place, in every social gathering, in the great cities and in the small towns. Sometimes I forget myself and get lost in my thoughts as I meander a small Kentucky town, admiring old architecture, only to be reawakened abruptly by the sight of a raving Kentucky beauty descending from a battered old pick-up truck.

Our more northern friends are in amazement, where upon their visit to Kentucky, they are greeted by an embrace upon meeting the feminine friends of their friend and then by an embrace by the women in attendance upon their departure. Kentucky women often practice this courtesy without regard to age. In my college years, the grandmother of one of my friends, who was in her eighties when I knew her, lived in a large home that accommodated many overnight guests. When we availed ourselves of her generous hospitality, she required an embrace and a kiss on her cheek when we entered her home, and at bedtime she would line us all up so that we could give her an embrace and a kiss before retiring. It is this way at my house, at my mother's house, at the homes of my sisters and everywhere else I might visit.

Kentucky women, I find, age well, moving easily from the beauty of their youth, to a handsome middle age, to a certain elegance in their elder years. That is the way I see it, and I choose to see the matter in no other way.

Bird Hunting

Sometimes I think the entire year is a prelude to the Kentucky fall sporting season. It is not based on the Julian calendar, the orbit of the moon or the rotation of the earth. Fall begins for us on the first day of September every year, and winter comes on Christmas day, which draws the fall sporting season to a close. Kentucky embraces the fall, and it is the best of times in Kentucky. No question about it, nothing compares with the sporting grandeur of Keeneland Race Course on any day in April or with the week of the Kentucky Derby at Churchill Downs in May. But, if a favorite four-month part of the year is in the debate, the answer is—the fall.

I have had the honor of counting many farmers in central Kentucky as my friends. The permission that they grant me to hunt their fields in the fall has been a lifetime of satisfaction. We are talking bird hunting here. The fast-flying mourning dove in September, the wary mallard duck in November and the cagey Canada goose in December are my quarry.

My association with hunting is exclusive to bird hunting. The magnificent game dinners that result from the hunt are warm, convivial evenings spent with childhood friends and comrades of the field. I find bird hunters to be a congenial lot who spend as much time grousing about the experiences shared in the autumnal fields and the frigid waters of our Kentucky rivers, streams, ponds and lakes as they do the actual shot. In character and by way of temperament, my bird-hunting companions have been and are, in an absolute sense, Kentucky gentlemen.

We like to sauté the doves in butter or marinate them overnight in orange juice and soy sauce, grill them outdoors with a sliver of hot pepper inserted into each breast with a half-slice of bacon secured with a wooden spear. Or we substitute the dove breast for beef in the Beef Masters recipe.

We filet the ducks, marinate them in butter and ground pepper and roast them on a very hot grill, medium rare.

The Canada is smoked by placing it on the cold side of the grill, covered, and basting it with butter, continuously, 30 minutes to the pound.

Masters Steak Sauce and orange bourbon sauce are at the ready. Fine aged Kentucky bourbon whisky is in the glass.

College Battle Cry

The college football season begins in Kentucky with the anticipation that this time, maybe, the boys on the gridirons across the commonwealth will find a winning formula. Alas, over the past century, our brave lads have all too frequently had to settle for the short end of the victory stick. Kentucky feeds on basketball, and football has had a difficult ride. But dauntless in the face of adversity, the college football faithful load up their vehicles and usher in the fall tailgating season.

An excellent bar has been stocked in the trunk of the car. The Benedictine, pimento cheese, pecan chicken salad and bourbon cheese are secure in the ice chest. Chips, crackers, sourdough bread and the condiments are in the food locker. In all honesty, I love going to our college football games. There is a drama full of hope and pathos, played out each week at our universities. In spite of all this, if Margaret Sue made me, I would be overjoyed to sit on a comfortable chair under a big fat tree on the college campus and listen to the game on the radio with a gang of fans in likewise sympathy. After all, the party is in the trunk.

Then, in a clash of resounding arms and to the drumbeat of war, basketball in Kentucky marches into the fall sporting season in December. In Kentucky, college basketball is a full-body contact sport, and every Kentuckian from the cities to the "hollers" has a voracious appetite for victory on the hardwood. Winning is the only acceptable result; no excuses are tolerated and no quarter asked or given.

In this rancorous atmosphere, the spontaneous battle cry is trumpeted to "come to the house and watch the game." And you may as well. The retail establishments are deserted; their owners and employees are listening to the game. Across the commonwealth it is the same. I have known priests to take their radio and headset into the confessional box on Saturday afternoon so as not to miss the play of their team. I am certain that the sinner across from him did, too.

In a Kentucky house, there is only room for one team. Those for that team are in on the invitation. Those who are in opposition are excluded, and that extends to marriages. This is serious business. McManus House is University of Kentucky; my neighbor is University of Louisville. They have never been to my house to watch the game, as there is no reason to set up an ugly situation. In Owensboro, they are all about Kentucky Wesleyan. In Bowling Green, it is Western Kentucky University; in Richmond, it is Eastern Kentucky University; and so forth.

Just as the season begins, it breaks for the Christmas holiday, the battle to join the Final Four to be resumed after the new year.

The "Voice From Old Kentucky"

"So you came back, after all, Colonel? When I saw you in Paris two years ago, you told me that Paris was your home. You said it fit you like an old glove; that the boulevards were made for you, and that you never expected to come over to this side of the pond again. How came you to change your mind?"

"I got homesick."

"Homesick? Homesick? Well, that's good. Like a schoolgirl, eh? What do you think of that, gentlemen? The Colonel got homesick! He, who hasn't had a home for thirty years — who has been roaming the earth ever since Lee surrendered. Touch the button, Colonel, the drinks are on you."

"With pleasure, Judge, but pardon me if I fail to understand the cause of your merriment. As the doctor says, it has been many years since I have known a home; but don't keep the boy waiting. A little bourbon for me. Yes, many years, gentlemen, many, many years. But, I was homesick, just the same. And I confess that the incident that sent me back will probably seem trivial and absurd to you. I had made my mind up to make Paris my home. For a wanderer like me it seemed like the proper haven. I like its ways. I like its playhouses. In fact, I like everything about Paris — except its taste in the manner of drinks. But you don't have to drink absinthe unless you care to, and I thought I was at last satisfied to settle down. I felt so thoroughly established that I began to think of doing some work, and actually did a little writing. This went on for a year or more, and I was fully determined to stay right there like an old hull on the beach, until the timbers fell apart.

"At last, some way or other, however, I began to feel a strong feeling of unrest. I got nervous. I began to worry about my liver. I consulted a doctor. He, the idiot, advised me to quit smoking, and I advised him to go to that place where people are supposed to smoke forever. I decided that I would run down to Rome and see the gay old town of dirty beggars and bid farewell to meat. It was just the time for the carnival, so to Rome I went. I didn't enjoy myself. I met many people I knew, but none for whom I cared. It's hard on a man to make merry all alone. I wondered what I had ever seen in the carnival before. I had a personal grievance against everyone who was enjoying himself. When someone threw a handful of confetti over me, I swore. I made up my mind to stay it out, however. I had a good window on the Corso, near the Piazza del Poplo, and there was no use running away. The blue devils would have followed me. You can imagine me sitting there all alone, biting a cigar, and frowning down upon the gay crowds in the Corso. Little girls pointed me out and threw confetti at me, and then, when I did not smile, said something about the evil eye and got away. The noise made my head ache. Some friends called out to me from passing carriages, and I almost forgot to return their salutations. But all of a sudden my ears caught a whiff of an old melody. At first, gentlemen, I was not sure. I thought the tune was just running through my mind. But someone was surely singing. I could catch the song and the tinkling of banjos away down the street. Very faint, but coming nearer:

16

'Weep no Mo', my lady,
O weep no mo' to-day,
For I'll sing one song ob de old Kaintucky home,
Ob de old Kaintucky home far away.'

"Doctor, I don't know what you would have made out of a study of my brain when I caught those words; but I knew that it darted electricity all through every nerve in my body. The singers were coming my way — four good, strong American boys (Woodford County boys, I'll bet). They were in an open carriage. When they got up under my window, I jumped up and gave a rebel yell that shook the Vatican. They looked up, laughed, and kept on singing. I strained my ears as they went down the Corso, and when I caught that last echo, hang it, gentlemen, there was a lump in my throat as big as your fist. I sailed for New York the very next week, and three weeks later I took a drink in Louisville."

"Well, here's to the boy. Everybody standing, please. Here's to 'The Old Kentucky Home!'"

— Anonymous

"My Old Kentucky Home"

The sun shines bright in the old Kentucky home
'Tis summer, the people are gay;
The corn top's ripe and the meadow's in the bloom,
While the birds make music all the day;
The young folks roll on the little cabin floor,
All merry, all happy and bright,
By'n by hard times come a-knocking at the door,
Then my old Kentucky home, good night!

Weep no more, my lady,
Oh weep no more today!
We will sing one song for the old Kentucky home,
For the old Kentucky home far away.

— Stephen Collins Foster, 1853

To My Darling Grand-daughter

I do not know what I would do without your mother;
For me there can never be another,
You know she was my very first, my own,
Always sweet, beautiful, loving, she has always shown.

I love all my grand-children you know;
But you are a little nearer and you do know,
In many ways by your loving care,
Just how much sweet love we share.

You are welcome to anything that I own;
Because you will take care, this you have shown,
It's all the little things that make life worth living,
Yet all the while you keep on giving.

That's what this world is all about,
after all is said and done;
Live life at its fullest and after the run,
You are a little bit different from all others I know,
Sweet, kind, loving and giving to others,
that's the show.

—Mama Sudie, 1989
Margaret Sue's birthday card from
her grandmother, Mama Sudie Holloway

Kentucky Benediction

Every day as a Kentuckian, I recite the Lord's Prayer,
Intoning in a loud, confident voice heard only by me,
"My Father, who art in heaven, hallowed be thy name."

Every day as a Kentuckian, I hear the song "My Old Kentucky Home";
I make the urgent appeal to "weep no more my lady,"
As I embrace the mother, sister, daughter, wife
That weave the tapestry of my life.

Every day as a Kentuckian, I thank Providence
That I have been granted the privilege of living a Kentucky life,
Living amongst the mountains and the bluegrass.

Every day as a Kentuckian, I revere my family and my friends
For their care and concern, their love and affection,
That grants my life meaning.

Every day as a Kentuckian, I feel honored to spend my time
The balance of my sojourn upon this earth
With Kentucky gentlemen and Kentucky gentlewomen
Who practice simple courtesy toward friends and strangers.

Every day as a Kentuckian, I celebrate
The breathtaking beauty, the stunning grandeur, the soaring majesty,
Of my commonwealth, my state, my Kentucky.

—Col. Michael Edward Masters, "The Host of Kentucky" SM
Kentucky Benediction© 2002, Michael Edward Masters

Genealogy

I am convinced that the younger generation should not research its ancestral lineage. I take this attitude so I will not suffer under the illusion that my offspring will spend even a moment considering where they came from. Youth is expended falling in love, competing for the winner's circle and recuperating from the effort of it all. Therefore, the joy in finding an interesting family-genealogy link pales in comparison. But to those of us who have passed the third pole in the four-pole race, it is an enjoyable pastime shared with many similarly minded cousins and remotely related kin.

I do not, in any way, take anything that I find in genealogy as serious business. I like the Kentucky family ties and have an interest in the Maryland and Virginia family lines. Our family was among the first to enter those lands, and I enjoy reading about those histories.

Our European royal ancestry has a certain fascination for me, but what I am to do with the information, I haven't a clue. A royal ancestor is a mixed blessing. If you proclaim a royal connection, there is a tendency toward disbelief. Those hearing the claim look for a mountain of money passed down from a royal treasury and, when the cash is not in evidence, scoff at the claim. No matter, the way I look at it, if those royal families had made it worth our time, we would still be "over there." And besides, the American stock is the blood I am proud to belong to.

However, Kentucky owes a great deal of its culture to England, Scotland and Ireland. When Daniel Boone and William Bryan cut the Wilderness Trail through the Kentucky forest to Boonesborough and Bryan's Station, they brought with them men like themselves, who had been displaced for one reason or another in prior generations and who were from some of the great and wealthy families of Britain. These pioneers possessed a cultural heritage that knew of and appreciated grand architecture, distilled spirits and sound horseflesh.

Consequently, our early homes are Georgian in appearance, our bourbon whisky is based upon the Highland art and science of distilling, and our horse-racing industry is the English and Irish model. The fact that we trumpet to the world that in Kentucky, we are known for fine aged bourbon whisky, fast horses and beautiful women should come as no surprise. Fate took the best of Europe and the world and brought it to America. Then we took the best of America and brought it to Kentucky.

Scotland

Alexander I, King of Scotland, 1078-1124, + Sybilla
David I, The Saint King of Scotland, 1084-1153, + Matilda
Malcolm IV, King of Scotland, 1141-1165
Fitzalan, Walter I, Steward of Scotland, d. 1177
William I, King of Scotland, 1143-1214, + Ermengarde
Alexander II, King of Scotland, 1198-1249, + Joan
Fitzalan, Walter II, High Steward of Scotland, d. 1230, + Angus
Alexander III, King of Scotland, 1241-1286, + Margaret Plantagenet
Stewart, James, High Stewart of Scotland, 1243-1309
Eriksdottir, Margaret, Queen of Scotland, 1282-1290
Balliol, John, King of Scotland, + Isabel of Warren, 1240-1313
Bruce, Robert I, "the Bruce," King of Scotland, 1274-1329, + Isabel
Marjorie Bruce + Sir Walter Stewart, 1293-1327
Robert Stewart II, King of Scotland, 1314-1390, + Elizabeth Mure
Robert Stewart III, Regent of Scotland, 1340-1419, + Murietta Keith
Marjorie Stewart, b. 1361, + Duncan Campbell, Lord of Argyll, b. 1453
Archibald Campbell, Earl of Argyll, 1446 -1513, + Elizabeth Stewart
Donald Campbell, Abbot Lord Privy Seal, + Margaret
Margaret Campbell, 1571-1632, + Alexander I Magruder, b. 1569
Alexander II Magruder, 1610-1677, + Sarah Braithwaite, b. 1638
Samuel Magruder, 1660-1711, + Sarah Beall, 1658-1743
Ninian Magruder, 1686-1731, + Elizabeth Brewer, b. 1690
Ann Magruder, b. 1732, + Thomas Claggett, 1713-1778
Ninian Claggett, 1750-1805, + Euphon Wilson, b. 1752
Mary Claggett, 1787-1857, + Thomas W. Prather, 1778-1857
John M. Prather, 1808-1894, + Demarius Brink
Henry W. Masters, 1824-1886, + Sarah E. Prather, 1826-1892
William Irvine Masters, 1856-1932, + Elizabeth Witt, 1862-1932
Vernon Elser Masters, 1893-1952, + Clara Alcorn, 1898-1976
Vernon Edward Masters, 1918-1996, + Barbara Gallagher, b. 1926
Col. Michael Edward Masters, b. 1949

England

William the Conqueror, 1027-1087, + Matilda of Flanders
Henry I, King of England 1088-1135, + Matilda of Scotland
Matilda, 1102-1135, + Geoffrey Plantagenet V
Henry II Plantagenet, King of England, 1133-1189, + Eleanor
Richard I Plantagenet, King of England, 1189-1199
John Plantagenet, King of England, 1199-1216, + Isabella
Henry III Plantagenet, King of England, 1216-1272, + Eleanor
Edward I Plantagenet, King of England, 1272-1307, + Eleanor
Edward II Plantagenet, King of England, 1307-1327, + Isabelle
Edward III Plantagenet, King of England, 1327-1377, + Philippa
Thomas Plantagenet, 1355-1396, + Eleanor de Bohun
Anne Plantagenet, 1383-1438, + William Bouchier
John Bouchier, 1412-1474, + Margery Berners
Humphrey Bouchier, 1432-1471, + Elizabeth Tylney
Margaret Bouchier, 1470-1551, + Thomas Bryan
Francis Bryan I of Ireland, 1490-1551, + Joan FitzGerald
Francis Bryan II, b. 1549, + Ann Smith
William Smith Bryan, b. 1604, + Catherine Morgan
Francis Bryan III, 1630-1677, + Sarah Brinker
Morgan Bryan, 1671-1763, + Martha Strode
William Bryan, 1733-1780, + Mary Boone
Mary Nancy Polly Bryan, 1771-1818, + David Hampton
Cynthia Hampton, 1798-1845, + Claiborne Cox
Mary B. Polly Cox, 1819-1900, + Allen Witt, 1816-1883
Elizabeth Witt, 1862-1932, + William Irvine Masters, 1856-1932
Vernon Elser Masters, 1893-1952, + Clara Alcorn, 1898-1976
Vernon Edward Masters, 1918-1996, + Barbara Gallagher, b. 1926
Col. Michael Edward Masters, b. 1949

Pioneer Kentucky Settlement

1763 Daniel Boone, 1734-1820, + Rebecca Bryan, 1738-1813
1765 Squire Boone, 1744-1815, + Jane Van Cleve, 1749-1829
1765 William Bryan, 1733-1780, + Mary Boone, 1736-1819
1773 John Strode, 1730-1806, + Mary Polly Boyle, 1739-1829
1775 Ninian Claggett, 1750-1805, + Euphon Wilson, 1759-1836
1775 Elisha Witt, 1759-1835, + Phoebe Dodd, 1759-1840
1782 Baruch Prather, 1742-1810, + Sarah Higgins, 1761-1844
1782 Walter Beall, 1740-1818, + Rebecca Tannehill, 1751-1791
1802 John Masters, 1778-1860, + Anna Holmes, 1780-1820

Pilgrim American Settlement

1622 Thomas Prather, 1604-1666, + Mary McKay, 1602-1680
1635 William Braithwaite, 1600-1649, + Margaret, b. 1610
1652 Alexander Magruder, b. 1605, + Margaret Braithwaite, b. 1638
1652 Ninian Beall, 1625-1717, + Ruth Moore, 1648-1712
1668 Thomas Masters + Margery
1670 Thomas Claggett, 1644-1703, + Mary Nutter, 1645-1692
1683 Edward Morgan, 1670-1736, + Elizabeth Jarman, 1670-1731
1702 John Witt, 1645-1715, + Anne Daux, b. 1647
1712 Morgan Bryan, 1671-1763, + Martha Strode, 1690-1747
1717 George Boone, 1662-1740, + Mary Maugridge

Elmwood

The master of Elmwood mansion, my father, known by all as Papa, delivered more than 10,000 babies in the span of his medical career. Papa felt very grateful to his patients. He believed that he took care of them and that they took care of him. After he retired, when asked by former patients if he missed the practice of medicine, he would proclaim that indeed he did: "The day before I retired, 2,000 women adored me; the day after, just one." This was said with a twinkle in his eye and a peripheral glance in the direction of his wife, Mimi.

The old patriarch never really retired; he simply found other ways to engage his numerous friends and admirers. He grew a garden of 450 rosebushes and sold the roses for fifty cents a stem, check made out to the medical school. Weddings and debutante balls could require as many as twenty-five dozen stems. No problem, he had it covered.

It would be a mistake to think of Mimi as only the supportive element in Papa's life or in the household life of Elmwood. Mimi had a mind and a career of her own. For many years, she was an international buyer for a major department store in Kentucky, traveling to New York each month and to the European markets each year. The politically powerful and successful businessmen that were entertained at Elmwood found in her the Southern charm of a great lady and an intellect that challenged their own.

Mimi had an enormous influence on the lives she touched. She was an accomplished hostess and entertained beautifully in the formal rooms of Elmwood. However, it was in her everyday life that she proved most remarkable. Her evening meal was a five-star dinner; if she knew you were coming, she would set a place at the table for you. She invited the single and the recently unmarried to Thanksgiving and Christmas dinners. At times, the group was so large that the sixteen-seat dining room table was insufficient and she hosted the dinner buffet-style. I can recount many times when the dinner swelled to thirty or more. Those who were in on these dinners have commented throughout their lives on their memory of the event to our family. Mimi did not want her friends or the friends of her brood to be alone on a festival day, unless it was by personal choice.

The magic and allure of Elmwood in Louisville, Kentucky, had a lot to do with the architecture and the age of the place. It was built in 1840 on a massive scale with fourteen-foot ceilings and extraordinarily wide floor and ceiling moldings. Papa and Mimi had only two kinds of furnishings: old furniture, dating prior to Adams, "the first one," and furniture crafted by Papa, who was proud to be known as a cabinetmaker of consummate skill. A tour of Elmwood conducted by the master himself was an adventure not to be missed. But I am telling you that the powerful charm of Elmwood was not so much in its voluminous rooms as it was in the sofas and wing-back chairs filled with family and friends who were attracted to the mansion to be in the excellent company of Papa and Mimi.

The bar at Elmwood was always open. A drink could be had for breakfast, if one were so inclined. But I cannot remember a time when the privilege was abused. The guests that came to Elmwood came to be with its stewards, to be embraced by an old style of Kentucky hospitality, chock full of simple courtesies and elegant manners.

Holloway House

There was a time in the early 1800s when a Kentucky farm was much more than the home place for a family. It was an economic center that produced nearly all the means and materials that a large, extended family group required to sustain its life and livelihood. Holloway House is an example of Kentucky life as it appeared in the emerging prosperity of the post-Revolution years.

Holloway House was constructed in 1820 by the architect John Rogers, who also built the Basilica of St. Joseph's Proto-Cathedral in Bardstown. The house is some 10,000 square feet, with a spiral staircase ascending to the third-story ballroom. The plantation upon which it was built produced all the brick and timber used in its construction. Most of the Holloway plantation outbuildings are extant, as they were constructed with the same three-brick-thick walls as the house. The smokehouse, icehouse and barns still stand next to the grand old mansion as sentinels to a time when the farm and plantation were the center of social and business life in Kentucky.

And it was here that Mama Sudie, Sue Carol's mother and Margaret Sue's grandmother, was queen of all that she surveyed. I did not have the pleasure of knowing E.T. Holloway, Mama Sudie's husband, but I wish I had known him. Mama Sudie was so fond of him. Every day living with Mama Sudie must have been an experience like no other.

27

Mama Sudie treated life as her playground; she rarely missed a social opportunity. To her life was about seeing her friends. Whether they were rich or destitute, educated or illiterate, powerful or weak was not a judgment she felt the need to make. She invited them all to Holloway House to visit with her, and if they were sick or had passed away, she went to visit them. I saw her buy clothes at Saturday yard sales, clothes that she felt were attractive and sized correctly, to take to children she knew who were without pretty garments to wear to church or school. And with equal aplomb, she would entertain a Kentucky governor or senator or a host of dignified guests later in the evening.

Mama Sudie was married to E.T. Holloway for thirty-five years. She lived on and worked a 1,500-acre plantation that had three dairies and extensive tobacco and timber acreage. Her sister-in-law, Margaret Holloway Veech, lived across the road on a 700-acre horse farm and also was married for thirty-five years. The two "sisters" lived the last thirty years of their lives with each other, their husbands having passed away. Every day, Aunt Margaret would travel to the store to purchase the dinner for the evening, she being selected because Mama Sudie considered her the rich one, and every evening Mama Sudie would cook dinner for the two of them. On Sunday, the Holloway family, the preacher, the recently engaged and various friends and lost souls would gather in the great parlors of Holloway House, which was filled with early Kentucky cherry and walnut furniture and massive Victorian pieces, to share luncheon after church services.

Preparing Sunday dinner, as it was termed, was a two-day enterprise at Holloway House that began on Saturday afternoon with Mama Sudie and Sue Carol baking cakes and vegetable casseroles. Early on Sunday morning, rolls, biscuits and breads were taken up and left in their baking pans to rise, filling the great house with the aroma of yeast and freshly kneaded dough. The Sunday dinner crowd would arrive at half past twelve. The men would fill the chairs and sofas to talk the conversation of rural Kentucky: weather, crop health, livestock and market conditions. The boys and girls would play outside on the lawn or in the third-floor ballroom if the weather was inclement. The women occupied themselves with the dinner, cooking the meal in both the summer and winter kitchens, the first being away from the house connected by a covered breezeway, the second inside the house. At three in the afternoon, the table was set, and a dining room table meant to seat eighteen would have twenty-five place settings of china plates, crystal glass and silver from the various generations of the Holloway family.

On the sideboard was a tremendous array of foods, seemingly without a plan as to whether or not they complemented each other. The obligatory country ham and fried chicken were there, as well as roast beef or turkey. Scalloped and mashed potatoes, broccoli casserole and corn pudding, baked oysters and stewed tomatoes, deviled eggs and banana croquettes were invariably present. A gallon of iced tea with four cups of sugar mixed in and coffee were the beverages. White cakes with creamy caramel icing were on hand, as well as double-layered jam cakes, the centers filled with strawberry or blackberry preserves. The breads were on the table, to be passed throughout the meal.

Sue Carol, after an hour at the table, would then organize the scullery. She would summon the guests to their stations. The roles of dish washing and hand drying were delegated to particular women, who had assumed their positions in the kitchen hierarchy decades in the past. The men would maneuver the furnishings back into their proper places. And then, to complete their tour of duty, the men would act as couriers, carting the crystal and silver from the washbasins back to their homes to the cupboards and pantry shelves. The entire work in progress was supervised relentlessly by Sue Carol, who required diligence from all her help. After the chores were completed, the Sunday dinner contingent would find the safe harbor of a favorite chair to spend the remainder of the day in pleasant discourse with those assembled.

I never tired of listening to Mama Sudie talk of the days when she and her mother would host similar dinners on the same kind of scale, without the benefit of running water or electricity. The heat for the ovens came from wood. The light for the rooms came from coal oil and candles. The water was hand pumped from the well. The meat came from the smokehouse and the poultry lot. And yet the same bountiful table was set, and the dining table was packed with dinner guests.

Margaret Sue and I were married on the front porch of Holloway House, amidst the great columns, with a soloist above us on the second-floor balcony to help create the proper mood. The wedding guests were on the lawn in front of us. As the preacher invoked "Gawd's" great mercy and blessing, we felt fortunate to have our love consecrated at Holloway House. Margaret Sue took my breath away, she looked so beautiful in her wedding gown. The fact that it rained toward the end of round one of the wedding ceremony, depriving the preacher of a full hour before us, did not dampen the happiness we felt on our wedding day. The folks on the lawn, all 200 of them, simply packed into the parlors of Holloway House to sample the coconut and pineapple upside-down cakes prepared by Mama Sudie and Sue Carol. Gracious, it was an elegant affair. A second reception was held later in the evening at my club for those inclined toward strong drink, sumptuous food and loud music.

McManus House

Bardstown, Kentucky, was occupied in the late 1770s by pioneer families who braved the hostile and dangerous conditions largely created by our nation's fight for independence from England. The American war with our English adversaries and their Indian allies cost many a frontier life without regard to age or gender. Out of these desperate times emerged a hardy, tough and resilient Kentucky breed of men and women, intent on making Kentucky their home. Almost a thousand miles from civilization, these Kentucky pioneers had to do for themselves.

It is amazing that under these harsh and hard circumstances, a town as beautiful as Bardstown could be built at the beginning of the nineteenth century using the scarce tools and only the wood and stone available from the forest. By 1820, the citizens of Bardstown had built a magnificent cathedral, a hotel, large estate homes, a courthouse, schools for boys and girls, a college and a business marketplace. Many of the houses and stores have at least one log room, and many of the houses, whether log, frame or brick, are supported in their floor, walls or roof with bark-on timbers, squared on the appropriate side with an adz.

The earliest houses, built before 1810, were constructed of a room or two at a time with low ceilings and huge fireplaces. The most common way to accommodate the growing family was to construct the first room of log, thereby securing the family against the advancing winter. The next addition placed a frame or brick room against the existing log room, and the following addition placed two rooms above those on the ground, creating a house plan of "two over two." If a level of affluence found favor with the owners of the property, an additional wing was added, usually another "two over two," giving the family four rooms up and four rooms down. This description fits the architectural history of our home, McManus House.

McManus House, which resides within the historic district of Bardstown, was also built in stages, the log room having been constructed in 1797, with frame and brick additions in 1820 and 1840. The property was originally owned by my ancestor, Walter Beall, who developed Bardstown after the Revolutionary War with England. Walter Beall sold the property to Charles McManus in 1796, who constructed our home.

McManus House has been the scene of many fine times. It is not the imposing mansion of Elmwood or of the grandeur of Federal Hill, the Old Kentucky Home state shrine. But it is almost as old as the commonwealth itself and possesses a charm that is remarkable. Margaret Sue and I entertain inside the house in the wintertime, with the old fireplaces roaring with heat and good cheer. In the other three seasons, we are on the lawn using the great trees as our canopy. Margaret Sue and I have created a home that is warm and welcoming. We offer our neighbors, our family and our friends a very old and congenial atmosphere in which to enjoy life with us.

Margaret Sue and I see ourselves as the beneficiaries of a tradition of Kentucky hospitality that traces our family roots back to the original settlers in Kentucky and to the first English families on the American continent. When I am sitting in front of my garden at McManus House under the redbud tree on a hot, humid Kentucky summer day, I am satisfied. I am content that although I am a modern man, I can still reach into my past for the solace that I belong to the family that first explored Kentucky and to a race of English people documented far beyond the Norman conquerors of that island. When I find myself in the soup of our Kentucky and English genealogy and share this history with my children, they rush to find other ways to occupy their time. This level of sentimentality is more than they can tolerate.

It is not by accident that we learn our hospitable way. Children, from the time they acquire language, are expected to rise to shake the hand of an adult entering the house, looking straight into their eyes, to show respect and to give a proper greeting. We address our children using "sir" and "miss," according to their gender, from the day of their birth. The children respond in likewise fashion using "sir" and "m'am." The cornerstone of our etiquette training is revealed in our language and is based in gratitude, using the words "please" and "thank you."

We include our children in our entertaining, teaching them the rules of courtesy and expecting them to make us proud with their polite behavior and respectful demeanor. We teach our children that they are the equal of anyone, regardless of their station or title, and to treat all ranks in the social order with a polite countenance. In this way, the doctor, lawyer and Indian chief, as well as the hunting guide, bartender and carpenter, are friends, each in their way. Once the social graces have been attended to, the party can begin.

Boonesborough, Bryan's Station

In 1763, Daniel Boone left his family home in the Yadkin Valley of North Carolina to explore the lands west of the Appalachians. The British Crown had expressly forbidden the exploration of these lands, fearing the expansion of Colonial influence so far away from British government and military control. The English army regulars stationed on the American continent had just concluded a protracted war with Native Americans, who were contesting Colonial settlement of their homelands and annual migration routes on the frontier. Another war with France seemed to be on the horizon, and a continuing conflict with Spain kept English military forces alert in Europe.

The Crown was beginning to feel the weight of the American Colonies' nascent expressions to separate from English rule. American dissatisfaction with English trade monopolies was becoming more ominous, and the rhetoric on both sides of the Atlantic Ocean was becoming increasingly inflammatory as the English placed restrictions on American trading and settlement ambitions.

The opportunities to claim or receive grants of large tracts of land east of the mountains were diminishing, much of the land having already been taken. Boone, restless and feeling enclosed living amongst his neighbors in the Yadkin Valley, declined to heed the admonishments of the Crown and decided to explore the uncharted wilderness west of the mountains. An earlier explorer of Kentucky, John Finley, had found a pass through these mountains and had revealed to Boone his discovery of vast meadowlands with a gentle terrain of rolling hills and an abundance of streams and rivers. Boone spent the better part of the next ten years exploring, hunting and trapping the region we know as Kentucky.

Returning to the Yadkin Valley periodically, Boone interested a land speculator, one Richard Henderson, in financing an expedition to the Kentucky country. The idea was to survey the ground where Boone had traveled and to trade with the Indians he had met. Boone thought the Indians would sell the settlers the claim the Indians believed they had on the land. The Henderson group would then petition the British Crown for a claim for millions of acres and, if denied, set up an autonomous government. The alternative plan, in the event of a separation from England, was to have the Commonwealth of Virginia, of which the Kentucky county was a part, recognize and record the surveyed claim. The plan was to erect a series of fortified stations to securely receive the settlers that would follow.

To this end, Boone gathered together men who shared his aspirations. Among these was William Bryan, who had married Boone's sister, Mary Boone. William Bryan and Mary Boone Bryan were my distant grandfather and grandmother of generations past. Daniel Boone then married William Bryan's niece, Rebecca Bryan, making Daniel Boone an ancestor by marriage and by blood.

Boone and Bryan, along with thirty other men, made the journey through the wilderness to build Boonesborough, the first fortified settlement in Kentucky in 1775. The following year, the brothers-in-law, Boone and Bryan, along with other men, returned to the Yadkin Valley and brought their wives and children to Boonesborough. Bryan, several years in the Boonesborough fortification, struck out with several of his brothers to build Bryan's Station in 1779, about twenty miles west of Boonesborough and about five miles from the fort at Lexington, which was built a year earlier.

In 1776, the Americans declared their independence from England, formed a government and set about the task of expelling the English from the North American continent. The English, determined not to lose the American Colonies, used their army to attack the eastern seaboard port cities, thereby severing the flow of supplies from Europe. The English strategy to attack the Americans west of the mountains was to launch the assaults from the English forts at Vincennes, Fort Sackville and Kaskaskia in the Illinois country and to enlist the support of the Indians centered around Detroit and Chillicothe in the Ohio country. From these bases, Kentucky could be attacked by Britain using English troops and their Indian allies. The stakes for the nations at war was immense, the control of the Northwest Territory east of the Mississippi River.

The fighting was ferocious. My grandfather seven generations back, William Bryan, and his son by the same name were killed in 1780 in the Battle of Bryan's Station in a savage attack by English and Indian forces led by the English commander Simon Girty. Mary Boone Bryan was recognized for her heroism during the siege of Bryan's Station; she left the fort to carry water from the spring, the guns of the British and Indians leveled upon her.

In 1783, the Americans signed a peace treaty with England, with the English ceding Kentucky and the Northwest Territory to the Americans. By their courage and sacrifice, the pioneers of Kentucky had weathered the storm of war.

Boonesborough was my family's first home in Kentucky in 1775, and our family were among the first Colonial inhabitants of Kentucky. Bryan's Station was our second home in 1779. Both had been cut out of the wilderness and defended with the lives of our family.

Waveland

The son of William Bryan and Mary Boone Bryan, Daniel Boone Bryan, built Waveland plantation in Lexington after the Revolution, with his heir, Joseph Bryan, completing the work in the mid-1800s. Waveland's 2,000 acres was a self-sufficient farming operation with a dairy, a grist mill, a distillery and a forge to support and process the agricultural production. Throughout the nineteenth century, Waveland was the center of horse racing and bloodstock breeding in Kentucky.

The Kentucky Colonel persona traces its origin to the beginning of the nineteenth century. Kentucky's contentious brand of politics after the Revolutionary War often settled different points of view with "iron and lead." The settlers coming to Kentucky after the war with England were made up primarily of a discharged army, armed to the teeth and ready to claim warrants of land in Kentucky.

During that period, the elected governors of Kentucky felt the need for personal protection and literally surrounded themselves with family and friends, no doubt fierce warriors on their own account, having fought the British and Indian for forty years. These loyal supporters were given the honorary title of Colonel by the governor's office and often wore militia uniforms. The need to secure the governor's safety was heightened throughout the Civil War and the Reconstruction period as Kentucky sons joined either the Union or Southern cause, then returned home, often bitter at the war's outcome. The assassination of Governor William Goebel in 1901 gave credence to the notion that the sectional feelings had not been resolved.

The Kentucky Constitutional Oath of Office, ratified in the Kentucky Constitution of 1891, addressed the concerns that affairs of honor were consuming what remained of the generation that had fought the Civil War. The Oath of Office is still used to this day.

> "I do solemnly swear that I will support the Constitution of the United States and the Constitution of this Commonwealth, and be faithful and true to the Commonwealth of Kentucky so long as I continue a citizen thereof, and that I will faithfully execute, to the best of my ability the office of _____ according to law; and I do further solemnly swear that since the adoption of this constitution, I, being a citizen of this state, have not fought a duel with deadly weapons within this state nor out of it, nor have I sent nor accepted a challenge to fight a duel with deadly weapons, nor have I acted as a second in carrying a challenge, nor aided or assisted any person thus offending, so help me God."

However, as the Civil War generation was laid to rest and as the commonwealth developed a professional state police force in the second decade of the twentieth century, the need diminished for a Kentucky governor to rely upon a personal militia.

In 1931, the Honorable Order of Kentucky Colonels was incorporated as a nonprofit charitable organization to promote Kentucky hospitality and to act as goodwill ambassadors throughout the world. The image of the Kentucky Colonel has always been one of a Kentucky gentleman planter and was given form by the worldwide fame of the novelist Mark Twain, who wore the white suit and string tie to his speaking engagements. His cousin, Henry Watterson, the nationally famous and notoriously pithy editor of the *Louisville Courier-Journal*, sported the classic mustache and goatee, fashionable in the antebellum South. And the Louisville scion of military and business affairs, General John Breckinridge Castleman, had the photogenic bearing and grace of the benevolent and worldly Kentucky gentleman.

Those of us who assume the title of Colonel do so out of respect for the Commonwealth of Kentucky and the Honorable Order of Kentucky Colonels. It has been my privilege, as an ambassador of our commonwealth, to promote Kentucky goodwill and *Hospitality – Kentucky Style* where-ever and to whomever will stand their ground to my exhortations.

General John Breckinridge Castleman
Cherokee Park, Louisville

Kentucky Heritage Grand Tour

The people of the Commonwealth of Kentucky periodically have had the opportunity to save a building or a piece of land that is significant to our history. Many of these buildings were in disrepair after many generations of use and have lost future economic viability. Without the intervention of our government or private initiatives, these historical structures would have been destroyed. Historically profound tracts of land are often under threat of high-impact development that removes it from the public use and destroys the historically significant features.

Occasionally, however, an historically significant building or land tract presents itself for salvation. These opportunities invariably come to us as ghosts out of our Kentucky past needing substantial reinvestment to preserve the structure or the integrity of the land. In other words, that piece of architecture or that piece of land needs an angel to save it.

The winds of historical preservation blow with an intermittent force. The one constant is that we as a people hold our Kentucky home place as sacred and inviolate. In our frontier past, that home may have been a remote, tiny log cabin that the settler family often, literally, would defend with their lives. Or the Kentucky home might have been a refined plantation house. Sometimes the preservation of the Kentucky home has come by accessing local and state treasuries, but just as often, it has been by collecting small donations from every soul in the community, from schoolchildren to pensioners. And at times, it has been a partnership of state and local government and community interest groups. We celebrate and hold dear the cabin of Lincoln as well as the mansion My Old Kentucky Home.

Early Kentucky architecture was in many ways a frontier adaptation of Virginia design. Prominent Virginians with political and family ties to Governor Patrick Henry and Thomas Jefferson were the recipients of the first warrants for Revolutionary War military service, and these warrants were executed on the prime land, surveyed by the warrant holders in the years before the conflict.

The first buildings in Kentucky had a lot to do with log shelter and fortification. The second period was the era dominated by the great builders and architects. John Rogers of Bardstown built the Basilica of St. Joseph Proto-Cathedral, the Church at Nazareth and many of the great manor and plantation houses in the Bardstown area in the Greek Revival style. Robert Russel Jr. built the early grand buildings at Centre College and many fine homes in Danville and Harrodsburg. John McMurtry and Thomas Lewinsky developed the Italianate design in Lexington, Paris and Richmond. Gideon Shryock's courthouse and statehouse work in Louisville and Frankfort and Old Morrison in Lexington were prominent.

The homes and government structures we have preserved, the museums we have created, the land tracts we have conserved are all a part of the matrix that we in our commonwealth have fashioned to honor the ancestral Kentucky home. The Kentucky Heritage Grand Tour is the journey that I suggest each of us must make to discover Kentucky and our own Kentucky homes.

Louisville
Cave Hill National Cemetery

Cave Hill National Cemetery was incorporated in 1848 and is an absolutely stunning arboretum with almost a thousand plant varieties. Many of the monuments, crypts and vaults that grace the gravesites are the work of world-renowned stone sculptors. Robert E. Taunitz, "the father of monumental art in America," crafted many of the late-nineteenth-century memorials.

The cemetery has a vast number and many species of wild ducks, geese and swans on the ponds and lakes that are scattered throughout the property. Naturalists from all over the world visit Cave Hill to observe the wildlife spectacle in the managed woodland setting of Cave Hill, situated in the heart of the Louisville metropolis.

The giant of American history, west of the Allegheny Mountains, General George Rogers Clark, has his hallowed resting place within this ground, as do many of the prominent personages of early Kentucky and the city of Louisville. Many Union and Confederate soldiers, as well as soldiers from the later world wars, are buried in Cave Hill.

Cave Hill National Cemetery is owned by the Cave Hill Association Trust.

Louisville
Speed Museum and
University of Louisville

The Speed Museum, located adjacent to the University of Louisville campus, is a nationally recognized art museum with outstanding collections of Kentucky, American, European and African art.

The Kentucky collection has several important paintings: a portrait of James Speed, U.S. attorney general under President Lincoln; the oil-on-canvas depiction of the Oakland Racecourse; a portrait of Daniel Boone by Chester Harding, painted a few years before his death; several portraits by Matthew Harris Jouett; and a portrait of Robert E. Lee.

The University of Louisville dates back to 1798, when the frontier town of Louisville chartered the Jefferson Seminary. In succeeding years medical, law and graduate schools aligned their interests with the ideal of a formal university structure. In 1846 the University of Louisville received its charter, bringing together many of the disparate professional schools of medicine and law in the Commonwealth of Kentucky. The bronze statue *The Thinker* by Auguste Rodin, a gift of the Hillman Hopkins family, is ensconced before the steps of the Rotunda, the administration building for the University of Louisville.

The Speed family of Louisville, who generously endowed this great museum, are from the same stock that once resided at Farmington. John and Lucy Speed and their sons, James and Joshua Speed, were Abraham Lincoln's friend and advisors and constituted a very prominent family in Louisville's first century. Succeeding generations of the Speed family have taken a great interest in the growth and development of the Speed Museum.

Louisville
Farmington, circa 1810
National Register of Historic Places

Farmington was built by Judge John Speed and Lucy Fry Speed on a design given to them by Thomas Jefferson. Their sons, James and Joshua Speed, were educated at St. Joseph College in Bardstown and Transylvania University in Lexington. Both James and Joshua Speed were confidants and friends of Abraham Lincoln, who as president, named James Speed to the office of U.S. attorney general in 1864 and relied upon Joshua Speed as his lifelong Western adviser. Abraham Lincoln was a frequent guest at Farmington.

Throughout the early months of the Civil War, Lincoln relied on James and Joshua Speed to keep Louisville, the economic center of Kentucky and the military gateway to the South, out of the hands of the Confederacy.

Farmington is furnished in the period and has a fine collection of Speed family heirlooms and accessories. The home is owned by the Historic Homes Foundation.

Louisville
Locust Grove, circa 1790
National Historic Landmark

L ocust Grove was built by Major William Croghan and his wife, Lucy Clark Croghan, the sister of General George Rogers Clark. It was an important house in early Kentucky military and political affairs, receiving, among the many notable guests, Presidents James Monroe, Andrew Jackson and Zachary Taylor; the Speeds of Louisville; and the Clays of Lexington. The brother of Lucy Clark Croghan and General Clark, William Clark, received Meriwether Lewis at Locust Grove to plan the start of their epic expedition to the Pacific Ocean in 1803. Lewis and Clark returned to Locust Grove in 1806 at the conclusion of their "Expedition of Discovery."

General Clark moved to Locust Grove in 1809, adding brilliance to the house by way of his legendary reputation as an Indian fighter and army commander and his national prominence as the "George Washington of the West." General Clark went to Locust Grove to live with his sister, Lucy Clark Croghan and died there in 1818.

Locust Grove is owned by the people of Jefferson County and is managed by Historic Locust Grove.

Louisville
Whitehall, circa 1855

Whitehall, one of the venerable mansions in Louisville, was built originally on twenty acres of land in 1855, on the newly formed Lexington Road, which had been developed as a bypass to the highly congested Frankfort Avenue. During the Civil War, the house saw service as a field hospital

Whitehall is an excellent example of an Italianate, antebellum estate home built on the four-room-over-four architectural plan that received a Classical Revival style makeover during the opulent times after the Civil War and Reconstruction.

Visitors can view this completely furnished estate house, replete with the massive Victorian pieces and great framed oil paintings that characterized a grand Louisville lifestyle in the late nineteenth century. The formal gardens, under the canopy formed by the towering hardwood trees, is a very elegant tour.

Whitehall was bequeathed in 1992 by Hume Logan Jr., to the Historic Homes Foundation Inc. It is a living museum of our Louisville past. Whitehall is a host to many weddings and social events throughout the year, in the house and on the grounds, catered on the grand scale.

Louisville
Zachary Taylor National Cemetery

Zachary Taylor (1784-1850), the twelfth president of the United States, was born to Colonel Richard and Mary Strother Taylor at Springfields Plantation in Louisville, Kentucky. The estate was considerable, and the income derived from Springfields made Taylor a very wealthy landholder. Taylor spent little time at Springfields Plantation, however, having chosen a military career, though he considered Springfields his home throughout his life. Springfields mansion is now a private home.

Taylor was commissioned an officer in the Army of the United States in 1808. He saw action in the war with England in 1812, in the Black Hawk War of 1832 and Seminole War of 1837, where he served with great distinction.

He was commissioned a general officer and commanded the Army of the Rio Grande in the Mexican War, achieving victory against vastly superior forces at the battles of Palo Alto, Monterey and Buena Vista and winning the nickname "Old Rough and Ready." As a result of his national acclaim he earned in the Mexican War, "The Kentucky Warrior" ran for the presidency in 1848, narrowly winning the office, only to die sixteen months later.

President Taylor's daughter, Sarah Knox Taylor, married Jefferson Davis, the future president of the Confederate States in 1835. His son Richard Taylor, became a Confederate general.

President Taylor is entombed in the national cemetery that bears his name. His statue on a sixty-foot column and his crypt are his only memorials. I would like to see more, learn more, teach more about this twelfth president of the United States. Taylor did not attend school and never cast a ballot in a political race, yet he became our nation's most accomplished warrior and the commander in chief of our fledging nation.

Louisville
Riverside (Farnsley-Moreman Landing), circa 1837

Built by Gabriel Farnsley and later occupied by the Moreman family, Riverside is a striking example of plantation life along the Ohio River in nineteenth-century Kentucky. This fully furnished house and detached kitchen depict the household life of a working farm and riverboat landing. This farm did a large volume business supplying the passing steamboats with wood for its boilers and food stores for its crew and passengers. The landing also operated a ferry, transporting people and commerce between Kentucky and Indiana. At one time Riverside and the Moreman family managed the largest farm in Jefferson County.

Riverside is an archaeology site that receives much attention from the academic community. Robust and diverse economic activity was practiced at Riverside at the river's edge during the nineteenth-century and the site gives scholars a unique opportunity to discover and reveal Kentucky agricultural culture just below the Falls of the Ohio.

Riverside is a wonderful example of the transition in style from the Federal to Greek Revival. It is not a house built by a wealthy merchant to showcase accumulated wealth. Rather, Riverside is a wonderful farmhouse built by a hard-working and affluent Kentucky family. Riverside is owned and preserved by the people of Jefferson County, who operate this home as a museum that gives homage to Louisville's Ohio River heritage.

Louisville
Jefferson County Court House, circa 1836
National Register of Historic Places

The Jefferson County Court House, built on a Gidgeon Shyrock design and completed by Albert Fink, is a masterpiece of a government building. It is the Greek Revival style in full form. The interior superstructure is graced by beautiful iron staircases and floor-to-ceiling windows that provide vast streams of light. A glass rotunda in the roof above the staircase provides a cascade of angled lighting that shines upon Kentucky sculptor Joel T. Hart's marble statue of Henry Clay. The public viewing areas in the fiscal court chamber are balconies ascending to balconies that surround the chamber, allowing the public to stand and witness the monthly meetings of their elected representatives.

Louisville was founded in 1778 on Corn Island by General George Rogers Clark on orders from Governor Thomas Jefferson. Louisville was named after the great benefactor of the American Revolution, King Louis XVI of France. Jefferson County was founded in 1780 and so named to honor Thomas Jefferson, writer of the Declaration of Independence, governor of Virginia, author of the Kentucky Resolutions and future president of the United States. The statues of Louis XVI and Thomas Jefferson by the sculptor Moses Ezekiel are on the Jefferson County Court House steps.

In Louisville and Jefferson County we honor Louis XVI, George Rogers Clark, Thomas Jefferson and Henry Clay as champions of our city, our county, our commonwealth and our nation.

Louisville
Fort William, circa 1785

Colonel William Christian came to Kentucky from Virginia bringing his wife, Anne Henry, Patrick Henry's sister, and his children. He built Fort William, a home of stone three feet thick. His daughter, Priscilla, married Colonel Alexander Scott Bullitt. Within a year of building their home, Fort William, Colonel Christian was killed by Indian attack. The significance of Fort William is that its presence is a gateway to our Louisville pioneer past and represents for me the little stations that constituted the thin, perilous defense of Louisville settlement.

Colonel Alexander Scott Bullitt and Captain Thomas Bullitt had come to Jefferson County in 1774 to survey land along the Ohio River. When Indian predation began, they, along with Colonel John Floyd, Colonel Richard Chenoweth and Captain William Harrod, under the direction of General George Rogers Clark, formed the militia command in 1778 with Corn Island, Fort Nelson, then Louisville as the principal fortification. Extending out from Louisville were the pioneer stations along the Beargrass Creek: Floyd's, Low Dutch, Spring Fort, A'Sturgus and Linn.

I pray that we have the communal wisdom to learn more about the men and women that founded Louisville and the spirit to preserve and memorialize their contributions. I am not satisfied with passing comment and highway markers. Fort William is privately owned.

Louisville
Churchill Downs, circa 1875
National Historic Landmark

This legendary racetrack in Louisville is home to the Kentucky Oaks for fillies and the Kentucky Derby, run on the first Friday and Saturday in May each year since 1875. The twin spires atop the grandstand roof are one of the most familiar trademarks in the world. Churchill Downs is at the center of the entertainment and hospitality culture in Louisville and in Kentucky.

Churchill Downs was built on land owned by John and Henry Churchill. In 1870, Louisville was faced with an unimaginable notion, that for virtually the first time in Louisville's history, there would be no horse racing. Oakland Race Course had ceased operations a decade before, and the last track remaining, Woodlawn, the Seventh Street track, had just closed its doors. The Churchills' nephew, Colonel Meriwether Lewis Clark, a descendant of both the Lewis and Clark families of explorer and military renown, seeing a business opportunity, had researched English- and Irish-style horse racing and wagering. Having viewed the Epsom Derby in England, Clark felt that Louisville could sustain a high-profile race that would focus worldwide attention on the racetrack and help to build the racing patrons' interest in the Thoroughbred breed of horse. Clark built Churchill Downs, founded the Kentucky Derby and flamboyantly led the track for 20 years.

In 1903, Colonel Matt Winn was named president of the track and became the fabled world-class promoter of Churchill Downs who helped turn American horse racing into a premier American sports attraction. Winn was instrumental in developing the mechanical parimutuel betting system and in institutionalizing the recording of Thoroughbred bloodlines. Winn's ability to draw the great names in the American entertainment industry to Churchill Downs and the Kentucky Derby gave the race the high profile and glamour envisioned by Clark and made the Kentucky Derby into "the greatest two minutes in sports."

There is very little in this world as exciting and alluring as a visit to Churchill Downs for the spring race meeting. The taste of Kentucky bourbon, a sumptuous luncheon, a full complement of beautiful women and the thrill of watching the fastest racehorses in the world is the best of times for this old Kentucky gentleman.

Louisville
Louisville Life Saving Station, circa 1848
National Historic Landmark

The historic Ohio River is a water course that travels from Pittsburgh to the Mississippi River, a 970-mile journey that is obstructed only by the Falls of the Ohio at Louisville. In the last quarter of the eighteenth-century, the Ohio River invited explorers, pioneers and settlers to discover Kentucky. The Falls of the Ohio was a treacherous passage, and in the early days many chose to portage and ferry their goods and persons around the falls. Louisville became a booming river town attracting the commerce and migration of America as it moved west.

The Louisville Life Saving Station was established to provide immediate rescue assistance to vessels wrecked while attempting to pass over the Falls of the Ohio. Locks

were built in 1845 to allow vessels to bypass the falls, however, flatboats, sailboats and stern-wheelers missing the lock channel faced a very dangerous and uncertain navigation of the falls. The United States Coast Guard operated the station for more than a century. The Louisville Life Saving Station stands at the foot of Fourth Street, at a place known for almost two centuries as the Louisville Wharf, as a proud old sentinel standing guard over the river, its travelers and sailors.

The Louisville Life Saving Station now serves as the administrative offices for the Belle of Louisville, the tall stack stern-wheeler cruise ship that is the worldwide symbol of Louisville as a great inland marine city.

Louisville
Filson Historical Society
Ferguson Mansion, circa 1901

The Filson Historical Society is a private nonprofit organization dedicated to preserving the significant documents in Kentucky's pioneer and antebellum past. With almost 2 million manuscripts, it is an outstanding depository of Kentucky history and genealogy. The Filson Historical Society is named for John Filson (1753-1788), an early writer of Kentucky history who, in 1784, published *The Discovery, Settlement and Present State of Kentucke.* His second publication, *The Adventures of Col. Daniel Boon,* was widely read and contributed substantially to the Boone legend. John Filson disappeared in 1788, likely killed by marauding Indians.

The Filson Historical Society was founded in 1884 in Louisville by business and academic leaders headed by Colonel Reuben T. Durrett (1824-1913), who was president of the club until his death. The succeeding president, R.C. Ballard Thurston, guided the club from 1923 to 1946, leaving the Filson Club his substantial Kentucky collection.

In the archive are many of the original wartime communications of Daniel Boone, George Rogers Clark, Patrick Henry and Thomas Jefferson. The museum has portraits and artifacts relating to Boone and the early Kentucky explorers. The tree trunk where Boone inscribed "D. Boon killed a bar" is preserved in the Filson Museum.

The library stacks and archival files hold primary source materials on all aspects of Kentucky life with great concentrations in the pioneer, antebellum and Civil War periods of our commonwealth. The Lewis and Clark expedition was staged and outfitted at the Falls of the Ohio at Louisville, and a good deal of this correspondence is housed in the Filson Library. The photograph, engraving and print collection is vast and visually documents the persons and events throughout our Kentucky history.

Louisville
National Society of the Sons
of the American Revolution

The general offices of the National Society of the Sons of the American Revolution are located in this great Southern city. The SAR, as it is known, is one of the principal genealogy organizations in the United States.

The role of this noble order is to research, preserve and celebrate the American patriots who fought and served in the cause of American independence. The SAR maintains a registry of those patriots who served in the American Revolution and documents genealogical descent. There are more than 26,000 members of the SAR in more than 450 chapters.

The SAR genealogy library is a great repository of American Revolutionary history. The library has excellent reading collections on George Washington, his officer corps and the battles and military engagements that wrested America from the British. The SAR has made every effort to provide reading and research material on matters relating to the original signers of the Declaration of Independence.

A visit to the SAR museum and library is a humbling experience. It is not the kind of humbling experience one gets standing before the Lincoln Memorial or the memorials at Blue Licks or Perryville. Rather it is an opportunity to experience the deep reverence that this organization holds for the American patriots who fought and died in the struggle for American liberty.

The genealogical descendants of these Revolutionary War patriots celebrate their ancestors through their membeership in the SAR. In this way, the membership of the SAR maintains a deep respect for the historical symbols of American liberty.

Louisville
Bank of Louisville, circa 1837
National Historic Landmark

Built on a design by Gideon Shryock, the Bank of Louisville was the first nationally chartered bank in Kentucky and was Louisville's first attempt to bring financial liquidity to its burgeoning Ohio River trade with New Orleans.

The bank was created to provide a clearinghouse for converting various money species into gold or silver, a daunting task on the western frontier. The downriver buyers of Kentucky agricultural goods and whiskey paid in French, Spanish and English note and coin. After the Civil War, when a United States currency became commonly accepted legal tender the Bank of Louisville gave way to state chartered banks.

This remarkable bank temple, a Greek Revival structure, was built to honor and serve Louisville commerce and is a proud beacon to the prosperous city of Louisville. Actor's Theatre, Kentucky's designated repertory theater, now owns the property. Upon these stages are produced world-class plays, and its New American plays series is acclaimed throughout the world.

Bardstown
St. Thomas Church, circa 1811

Pioneer settlers began clearing land for cabins in the area we know as Bardstown in the fall of 1775. The cold Kentucky winter was near. Half-faced cabins, built low to the ground with a fire set before the opening, were essential to the families' survival. The settlers, from Maryland and Virginia, were full of hope and faith in their future prospects. They came as Catholic families with ideas of building a community of the faithful in the middle of the Kentucky wilderness.

Learned, scholarly men came to Bardstown from the Baltimore diocese in the early days of the migration to nurture the small nascent Catholic community. In 1808 New York, Boston, Philadelphia and Bardstown joined Baltimore as four-additional diocese of the Catholic Church in America. The see at Bardstown had administration over most of the territory west of the Allegheny Mountains to the Mississippi River, north of New Orleans and south of the Canadian border.

Bishop Benedict Joseph Flaget traveled to the Bardstown see in 1811, erected St. Thomas Church and made plans to erect a cathedral that would demonstrate the growing prestige of the Catholic Church on the western frontier of American settlement. The Basilica of St. Joseph Photo-Cathedral was the result. Over the next 30 years, Bishop Flaget, created or assisted in the creation of scores of parishes, schools, seminaries, convents and hospitals across the South and Northwest Territory of American settlement. All of this emanated, from the seed parish of St. Thomas Church.

Bardstown
Basilica of St. Joseph Proto-Cathedral, circa 1816
National Historic Landmark

The Basilica of St. Joseph Proto-Cathedral in Bardstown was built by the architect John Rogers under the direction of Bishop Benedict Joseph Flaget. The basilica was the first Roman Catholic cathedral built west of the Allegheny Mountains. Called the "Cathedral in the Wilderness," it was the archdiocese of the Catholic Church west of the Allegheny Mountains from 1816 until 1841, when the see was moved to Louisville.

This Roman Catholic church is remarkable in that it was constructed of brick on a massive scale in a time when log construction was still the construction material of choice. The beams that support the vaulted ceiling are whole tree trunks with a plaster overlay.

The Basilica of St. Joseph Proto-Cathedral was the beneficiary of several paintings and numerous gold and silver ornaments given to the church by King Louis-Philippe and his family, who visited Bardstown on May 18-21, 1797. The paintings are credited to the schools of Van Bree and Van Eyck. Louis-Philippe was king of France from 1830 to 1848.

Bardstown
Nazareth Church, circa 1822

Nazareth Church and the convent of the Sisters of Charity originated at the St. Thomas Plantation and was moved to its present location in 1812. Nazareth was hewn out of the wilderness by Bishop Benedict Joseph Flaget and Sister Catherine Spalding, the first mother superior of the Sisters of Charity, and her sisterhood to train teachers and nurses. Nazareth College was founded on this site.

The Sisters of Charity operate Spalding University in Louisville, founded in 1839, and numerous hospitals throughout America.

Visitors to the Nazareth campus find solace and peace. It is a feeling that is engendered by taking long reflective walks around the grounds and meeting the sisters that one encounters along the pathways. Sitting with the sisterhood at Sunday service, in my view, is to worship and commune with earthbound angels.

Bardstown
Gethsemani Abbey, circa 1856

The Trappist Cistercians, who date their order's founding to 1098 in France, are often cloistered and practice a life of prayer, labor and silence.

Gethsemani Abbey is the destination for thousands of thoughtful and prayerful people who go there to meditate and to enjoy the peace of the place. Many of the faithful make the pilgrimage to Gethsemani to enjoy the simple hospitality offered by the monks in their retreat program. The program has allowed the outside world to experience for a few days the monastic spiritual world of Thomas Merton, the modest and retiring monk and author.

The monks of Gethsemani rise at two o'clock in the morning to begin prayer and then spend the remainder of the day working. The evening is spent in prayer and meditation.

The abbey supports itself by selling the agricultural products produced in its dairies and bakeries. The fruitcakes, cheeses and candies made by the monks are exported all over the world.

Bardstown
Federal Hill, circa 1795-1818
State Shrine, State Historic Site, State Park

The plantation home of John Rowen in Bardstown, Federal Hill, is the state shrine of the commonwealth and is known as My Old Kentucky Home, so named in honor of the Stephen Foster plantation song by the same name. It is said that in our adoration for Federal Hill, "every Kentuckian has a home."

Stephen Collins Foster (1826-1864), the world-renowned writer of minstrel tunes, wrote some of the more memorable music ever penned by an American. His plantation songs and love ballads are classics. In 1853, after a visit to John Rowen's plantation, he wrote "My Old Kentucky Home, Goodnight." The song was so beloved in Kentucky that Federal Hill, the scene and inspiration for the tune, became the state shrine in 1923, and the plantation tune became the state song in 1928.

We like to sing "one song for the old Kentucky home" before our sporting and official events, or whenever a sense of nostalgic majesty is required. Whenever the song "My Old Kentucky Home" is lifted to the heavens, I promise you, there is not a dry eye in the house.

A visit to Federal Hill is time well expended. The mansion is elegant, beautiful and very well appointed and furnished. If you have not made the pilgrimage to our state shine, known throughout the world as My Old Kentucky Home, you have not discovered "who we are, why we are, the way we are, in Kentucky."

Bardstown
Spalding Hall, Getz Museum, circa 1826

Spalding Hall was built as St. Joseph College by the architect John Rogers for Bishop Benedict Joseph Flaget. Cassius Marcellus Clay, the "Lion of White Hall," and James and Joshua Speed were educated here.

The hall was named in honor of Bishop M.J. Spalding. Jesuits operated the college from 1848 to 1868. Spalding Hall was used as a military hospital during the Civil War and then as an orphanage. From 1911 to 1968, Spalding Hall was St. Joseph Preparatory School, a nationally acclaimed academy of the Xaverian Brothers. It now houses the Getz Museum, an internationally recognized museum of Kentucky bourbon whisky history.

The proud history of Spalding Hall is not yet complete. Each year Spalding Hall plays host to numerous fund-raising events and community events important to Bardstown. The Bourbon Festival is held here, and in that week, journalists from all over the globe travel to Bardstown, "The Bourbon Capitol of the World," to discover and write about this American spirit.

Every old home and commercial building in Kentucky must find angels who love them, if they are to be saved and restored. Spalding Hall, so vital to the social life of Bardstown, came close to destruction as an obsolete building. The building was saved, and it was restored because Spalding Hall found angels in the form of a few magnificent Bardstown citizens.

Springfield
Washington County Court House, circa 1816

The Washington County Court House is the oldest Kentucky courthouse still in active use. Springfield, the county seat, is a charming small Kentucky town on the southern edge of the Bluegrass. It is here that the paths of the Civil War presidents, Abraham Lincoln and Jefferson Davis, came into close proximity.

The Washington County Court House archives record the marriage bond between Thomas Lincoln and Nancy Hanks, the parents of Abraham Lincoln. A short distance away is the Hanks farm and Lincoln Homestead State Park, where Thomas Lincoln courted and learned his carpentry trade. Lincoln and Hanks family connections are everywhere in Springfield.

The young Jefferson Davis came to Springfield to attend St. Rose Priory, the oldest Catholic school, west of the Allegheny Mountains. The priory still stands on a hill overlooking the town, proud and magnificent.

The St. Catherine Mother House is on the rolling hills outside of town. Established in 1822, the convent is the first home of the Dominican Sisters in America and is the campus of St. Catherine College.

Springfield
Lincoln Homestead, circa 1782
State Park

The parents of Abraham Lincoln, Thomas Lincoln and Nancy Hanks Lincoln, were married in this home. The wedding service was performed by the Reverend Jesse Head of the Methodist faith on June 12, 1806.

The Hanks family home is the place where Thomas Lincoln courted his wife, Nancy Hanks. Thomas and Nancy Hanks Lincoln lived on the Hanks' property for two years after their marriage. During this period of time, Thomas Lincoln learned the carpenter and blacksmith trades from Richard and Francis Berry in the log buildings preserved on this property.

The Lincoln Homestead is a unique Kentucky monument to Nancy Hanks, the mother of Abraham Lincoln, who arguably is one of the towering mothering figures in the history of Western civilization. The log homes and outbuildings are furnished in pioneer furniture of the period.

Elizabethtown
Brown-Pusey House, circa 1825

The Brown-Pusey House was a hotel for many years operated by "Aunt Beck" Hill. General George Armstrong Custer and his wife were guests in this house. Custer's assignment was to eliminate illegal distilling in central Kentucky, to his chagrin, an almost impossible military task. An original oil painting of the general, signed by Mrs. Custer, hangs in the Brown-Pusey Museum.

The Brown-Pusey House has an excellent genealogy library and maintains documents and memorabilia from the settlement and the Civil War era in and around Elizabethtown. The Brown-Pusey House was willed by the Pusey/Brown/Hastings family in 1923 to the community of Elizabethtown. A replica of Dr. William Pusey's medical office has been faithfully reconstructed and is part of the museum.

This beguiling Federalist mansion of classical proportion serves Elizabethtown as a social meeting place, hosting weddings and family reunions. The board that governs the Brown-Pusey House has chosen to charge only a nominal fee for the use of this great house. Above the foyer in the hallway are words penned by Oliver Wendell Holmes:

> "There is no time like the old time
> When you and I were young.
> There is no place like the old place
> Where you and I were born."

Hodgenville
Knob Creek Farm, circa 1811 State Park

Knob Creek Farm was Abraham Lincoln's boyhood home for seven years. Lincoln maintained that at Knob Creek Farm were "my first boyhood memories."

The forebears of Abraham Lincoln began their American journey in 1637 when they arrived upon the Massachusetts shore. In succeeding generations, the family migrated to New Jersey, Pennsylvania, Virginia, North Carolina then to Kentucky through the Cumberland Gap. In 1782 Abraham and Bersheba Lincoln settled in Louisville, where, in 1786, Abraham Lincoln was killed by marauding Indians with his 10-year-old son Thomas Lincoln by his side. The widow Bersheba Lincoln then moved her family to Springfield, Kentucky.

Bersheba Lincoln's son, Thomas, met and married Nancy Hanks in this country, lived with her parents for several years and eventually purchased the Sinking Creek Farm. Abraham Lincoln, the savior of our union, was born in the little cabin at Sinking Creek Farm on February 12, 1809. In 1811 Thomas Lincoln moved the family to Knob Creek Farm, where they lived until 1816. The Lincoln family then moved to Indiana and Illinois, thereby creating "The Lincoln Trail."

Hodgenville
Abraham Lincoln Memorial
National Park

Inside this massive marble and granite monument, designed by John Russell Pope, the designer of the Jefferson Memorial in Washington, D.C., is the cabin believed to be the birthplace of President Abraham Lincoln. Lincoln was born February 12, 1809, to Thomas and Nancy (Hanks) Lincoln in this log cabin on this land that his father, Thomas Lincoln, called Sinking Creek Farm.

In 1906, Robert Collier, Mark Twain, William Jennings Bryan and Samuel Gompers formed the Lincoln Farm Association to purchase the Sinking Creek Farm to preserve the Lincoln heritage. A subscription drive among schoolchildren raised the necessary funds to build the memorial. President Theodore Roosevelt laid the initial cornerstone in 1909, and President William Howard Taft delivered the dedication in 1911.

Near this monument is the childhood home of Abraham Lincoln, Knob Creek Farm, where he spent the first seven years of his life. Lincoln had deep roots in Kentucky. His wife, Mary Todd, was from Lexington; his best friend was Joshua Speed of Farmington, outside of Louisville; Henry Clay of Ashland, outside of Lexington was his political mentor; and William Herndon of Greensburg was his law partner from 1844 to 1860 in Springfield, Illinois.

This wooded and forested historic ground is hauntingly beautiful. The memorial is imposing, presidential and august. By contrast, the Lincoln cabin within the memorial is simple, plain and small. To realize that this humble cabin, hewn from the rugged Kentucky frontier, could produce a man as extraordinary as Abraham Lincoln makes one somber and introspective. That this cabin could conceive a child that would in his time preserve the American nation in Civil War and rescue the democratic ideal from self-destruction is almost unimaginable. I stand before this cabin, inside the granite monument that protects it, silently, in awe and in respect for this remarkable son of Kentucky.

Abraham Lincoln made few references to his father, Thomas Lincoln, failing even to attend his funeral in 1851. He did, however, make fond references to his mother, Nancy Hanks Lincoln, who died in 1818 and whose life is memorialized at the Lincoln Homestead State Park in Springfield. He also made affectionate remarks about his stepmother, Nancy Bush Johnson Lincoln, who lived in Elizabethtown when she married Thomas Lincoln in 1919, thus becoming the most famous stepmother in American history.

Fairview
Jefferson Davis Monument State Historic Site
State Park

One of the tallest obelisk monuments in the world, rising 351 feet, marks the birthplace of Jefferson Davis, who was born on June 3, 1808, and died December 6, 1889, the only president of the Confederate States of America. The monument was erected after General Simon Bolivar Buckner suggested at a reunion of the Orphan Brigade in 1901 that the obelisk be raised to the memory of the late Confederate president.

The family of Jefferson Davis moved from Georgia to Nelson County, Kentucky, in 1793, and he attended school at St. Rose Priory and St. Thomas Aquins in Springfield. Davis later attended Transylvania College in Lexington, before finishing his education at West Point.

His first wife, Sarah Knox Taylor, was the daughter of Zachary Taylor, the twelfth president of the United States. They married in Louisville in 1835, but Sarah Taylor died three months later of malaria.

Davis moved to Mississippi after the death of his wife. He won election as U.S. representative in 1845 but resigned in 1846 to join the army being assembled to invade Mexico. He fearlessly charged the enemy works at Buena Vista and became a national hero in the aftermath of the Mexican War.

In 1847, Davis became a U.S. senator, but he resigned in 1851 in protest over Henry Clay's Compromise of 1850. Davis was a rigid interpreter of the Constitution, maintaining that the states held all rights not specifically delegated to the federal authority. Davis was a highly principled man who held firmly to the assertion that the states had the right to choose their level of commitment to the federal government, as the states were sovereign governments.

President Franklin Pierce appointed Jefferson Davis U.S. Secretary of War in 1853. In 1857, Davis was again elected to the U.S. Senate, and he resigned in January 1861, when Mississippi seceded from the Union. Davis was appointed president of the Confederate States of America on February 8, 1861. The Civil War ended for Davis on May 10, 1865, with his capture by Federal troops. He spent the last years of his life in business pursuits, admired and beloved by a Southern nation that had seceded from the United States and that had fought a "lost cause" for sectional honor and sovereignty.

Frankfort
The Capitol of the Commonwealth of Kentucky
circa 1910

The Capitol of Kentucky, situated in Frankfort, settled a bitter rivalry between Louisville and Lexington in the years preceding statehood in 1782. Both of these two great towns maintained that their prominence in business and politics demanded that the capitol be in their city. The Capitol is the fourth structure built as a state house, the one prior being the Old State House, which now houses the Kentucky Historical Society.

Frank Mills Andres designed the Capitol in the Beau Arts style following the Benjamin Latrobe design of the national capitol in Washington, D.C. The magnificent rotunda rising above the capitol was modeled after the dome at the Des Invalides in Paris, France, that covers the tomb of Napoleon Bonaparte. The State Reception Room replicates the Marie Antoinette drawing room at the Palace of Versailles. I am enthralled by our Capitol, which for me, is a lifetime of continuing adventure, full of discovery.

The north entrance is graced by Lady Kentucky being attended by Progress, History, Plenty, Law and Art. Great murals painted by T. Gilbert White, grace the top of the staircases leading to the chambers of the House of Representatives and Senate. The House mural depicts Daniel Boone leading pioneers into the Bluegrass. The Senate mural above the staircase illustrates the Treaty of Sycamore Shoals between the Translyvania Company and Cherokee Indians that led to the purchase of Kentucky. Statues of President Abraham Lincoln, Jefferson Davis, Honorable Henry Clay, Vice-President Alben Barkley and Dr. Ephraim McDowell stand vigilant over our commonwealth under the rotunda. And I assure you, there is much more.

I am well pleased upon my visits to our Capitol, a pilgrimage I make annually, sometimes for business, sometimes for pleasure. A Kentuckian is heir to two phenomena relating to our governance: a very rough and contentious brand of politics, practiced without mercy toward colleagues and constituents alike, and quite simply, the most beautiful, the most elegant, the most artistically satisfying state house in our Union, with no peer. Contrasting ideals? Absolutely.

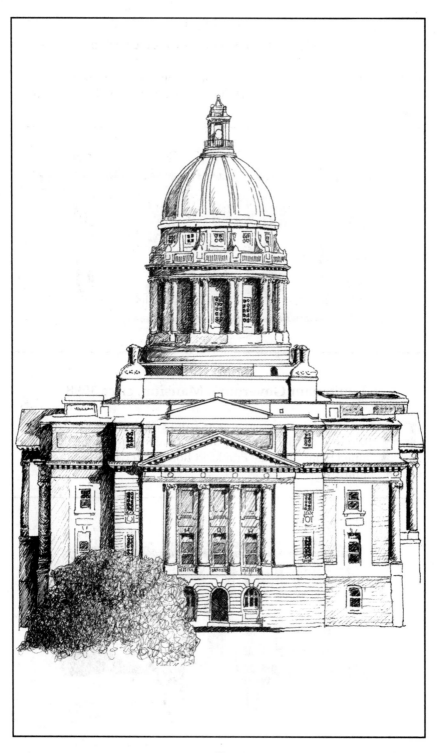

Frankfort
The Governor's Mansion, circa 1915

The sitting Kentucky governor and family reside in this home when they are in Frankfort. It is modeled after the Petit Trianon, Marie Antoinette's summer villa.

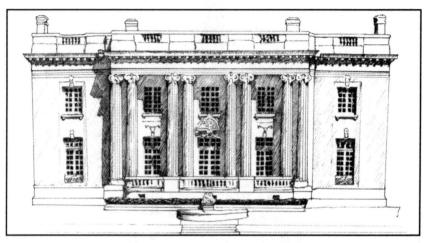

Frankfort
Lieutenant Governor's Mansion, circa 1798

Home to 33 Kentucky governors from 1798 to 1914, this house is the oldest official state executive home in continuous use in the United States. It is the Frankfort home to the lieutenant governor and family.

Frankfort
Old State House, circa 1827
State Shrine, National Historic Landmark

Kentucky's third capitol building was designed by architect Gideon Shryock, who introduced the Greek Revival style to Kentucky. The Old State House remained in active service as the seat of Kentucky government until 1909, when the fourth and present capitol was completed.

The Old State House continues to stand vigil over the Commonwealth of Kentucky. The interior is spectacular in design and has a staircase set on keystone arches that is singularly interesting. The oil paintings that adorn the granite walls are a real step into early Kentucky history. Oil-on-canvas portraits of legendary Kentuckians are on these walls: John Rowen of Federal Hill in Bardstown; John Fitch, the inventor of the steamboat, of Bardstown; the fabled Kentucky explorers and longhunters Daniel Boone and Simon Kenton; Robert Patterson, the founder of Lexington; Henry Watterson, the internationally famous editor of the *Louisville Courier-Journal*, whose editorials helped to end the repressive Yankee Reconstruction of the South. Also on the walls are wonderful portraits of: Simon Bolivar Buckner, John Cabell Breckinridge, John Hunt Morgan, John Castleman and Hardin Helm, the Civil War generals; President Jefferson Davis and President Zachary Taylor; Henry Clay, "The Great Compromiser"; and John Jordan Crittenden.

The Old State House is a magnificent Kentucky shrine and museum and is managed for the people of the commonwealth by the Kentucky Historical Society.

Frankfort
Frankfort Cemetery
State Historic Site

The Frankfort Cemetery celebrates, memorializes and dedicates its burial ground to the men and women who have represented our commonwealth in war and in our political history. Many of the monuments that honor the battles, wars and heroes of our Kentucky past reside here.

The Daniel Boone Monument that marks the grave of Daniel Boone and his wife, Rebecca Bryan Boone, is here. The Daniel Boone Monument represents for all Kentuckians the incredible courage, sacrifice and patriotic vision possessed by thousands of individual pioneer families who entered Kentucky between 1774 and 1814. Many Kentucky pioneer families perished in their resolve to establish their Kentucky homes. It is estimated that one half of the first 10,000 pioneers to Kentucky died from exposure to the elements, starvation, Indian attack, war and pestilence. We can only imagine the travail and danger faced each moment of the day by a pioneer family trying to settle the howling wilderness of Kentucky.

The State Mound, a sixty-two-foot marble column topped by the victorious Goddess of War, recognizes many of Kentucky's fallen heroes of the British and Indian wars, from 1774 to 1824, and the Mexican War. Numerous monuments in the Frankfort Cemetery are dedicated to and list many of the patriots who fought and died in the Revolutionary War.

The Frankfort Cemetery was organized in 1843; it overlooks the Kentucky River as it bends around the city. The pastoral grounds of the Frankfort Cemetery, canopied by great hardwood trees shading the weather-worn markers, memorials and gravestones of early Kentucky historical figures is a wonderful, sentimental hour of touring. Touch the simple stone memorial that covers the gravesite of Daniel and Rebecca Bryan Boone—and thank them for giving you Kentucky.

Frankfort
Kentucky Historical Society

The Kentucky State Historical Society was founded April 22, 1836, to collect and maintain items of historical interest of and about Kentucky. The original state seal and flag of the commonwealth of Kentucky are in the care of the society and are on display in the Kentucky History Center. The Commonwealth of Kentucky motto, "United We Stand, Divided We Fall," was proposed by Governor Isaac Shelby in 1792 from a song favored by him, "Liberty Song," written in 1768 by John Dickerson. The song intoned, "Then join hand in hand, brave Americans all, by uniting we stand, by dividing we fall."

The first president of the society was John Rowen of Federal Hill in Bardstown. The years following the Civil War created political problems for the Kentucky State Historical Society, for the radical Yankee Reconstruction government had no interest in preserving a Kentucky record of the Civil War or the times subsequent to that sectional conflict.

The Kentucky Historical Society was reincorporated in 1878 and moved its collection to the Old State House. The society, continually strapped for funds, had another difficult twenty years. In 1896, the society found an angel in the person of Jennie Chinn Morton (1838-1920) and in the patriotic organization of the Frankfort Chapter of the Kentucky Colonial Dames of America. Morton and the Frankfort Colonial Dames reorganized the society and rescued it from a dismal state by providing desperately needed funding. Morton worked diligently all her life to make the society an organization that encouraged scholarship, research and preservation, all critical to our understanding of Kentucky's past. In 1902, she founded the *Register of the Kentucky State Historical Society* and was editor of that historical quarterly until her death in 1920.

The Kentucky Historical Society is an independent agency of the Commonwealth of Kentucky. It operates the Kentucky Military History Museum, the Kentucky History Center and the museum of the Old State House, all in downtown Frankfort.

The Kentucky History Center, next door to the Old State House houses the Kentucky Governor's Portrait Gallery, the Kentucky History Library, the Kentucky Genealogy Library and the interactive *A Kentucky Journey*. Carve out a day for this visit. You will want to stay longer.

Frankfort
The Old State Arsenal, circa 1850

The Old State Arsenal, situated on the bluffs above Frankfort, has stood guard over the capitol city since 1850. The arsenal, built to safely warehouse the munitions and ordinance of the Kentucky Militia, was constructed on this site to minimize the risk of explosion and damage to the government buildings.

The Kentucky Military Museum is housed in the Old State Arsenal. The museum collection emphasizes the contribution made by the militias, State Guard and volunteer support organizations that have defended Kentucky and our nation from the time of the Revolutionary War to the present. Displays in the museum include large numbers of vintage firearms, cutlery and artillery. Kentucky military uniforms and flags are on review.

Be sure to find Daniel Boone's Kentucky Long Rifle, "Ticklikker." It is certain that this weapon, held in the steady hand of its master, found many a mark in the Kentucky wilderness.

The Kentucky Military History Museum is operated by the Kentucky National Guard and the Kentucky Historical Society.

Frankfort
Liberty Hall, circa 1796
National Historic Landmark

L iberty Hall was built by John Brown (1757-1837), a man who, along with Isaac Shelby, charted the Kentucky political course from a Virginia district to statehood, writing and debating the issues that would lead to Kentucky independence from Virginia. Brown studied law with Edmund Randolph, Thomas Jefferson and Andrew Wythe. He came to Kentucky in 1783 and was immediately appointed as the Kentucky delegate to the Virginia Senate of the Continental Congress. He was Kentucky's first U.S. representative in 1789-1792 (representing Virginia) and Kentucky's first U.S. senator from 1892 to 1805.

Liberty Hall was at the heart of Kentucky political life. Many of the early sessions debating and writing the Kentucky Constitution were held in this house. Liberty Hall was host to Presidents Monroe, Taylor and Jackson. General Lafayette, on his grand tour of the United States in 1825, was entertained by Brown in this home.

Liberty Hall is owned and maintained as a museum by the Colonial Dames of the National Society of the Colonial Dames of America in the Commonwealth of Kentucky.

Lexington
University of Kentucky
Young Library

Even as the enemies of the Kentucky pioneer settlements were attacking, Kentuckians were dreaming of creating a university for the intellectual and professional development of its citizens. In 1780 the Commonwealth of Virginia granted Transylvania Seminary a charter to build an institution of advanced learning in central Kentucky. This charter was the seed that spawned Kentucky's drive toward education excellence.

Transylvania Seminary began in Danville in 1785 but as Lexington proved a more rapidly growing city, Transylvania Seminary moved to Lexington in 1788. However, by 1858, many in Kentucky, who belonged to diverse religious faiths saw that the only way to build support for a successful statewide university was to form a non-sectarian publicly funded college apart from the Transylvania Seminary.

The great visionary, John A. Bowman, led the leading citizens of Lexington to purchase 324 acres of the Henry Clay estate, Ashland, for the development of a state supported university. John A. Bowman became the first chancellor of a newly chartered Kentucky Agricultural and Mechanical College with much of the western half of the Ashland estate as the campus. This quickly gave way to the State College of Kentucky in 1878, the State University of Kentucky in 1908 and the University of Kentucky in 1916. In 1918, as a part of its agrarian mission, the University of Kentucky formed the University of Kentucky Cooperative Extension to provide a framework of higher education throughout rural Kentucky.

The University of Kentucky is recognized throughout the world as a premier research and teaching facility in equine and crop agriculture, medicine, law, architecture and journalism.

Lexington
Waveland, circa 1840
State Historic Shrine

Waveland stands as the historic legacy of the Bryan family of Lexington the founders of Boonesborough in 1774 and Bryan's Station in 1779.

William Morgan Bryan and Mary Boone Bryan followed their famous brother-in-law and brother, Daniel Boone, through the Cumberland Gap to found and fortify the forts at Boonesborough and Bryan's Station. William and Mary Bryan had nine children, one of whom is named Daniel Boone Bryan. Daniel Boone, having completed innumerable surveys of the Bluegrass country, helped to perfect the claim of his nephew, Daniel Boone Bryan, to a 2,000-acre plantation tract he named Waveland.

Waveland Plantation was the premier equine bloodstock operation in Lexington throughout the nineteenth-century. The Bryan family was very prominent in the early development of Lexington's horse-racing culture. At the height of its prestige, Waveland was a model Kentucky plantation: self-sufficient and included horse, cattle, hemp, blacksmith, gunsmith, powder, distilling, gristmill and paper operations. Waveland is now a Kentucky State Shrine that depicts plantation life. Do take a tour of Waveland and meet the Bryan family.

I, Colonel Michael Masters, "The Host of Kentucky" and the author of *Hospitality – Kentucky Style,* am a descendent of the pioneers William Morgan Bryan and Mary Boone Bryan, the parents of Daniel Boone Bryan, the founding master of Waveland Plantation. If you come to know them, you will know me.

Lexington
Old Morrison, Transylvania University, circa 1833
National Historic Landmark

Transylvania University has the distinction of being the first college west of the Allegheny Mountains. Chartered by the Virginia legislature in 1780, Transylvania represented the nascent philosophic and education aspirations of pioneer Kentucky, as the forts and stations at Boonesborough, Danville, Lexington, Harrodsburg and Paris turned their attention to the spritual and academic edification of its citizens.

Over the next half-century, Transylvania became "The Athens of the West" attracting some of the most brilliant scholars in American law, medicine, botany and letters. Early graduates were Jefferson Davis and Cassius Marcellus Clay, "The Lion of Whitehall," men who would, in opposition to each other, shape the destiny of America, defined and resolved by the Civil War.

Old Morrison was commissioned by Colonel James Morrison, a founder of Lexington, and was designed by Gideon Shyrock in the Greek Revival style to house the professional schools of the college. Henry Clay, a professor of law and a trustee of Transylvania, supervised the construction. Old Morrison was, alternately, a hospital for the Confederate and Union armies during the Civil War as these forces traversed Kentucky.

Lexington
Lexington National Cemetery
National Register of Historic Places

The Lexington Cemetery is a beautiful pastoral burying ground set in the heart of Lexington. This national cemetery embraces much of the history of this Southern city as it developed from a Kentucky frontier station, to a political center of American western expansion, to the axis of the Civil War maelstrom in Kentucky. Within this national cemetery lie the mortal remains of many of the heroic political and military figures in Kentucky history. Many of the pioneer founders of Lexington also have found their rest within the walls of the Lexington Cemetery.

Levi Todd, the grandfather to Mary Todd Lincoln and one of the five original delegates to the first Kentucky constitutional convention held in Danville, is here. Robert Todd, her father, is also here.

The Henry Clay Monument, a limestone column of 120 feet, capped by a statue of "The Great Compromiser," is just beyond the cemetery gate. This massive monument is a fitting and stirring tribute to the man who variously represented Kentucky for fifty years in Congress and who ran for president in 1824, 1832 and1844.

The Civil War tore Kentucky families apart, often pitting brother against brother. Both Confederate and Union soldiers rest within the hallowed grounds of the Lexington Cemetery. The Confederate general and vice president of the United States, John Cabell Breckinridge, is entombed here, as well as General John Hunt Morgan, the "Confederate Raider." Morgan's brother-in-law, Basil Duke, who assumed command of Morgan's Raiders after the general's death in 1864, wrote the history of the mounted troop. Duke is here also.

Kentucky women led the national suffrage movement at the end of the nineteenth-century. Sophonisba Breckinridge, Madeline McDowell Breckinridge and Laura Clay were founders of the Kentucky Equal Rights Amendment, awesome women in their time. One of the four founders of the Daughters of the American Revolution, Mary DeSha, has a monument in the Lexington Cemetery. These women transcend their era and are giant figures in Kentucky and American constitutional history, and they are interred in the Lexington Cemetery.

"Throughout the South great sorrow followed the Civil War as families faced reconstruction without their fathers, husbands and sons."

—Lexington Cemetery

Lexington
Hopemont, The Hunt-Morgan House, circa 1814

This house is the family home of General John Hunt Morgan (1825-1864), the "Thunderbolt of the Confederacy." Morgan led his Lexington Rifle Company to the Confederate cause in 1861. This mounted cavalry played havoc with Union supply lines, conducting warfare operations throughout the Western theater of the war. After fighting in the Battle of Shiloh, the Lexington Rifles became the 2nd Kentucky Cavalry. This troop destroyed rail lines, bridges and tunnels and stored Union material throughout Kentucky and Tennessee.

Morgan's raids, battle escapes and engagements are part of Kentucky military folklore. His dashing Confederate persona, coupled with his stunning victories against far superior Union forces, have assured him an honored place in the heart of the South and in the soul of Kentucky. He was killed in Greenville, Tennessee, in 1864.

Hopemont, The Hunt-Morgan House, has a substantial holding of nineteenth-century Kentucky oil paintings and is the home of the Alexander T. Hunt Civil War Museum. Hopemont is such a serious museum for furnishings during the Kentucky Antebellum period that it is a must-see.

The house and the museum are owned by the Blue Grass Trust for Historic Preservation.

General John Hunt Morgan,
"Thunderbolt of the Confederacy"
Lexington - Old Courthouse Lawn

Lexington
Mary Todd Lincoln House, circa 1803
National Register of Historic Places

Mary Todd, the future wife of President Abraham Lincoln, moved to this house in 1832 when she was thirteen years old. Her parents, Robert Todd and Mary Parker Todd, were descended from the founding families of Lexington; her grandfather, Levi Todd, along with Robert Patterson, was one of the founders of Lexington who named the town after hearing that the Colonials had engaged British regular troops at Concord and Lexington, Massachusetts.

Mary Todd's family was prosperous and politically influential. The presidential aspirations of Henry Clay, who "would rather be right than president"; the abolitionist views of Cassius Marcellus Clay; and the presence of the leading political minds in Kentucky were all a part of the life of this household.

Mary Todd Lincoln (1818-1882) was fluent in several romance languages and well-read in history and classical literature. She was acclaimed in her day as a brilliant woman and one of the better educated women in the South. Observers of her generation often surmised that her husband's political career was ably guided and nurtured by the astute mind and political connections of his wife, Mary Todd Lincoln.

The Civil War had a devastating effect on Mary Todd Lincoln. Her husband was commander-in-chief of the Union; her three brothers were Confederate officers. In 1863, she brought her sister, Emile Todd Helm, the widowed wife of Confederate General Benjamin Hardin Helm, who was killed at the Battle of Chickamauga, to the White House to live. President Lincoln's political opposition gave him many a sleepless night over allegations that his wife was sympathetic to the South and therefore a traitor to the North. But, Mary Todd Lincoln was a steadfast Unionist and an important political adviser to her husband in the two decades before the outbreak of Civil War. Her life became a personification of the political rift and sectional schism tearing apart Kentucky families during the Civil War.

The great Civil War killed Mary Todd Lincoln's extended family. Her husband was assassinated while sitting at her side in Ford's Theater. Three of her four sons died prematurely; her remaining son was hostile toward her late in her life. Her Kentucky wealth was consumed by the war. The radical Yankee administration that followed the conciliatory Lincoln's death wreaked revenge upon her because of her Southern birth, initially denying her a pension and leaving her penniless for several years after the war. Mary Todd Lincoln's episodes of depression and mania are cited by some as evidence of an unstable personality after the Civil War.

Be kind and gentle toward Mary Todd Lincoln. Her mood and mind-set reflected that of our commonwealth and our nation, split in half. Mary Todd Lincoln went to the White House a triumphal Kentucky belle and left a broken and battle-scarred Southern lady. She deserves all the sympathy a Kentuckian can muster and all the honor that can be bestowed upon an extraordinary daughter of Kentucky.

The Mary Todd Lincoln House is the first house in the United States to honor a first lady. Kentucky pays tribute to Beulah Nunn, the wife of Kentucky Governor Louie Nunn, for saving this property and acting as this home's angel of restoration. The Mary Todd Lincoln House is replete with period furnishings, many of which have come back to the home from the Todd and Lincoln families. It is a precious Kentucky treasure.

The Mary Todd Lincoln House is owned by the Commonwealth of Kentucky and operated by the Kentucky Mansions Preservation Foundation Inc.

Lexington
Ashland, circa 1806
National Historic Landmark

Henry Clay, the "Great Compromiser," built this house and developed this estate from 1806 until his death in 1852. Clay's wife, Lucretia, is credited with managing the estate during the political absences of her husband. The plantation excelled in the science of livestock breeding, a lifelong pursuit of Clay's; he imported European sheep and cattle to improve the American stock.

Ashland was designed in the Federal style by the nation's first architect, Benjamin Henry Latrobe, who also designed the John Pope House in Lexington. Later work included Italianate accents by the architect Thomas Lewinski. The current house is a reconstruction of Henry Clay's original house, an endeavor undertaken by his son, James Brown Clay, after his father's death. The 300 acres that surround Ashland were sold by Henry Clay's heirs in 1917 as "the Ashland Addition," a subdivision of property by the renowned Olmstead brothers, who gained national attention as the developers of Central Park in New York and the system of parks in Louisville.

Henry Clay (1777-1852) was a towering figure in Kentucky and American politics for more than fifty years. He was a seven-term U.S. representative and for fourteen years Speaker of the House. He served in Congress under seven presidents. He ran for president of the United States three times, losing his last race to James K. Polk his greatest political disappointment.

His political years, 1799-1852, were the years that questioned and tested many of the rights and truths that Americans hold precious. He stood for a strong union, the gradual emancipation of slaves and a federal system of roads and canals. The principle of the federal government's constitutional authority over all the states was a strong political tenet in the industrialized North. The Northern states held fundamentally that the United States was a union of states and that Congress could establish laws for all the states. The agrarian South diametrically opposed this view, maintaining that the individual states created the federal government, and, therefore, the states were sovereign and could opt out of the Union. At the center of the controversy was the abolition of slavery. Henry Clay's Compromise of 1850 was an attempt to preserve the Union and to prevent a schism along Northern and Southern sectional lines.

Ashland is owned by the Henry Clay Memorial Foundation as a historic house museum.

Clay gave two gifts to the nation, as he articulated and framed the important questions of the day. He stood strong for the supremacy of federal constitutional law, which brought the issue of slavery into open political debate, and he was available to Abraham Lincoln early in his career as a political mentor. Clay's federal and abolition principles and his failed attempts at compromise in 1850 helped Lincoln answer the question of whether our nation should be governed by a federal government and the U.S. Constitution or by the laws enacted by each state. Clay's political and philosophical principles were the bedrock of Lincoln's resolve that the United States be free of slavery and one nation.

"I can with unshaken confidence appeal to the Divine arbiter for the truth of the declaration that I have been influenced by no impure purpose, no personal motive, have sought no personal aggrandizement. But that in all my public acts, I have had a sole and single eye and a warm devoted heart, directed and dedicated to what in my best judgement, I believe to be the true interest of my country."

—Henry Clay, 1852
Inscription upon his sarcophagus, ensconced
within the Henry Clay Memorial in the Lexington Cemetery

Lexington
General John Cabell Breckinridge, CSA

There are a few families in the history of Kentucky that have shaped and formed our commonwealth and have left a legacy of honorable service shining infinitely bright. John Cabell Breckinridge (1821-1875) was from one of these families. He served Kentucky in the U.S. Congress as a representative and senator, then as vice president under James Buchanan, 1856-1860. He ran for president on the Southern Democratic ticket in 1860 and was defeated by the Republican Abraham Lincoln.

Feeling that the South needed to secede from the union to form an independent nation, Breckinridge left the Senate to accept a Confederate States commission as general. He fought in the battles of Shiloh, Baton Rouge, Murfreesboro, Chattanooga and New Market. In February 1864, he was appointed secretary of war in the cabinet of President Jefferson Davis. He arranged for the surrender of the Army of Tennessee in North Carolina, the evacuation of Richmond under siege and the evacuation of the Confederate government to Georgia.

To identify the Breckinridge relations is to recount many of the leading forces in our Kentucky political, education, religion and constitutional life during its first century.

The Kentucky Breckinridge progeny has defined our Kentucky life. In politics and education we look to the pioneer legislator John Breckinridge; his sons, Joseph Cabell and Robert Jefferson Breckinridge; his grandsons, General John Cabell Breckinridge, William Campbell Breckinridge and Robert Jefferson Breckinridge; his great-grandson, Clifton Rodes Breckinridge; and his great-great-grandson John Bayne Breckinridge. In the battle for women's rights, we find Sophonisba Breckinridge and her sister-in-law Madeline McDowell Breckinridge. In the founding of the Frontier Nursing Service, we find Mary Breckinridge. The history of the Breckinridge family is a Kentucky treasure. Discover them through your reading. I am proud to have known them and proud to have known of them.

General John Cabell Breckinridge
Lexington - Old Court House Lawn

Lexington
Keeneland Race Course
National Historic Landmark

Keeneland, the plantation of the Keene family, originated as a land grant, signed by Patrick Henry and awarded to John Keene for his service as an officer with LaFayette during the Revolutionary War. Keeneland Plantation remained in the Keene family until 1936, when it was sold to the Keeneland Association for development of the Keeneland Race Course. The purpose of Keeneland is to promulgate premier Thoroughbred breeding, training and racing in a pastoral setting that presents "horse racing as it was meant to be."

I have made an annual pilgrimage to Keeneland every year of my adult life. I come in the spring to bask in the sun and to walk amongst the hundreds of leafing hardwood trees and the great privet hedges. I come to enjoy the limestone-facade clubhouse. I come to sip fine aged Kentucky bourbon whisky in a gloriously genteel setting. I come to stand at the "Keeneland green" rail at the track's edge next to breeders, trainers, groomsmen, jockeys and racehorse fans, all of us pressed together watching the horses run.

Between races, as one turns from the elegance and beauty of hard running, magnificent horse flesh, one becomes aware of the human pageantry. Beautiful women and gallant men from Kentucky and around the world are at Keeneland throughout the spring race meeting, resplendent in colorful, flowing spring dress and sporting attire. Listen to the old Colonel. If you miss the spring meet at Keeneland, you miss much and have only yourself to blame.

Georgetown
Kentucky Horse Park

The park is dedicated to the celebration of the horse in a beautiful horse-farm setting. The American Saddlebred Museum is on the park grounds, as is the International Museum of the Horse, the largest equestrian museum in the world. The magnificent Thoroughbred stallion, Man O' War, winner of 20 of 21 races, is buried here, along with Isaac Murphy, the greatest jockey of all time, who won 628 of 1,412 races. Both the horse and the rider are honored with memorials worthy of a visit.

The Kentucky Horse Park is owned by the people of the Commonwealth of Kentucky.

Carlisle
Blue Licks Battlefield
State Historic Shrine, State Park.

Daniel Boone had followed the path, known as the Buffalo Trace, to the salt deposits at Blue Licks and had shown these deposits to the leaders of the stations. Boone knew this Licking River crossing intimately. He had rescued his daughter, Jemima, and her friend, Flanders Calloway, from Indian capture at the Blue Licks in 1776. In 1778, while boiling down salt, Boone was captured by Indians, who used the low-lying hills to hide their presence, though he later escaped. Daniel Boone's knew the Licking River crossing and the topography perfect for ambush.

The infamous and inscrutable Simon Girty, in command of a mixed British and Indian force, had once again attacked Bryan's Station. He had laid siege to Bryan's Station in 1780, killing William Bryan, the station's founder, but was otherwise repulsed. On August 16, 1792, he and his Indian allies attacked Bryan's Station again, finding the same obstinate, determined defense. His retreat this time, however, was different. He wanted to be followed by the militia that had assembled to pursue his mixed force of Canadians, Shawnee, Wyandot, Miami and Cherokee, 400 in number.

Colonel John Todd came from Lexington, Colonel Stephen Trigg and Major Hugh McGary came from Harrodsburg, and Colonel Daniel Boone came from Boonesborough, all leading militiamen, 150 in number. Colonel Benjamin Logan from Logan's Station was mounted and a day away.

Following the Simon Girty ruse, the Kentuckians approached the area known as the Lower Blue Licks and spotted several Indians. Boone cautioned the troop to wait for Logan, the better to flank the enemy he felt certain lay behind hills along the banks of the Licking. Todd and Trigg agreed with Boone, but McGary, renowned as vain and fierce, derisively spurred the advice and counsel of his fellow officers. He insinuated that the caution was cowardice and drove his horse into the Licking River. The ambush was complete. In a matter of moments, the guns of Simon Girty and his marauders were emptied into the Kentuckians. The Kentuckians, barely able to volley, waist deep in the river water, fought unprotected and in the open against an entrenched enemy. Seeing the matter hopeless Boone ordered the force to retreat.

That day, 77 of the 150 Kentucky militia were slaughtered, devastating an already slender defense of the Kentucky frontier. The men at Blue Licks died in a moment of heated judgement. The Battle at Blue Licks was the worst defeat suffered by the Kentuckians on the frontier and was the last major engagement in the Revolutionary War.

Honor the Blue Licks Battlefield; honor the Kentuckians that perished there; honor August 19, 1782.

Perryville
Perryville Battlefield
State Shrine, National Historic Landmark

President Jefferson Davis was anxious to bring a Confederate army to Kentucky. The immense popularity of General John Hunt Morgan, "The Thunderbolt of the Confederacy," and General John Cabell Breckinridge the former vice president of the United States, both prominent citizens of Lexington, seemed to ensure the recruitment of many soldiers to the cause of Southern freedom. Davis knew, as did President Abraham Lincoln, that the Southern fortunes in this civil conflict depended upon Kentucky's siding solidly with Confederate arms. As Lincoln said so often, "To lose Kentucky is to lose the war."

In the summer of 1862, Kentucky was in a severe state of drought. The streams were dry, the land long gone to dust. The heat was still oppressive from the remaining days of summer. A Confederate army led by General Kirby Smith marched on Lexington and Frankfort, sending the legislature and the state government to Louisville. Confederate General Braxton Bragg's army came up from the west and marched toward Louisville. Union General Don Carlos Buell in Louisville sent 20,000 men to engage Smith in central Kentucky while he sent 50,000 men to Bardstown to engage Bragg's rebel forces. Both sides skirmished throughout September, keeping their adversary from the available water courses still flowing.

The armies collided at Perryville on October 8, 1862. There were no entrenchments, redoubts or barricades for either side. The Confederates threw 18,000 men into the conflagration against the Union's 20,000 — all desperate with thirst. The battle raged all day. As night silenced the guns, the Confederate Army slipped away to escape an overwhelming Union force marching from Bardstown. The carnage was horrible. A full 8,000 American men lay dead and dying. Survivors were cared for in the homes and public buildings of Perryville, Harrodsburg, Danville, Springfield and Bardstown for months after the battle.

I walk the fields of the Perryville Battlefield and try to hear and see the sounds and sights of that day. As I strain to envision that day in Kentucky, I am humbled, and I say a prayer. I pray for the United States, and I pray for America. The Civil War produced about 400 engagements, and of these, about 45 were fought in Kentucky. Honor the sacrifices these combatants made, both Confederate and Union. The men that stood on these firing lines were Americans, every one.

Washington
Simon Kenton Shrine, circa 1790
State Shrine

For the love of early Kentucky, visit Old Washington in the city of Washington, reminisce about this frontier village and imagine the pioneer time in days gone past. There are some fifty log, frame and brick buildings in Old Washington along Main Street that were constructed in the last decade of the eighteenth-century and in the first quarter of the nineteenth-century. The town of Washington was built on land purchased from Simon Kenton, the founder of the town and the in-some-ways-infamous, in-some-ways-illustrious fugitive, hunter, trapper, Indian fighter and Revolutionary War hero.

The state shrine to Kenton, the pathfinder, frontiersman, friend and companion to Daniel Boone, is in Old Washington, a very historic, venerable village. The Simon Kenton Shrine is disarmingly simple for one of Kentucky's truly monumental historical figures. Kenton explored the central Kentucky region throughout the 1760s. He was a solitary longhunter who followed and mapped the watercourses and noted the salt deposits and the geographical detail along the buffalo trails. Boone, challenged to explore Kentucky by the tales woven by the wandering Kenton, led the initial migration that would culminate in the settlement of Kentucky.

Old Washington is a Kentucky jewel of a living museum. Preserved is Mefford's Station, 1787; the birthplace of Confederate General Albert Sidney Johnson, 1797; the Marshall Key House, 1807, which houses the Harriet Beecher Stowe Slavery to Freedom Museum; the first U.S. Post Office west of the Allegheny Mountains, 1789; and many other interesting log and frame structures. Old Washington allows us to visualize the way a Kentucky frontier town developed, creating centers of government, justice, commerce, education and religion.

In recognizing Kenton, I find I also want to mention John Findley, "The Pathfinder." I raise the name of Findley in the shadow of Kenton, as both were extremely important to Boone in his early explorations of the Kentucky frontier. Findley made numerous solitary trading trips to Kentucky in the late 1750's, passing into the region by way of the Ohio River and by way of Dr. Thomas Walker's route through the Cumberland Gap. It is Findley who introduced Boone to the Cumberland Gap in 1769.

Paris
Duncan Tavern, circa 1788

uncan Tavern, situated on the Paris public square, is a wonderful old tavern that nurtured the Kentucky frontier with a safe respite, a congenial surrounding in which to debate and settle the land disputes and the political issues of the day. Major Joseph and Anne Duncan built this stone Greek Revival commercial building with walls two feet thick to act as a fortress if confronted with danger and attack. So many of the famous names in Kentucky pioneer and militia history were served at the Duncan Tavern that Anne Duncan named it the "Goddess of Liberty." The names of Boone, Bryan, Clark, Harrod, Todd, Patterson, Logan, and McAfee come to mind. I like to think of them raising a toast to Kentucky before the handsome fireplace.

The Duncan Tavern and the Anne Duncan House attached to it are owned by the Kentucky Chapter of the Daughters of the American Revolution. These fiercely proud and dignified women take great care in preserving the Duncan Tavern. They give the Duncan Tavern a place of patriotic honor by remembering for the benefit of all of us the history, the deeds and the exploits of those who fought for Kentucky and for America in the cause of liberty and freedom.

The Duncan Tavern also maintains an extensive genealogy library on Bourbon County families. The great Kentucky author John Fox Jr. was born near Paris, and his literary work and life are celebrated in the library named in his honor. I have appreciated his novels and recommend *The Kentuckians, Hell-Fer-Sartain, The Little Shepherd of Kingdom Come* and *The Trail of the Lonesome Pine.*

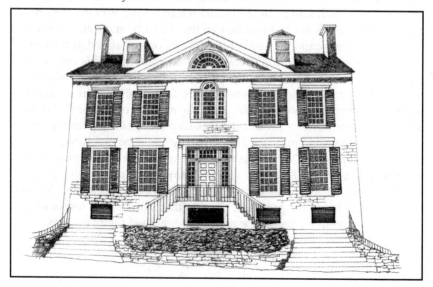

Richmond
White Hall, circa 1840
State Shrine and State Historic Site

The home of Cassius Marcellus Clay (1810-1903), the "Lion of White Hall," was designed by Thomas Lewinsky. Clay was a highly educated man of his time, having attended St. Joseph College in Bardstown, Transylvania University in Lexington and Yale University in New Haven, Connecticut. He began his career as an officer in the army leading Kentucky troops into battle in the Mexican War. He returned from that engagement a hero, famous among his Kentucky command as a courageous soldier.

Even in his college days, Clay's inflammatory abolitionist speeches branded him as an anti-slavery force to be reckoned with. Clay's combative, fierce and abrasive countenance led him to fire in more than a hundred duels. Clay termed himself a duelist, and in five or six instances, he caused the death of his opponent. An incident in 1849 had him charged with incitement to riot and murder when a political opponent pushed to an agitated heat of passion by Clay's emancipation rhetoric, initiated a brawl with him, stabbing Clay in the side. Clay responded by cutting his assailant from "throat to belly" with a small knife he kept in his boot, resulting in the assailant's death. His lawyer, cousin Henry Clay, convinced a jury to dismiss the charge on grounds of self-defense.

Cassius Marcellus Clay was a fearless abolitionist, having spoken against "that vile institution" in the twenty years before the advent of the Civil War. His newspaper in Lexington, *The True American*, so enraged his slaveholding contemporaries that his life was in constant danger. In typical Clay fashion, he met the threat by mounting several four-pound brass cannons inside his editorial offices aimed at the front door. Clay's strong abolitionist stance; his connections to his cousin, Henry Clay, the most important politician of his era; and his political support of Abraham Lincoln were very useful to the election of Lincoln to the presidency in 1860. In 1860, after the election of Lincoln, Clay led a Union civilian force to protect the U.S. Capitol against an imminent Confederate invasion until the Federal army could be mobilized.

Lincoln rewarded Clay for his unwavering support, appointing him minister of Russia in 1863. Clay was brilliant in that post, matching the arrogance of Czar Nicholas Alexander II. When commanded by the czar to remove his hat in his presence, Clay, without hesitation, responded that he only removed his hat for men who removed theirs for him.

White Hall was originally named Clermont and was the Federalist-style home of General Green Clay, a hero of the Revolutionary War who built an empire in central Kentucky of landholdings, gristmills, distilleries, ferries and goods transport. The rooms of Clermont are the interior rooms of White Hall, as Green Clay's son, Cassius Marcellus Clay, and his wife, Mary Jane Warfield, expanded the mansion to forty-four rooms to form the Italianate mansion.

It is inevitable that our observations are concentrated in the last measure of a person's life. Cassius Marcellus Clay was a magnificent Kentuckian, full of fight and fury. He was Kentuckian that spent his life looking for a fight, be it over a perceived insult or a constitutional injustice.

I am charmed by his wife, Mary Jane Warfield Clay. She was married to "The Lion of White Hall" for almost half a century, divorced him and participated in the women's suffrage movement that seemed to revolve around the Clays and Breckinridges of Lexington and Richmond. I have come to know her daughter, Laura Clay; Madeline McDowell Breckinridge, a grandaughter of Henry Clay; and her sister-in-law, Sophonisba Preston Breckinridge. All were central in the exciting national civil-rights movement of equal rights for women at the beginning of the twentieth-century.

Fort Boonesborough, circa 1775 replica State Park

The original Fort Boonesborough was built by Daniel Boone; his brother, Squire Boone; his brother-in-law, William Bryan; and others in April 1775 as the first fortified settlement in Kentucky. In May 1775, Richard Henderson, head of the Colony of Transylvania, held the first legislative assembly of the frontier settlements at Boonesborough under "the Divine Elm," along with delegates from Harrodsburg, St. Asaph and Boiling Springs. In October 1779, Fort Boonesborough became the first town to be chartered in Kentucky by the Virginia Assembly. Boonesborough was under constant attack from 1775 to 1882 and received settlers from the other stations during times of danger through 1818.

The town of Boonesborough did not survive past the middle of the nineteenth century, as Lexington and Winchester proved better crossroads to trade and migration. The present-day Fort Boonesborough is a historically accurate replica of the early fortress that received thousands of pioneers as they traversed the Wilderness Road. As a bastion of defense of the Kentucky frontier, Fort Boonesborough stands as a testament to Kentucky pioneer courage and resolve. That this small, log-hewn, picketed fort, defended by pioneer men, women and children, could stand against the weight of the British and Indian forces amassed and hurled against it for nearly forty years is almost beyond our ability to imagine. I honor this place and those pioneer ancestors of our great commonwealth.

Daniel Boone by Enid Yandell
Louisville, Cherokee Park,
Richmond, EKU Campus

Danville
McDowell House, circa 1786
National Historic Landmark

Dr. Ephraim McDowell (1771-1830) is known as "The Father of American Surgery" and was an eminent physician and teacher of medicine. In 1809, he performed the first successful laparotomy, abdomen surgery, on the second floor of this house. The Kentucky Medical Society purchased and restored McDowell House in the 1930s.

Danville
Old Centre, circa 1820

Built by the Greek Revival architect Robert Russel Jr. for Centre College, Old Centre is the oldest college building in the South. Centre College was founded by pioneer Kentuckians in 1819.

Danville
Jacobs Hall, circa 1855
Kentucky School for the Deaf
National Historic Landmark

Jacobs Hall is significant in the history of Kentucky. The settlement of Kentucky was hard. The Indians tried to destroy pioneer families with attacks launched from their compounds in the Ohio country. The British attempted to eradicate the Kentucky stations and forts from their strongholds in Canada. The lawyers came to seize Kentucky land titles that were won by pioneer hardship by obfuscating Kentucky surveys and land claims from their offices in Richmond. But in spite of all these travails, the Kentucky pioneer fought for a homeplace and yearned to be educated and spiritually elevated. Transylvania College in Lexington and Centre College in Danville were expressions of those needs.

The aspiration to found institutions of higher learning was strong in pioneer Kentucky. Transylvania Seminary was organized in 1780, even before cessation of hostilities with Britain. Classes began in Danville in 1785, but because of political necessity, Transylvania moved to Lexington in 1788. Centre College was established in 1819, with Isaac Shelby as chairman and his son-in-law, Dr. Ephraim McDowell, as board member. Centre College, as part of its mission, established the Kentucky School for the Deaf.

In 1824, the learned McDowell had used his political connection with Henry Clay to found and finance the Kentucky School for the Deaf. Jacobs Hall was designed to house the school and was built by John McMurtry and his son-in-law Thomas Lewinsky, the architects of White Hall. Jacobs Hall was the first building in the United States built specifically for the education of the deaf. Jacobs Hall was named to honor John Adamson Jacobs, who studied deaf education under Thomas Gallaudet in Hartford, Connecticut, and was superintendent of the school in its first forty years.

Jacobs Hall represents an early Kentucky desire to build exquisite institutions of higher learning. The Kentucky School for the Deaf has been independent of Centre College for over a century.

Danville
Constitution Square, circa 1782
State Historic Site

Virginia statute created the first Kentucky circuit court in 1785. Many of the initial sessions of the court were held here. Kentucky felt the need to form its own sovereign state, and many of the constitutional conventions were held at Boonesborough, Harrodsburg and on Constitution Square in Danville. The first courthouse west of the Allegheny Mountains was of log construction and is located on Constitution Square. Tradition holds that Danville boasted several taverns by 1785, thereby creating a properly hospitable environment for the vexing state constitution negotiations.

The Statesman and the Pioneer
Constitution Square, Danville

Stanford
Isaac Shelby Cemetery at Traveler's Rest, circa 1782
State Historic Site, State Shrine

Traveler's Rest was built by General Isaac Shelby (1750-1826), Kentucky's first and fifth governor and the leading officer in General George Rogers Clark's campaigns against the Indian in the Northwest Territory. Shelby stands as one of the founding fathers of Kentucky statehood; he sat as the first chairman of the first meeting of the Kentucky Constitutional Convention, which led eventually to separation from Virginia. Shelby is revered in Kentucky as a charismatic and gifted leader who lent his enormous military and social prestige to our fledgling, often politically contentious state.

Stanford
Sportsman's Hill, circa 1788
State Historic Site, State Park

Colonel William Whitley came to Kentucky with Colonel John Harrod. He led numerous campaigns against the British and Indians in Kentucky throughout 1776-1782 and provided leadership in defense of the stations during the Year of the Savage Sevens (1777). He led troops with General George Rogers Clark in the Northwest Indian campaigns in the 1780s, and he commanded a brigade of troops to the Tennessee Territory, defeating hostile Indian tribes. In 1813, at the age of sixty-three, Whitley volunteered to lead troops against the British and Indians in the Ohio country. He led the charge against Tecumseh at the Battle of the Thames. Both these great leaders were killed that day, October 5, 1813. Whitley is the personification of the Kentucky pioneer, "half man, half bear and all hell when trifled with."

Whitley laid out the first oval racetrack in Kentucky at Sportsman's Hill and, hating all things British, used clay instead of turf and ran the race counterclockwise, opposite to the British direction. Both practices stand today as traditional American racing formats. Sportsman's Hill is believed to be the first substantial house of brick construction in Kentucky. The escape hallways and hiding places from Indian attack should the walls be breached are very interesting.

The Commonwealth of Kentucky owns Sportsman's Hill and operates the site as a memorial to Kentucky frontier life. The house has a large collection of furnishings from the period.

Harrodsburg
Fort Harrod, circa 1774 replica
State Historic Site, State Park

Harrodsburg was the first settlement in Kentucky to become permanent. The fortification was erected by Colonel James Harrod and thirty of his followers and received the first families in September 1774. Fort Harrod was under continual attack by Indians from 1775 to 1786. Harrod accompanied General George Rogers Clark on his extremely arduous campaigns against the Indians in the Northwest Territories throughout the 1780s. Harrod also fortified Boiling Spring, the tract he claimed for his family home.

Fort Harrod dedicates many of the blockhouses and cabins inside the fort to Kentucky historical firsts that transpired at this fort and to the events and people that made Fort Harrod so critical to the Kentucky frontier. There are cabins dedicated to Clark, the first school and the first settler. One cabin is dedicated to the Bryan women, who left the Bryan Station fortification near Lexington to fetch water under the guns of the British and Indians during the Siege of Bryan's Station in August 1782.

Harrod, the legendary Kentucky commander, settler and Indian fighter, disappeared in 1792, having failed to return from a solitary hunting trip. His disappearance led to speculation that he encountered hostile Indian forces prowling the area.

There is a great national monument adjacent to the fort. It is a massive granite wall that honors in stone relief the arrival of Clark and the pioneers who faithfully followed him to Kentucky.

"Great things have been affected by a few men well conducted."

General George Rogers Clark

Harrodsburg
The Mansion Museum, circa 1830

The Mansion Museum is inside the Fort Harrod State Park and houses an interesting collection of early pioneer and Indian artifacts, as well as a collection of items pertaining to Abraham Lincoln. There is a pioneer weapons exhibit and a collection of Civil War relics. The Mansion is a fine museum of early American percussion and flintlock rifles and shotguns.

The Mansion is a beautiful restoration of the kind of Greek Revival manor house so popular and prevalent in antebellum Kentucky.

The Mansion Museum is under the direction of the Harrodsburg Historical Society.

Harrodsburg
Shakertown, circa 1824
National Historic Landmark

The Trustee House is part of the Shaker community at Pleasant Hill, one of the many major buildings still standing, along with numerous auxiliary buildings and outbuildings. The entire 2,700-acre boundary of Pleasant Hill constitutes the National Historic Landmark. The Shaker Kentucky communities, founded in 1806 at Pleasant Hill and in 1807 at South Union, were two of nineteen Shaker communities in the United States.

The Shaker communal life was a remarkable social experiment. Each family of "Believers" lived a life of shared property, shared labor and shared belief. The Shakers envisioned a high standard of industry and craftsmanship as their gift to God. Their handcrafted goods were prized for their quality and are still appreciated and sought by collectors today. The Shakers derived their name from their practice of vigorous "shaking and whirling" during their church services.

The Civil War decimated the pacifist Shaker community at Pleasant Hill. The Union and Confederate forces consumed the existing stores of meat and grain and appropriated all of the standing livestock, farm implements and tools. Situated within ten miles of the Perryville Battlefield, the Shaker community, with its 200 buildings, became a major field hospital and convalescent center for years after the battle was over, draining the remainder of the community's resources.

Celibacy and a failure to attract new members to the Shakers' austere lifestyle hastened the decline and end of the Society of Believers nationally. By 1912, Pleasant Hill had ceased operations.

Harrodsburg
Beaumont Inn, circa 1845

The Beaumont Inn is a great Kentucky mansion, built on a massive scale. The mansion was built in 1845, a time of affluence and economic prosperity for Harrodsburg. It was originally Greenville Institute, a proprietary school for the education of young ladies. In 1855 the mansion became Daughter's College, then in 1905 Beaumont College, both finishing schools of higher learning. The Dedman family has operated the mansion as the Beaumont Inn since 1918.

Beaumont Inn is the personification of Kentucky hospitality. It is located in the town that is Kentucky's oldest permanent settlement and a town that is one of Kentucky's architectural gems. Harrodsburg is replete with scores of wonderful old Federalist and Greek Revival homes, and the Beaumont Inn is of this style. The Southern grace practiced within the halls and rooms of this famous, historic hotel is internationally well known and appreciated. The Beaumont Inn has provided its guests with a respite that represents the best in Kentucky courtesy and manners.

When I find myself at the Beaumont Inn, I find a quiet pleasure sitting in the voluminous Kentucky-antique-appointed parlors. To dine upon the wonderful Kentucky fare of fried chicken, baked country ham, corn pudding, baked cheese grits and sweet potatoes in the wonderful old dining room endears me to the Beaumont Inn. I assure you, the Beaumont Inn is vintage Kentucky.

Kentucky Pioneer Spirit
Kentucky Confederate Stand
Kentucky Union Honor

For thousands of years, Kentucky had been the "dark and bloody ground" as indigenous tribes of American Indians followed and hunted the migrating herds of buffalo and elk. Inevitably, these hunter-warriors came into contact with each other with each tribe bent upon reserving the hunting ground for itself. The Indian tradition of annihilating competing human intrusion into Kentucky was well established by the time Daniel Boone and James Harrod led the first pioneer settlers to Fort Harrod and Boonesborough in 1774 and 1775. The settlement of Kentucky by men and women intent upon building permanent forts and stations along the big-game migration routes known as the Wilderness Road and the Warrior's Path placed every pioneer family at the crossroad of Indian attack.

The American move to separate from English rule in 1776 wrecked havoc on the Kentucky frontier, as the English allied with the Indian tribes in the Ohio and Illinois country to incite a savage war designed to destroy the forts and stations. For forty years Kentucky was under continual attack from marauding Indians, and due to geographic isolation, also from the starving, desperate, murderous brigands that roamed the land, preying upon the pioneer families traveling to Kentucky.

Kentucky and its commonwealth of citizens, as a result of these dangers and travails developed into a fierce, self-reliant populace. Because they were politically remote from the federal seat of power, Kentuckians exercised justice and government in a robust, vociferous manner at the county courthouse. The people of the commonwealth were Kentuckians by birth and allegiance and American by constitutional affinity.

In 1861 the secession of the Southern states from the American Union brought on conflicting sentiment. Families split along political lines. Forty thousand Kentuckians joined the Union army; 20,000 joined the Confederate army. The issue of whether the American states would unite or separate into northern and southern nations would be decided by an ensuing war between the sections.

The Union forces prevailed at egregious cost to Kentucky. Many of our fathers and sons perished in that conflict, and the Kentucky economy was destroyed as the Union victor imposed a cruel, oppressive Reconstruction government upon Kentucky. The issues of that politically pivotal American conflict have been resolved. It is proper that Kentucky honor our Kentucky fallen Confederate and Union ancestors.

Remember and Honor the Kentucky Forts and Stations

The forts and stations defended the Kentucky frontier at enormous sacrifice. So many of our Kentucky fathers, mothers, sons and daughters perished and were saved at the walls of these Kentucky wilderness outposts. Following are the forts and the stations, along with the years they were built.

Harrodsburg, 1774	Corn Island, 1778
Boonesborough, 1775	Fort-on-Shore, 1778
McClelland's Station, 1775	Louisville, 1779
Leestown, 1775	Spring Fort, 1779
Boiling Spring, 1775	Fort William, 1779
Ruddle's Station, 1775	Beargrass Station, 1779
Logan's Station, 1775	Floyd's Station, 1779
Crow's Station, 1775	Painted Stone, 1779
Martin's Station, 1777	A'Sturgus Station, 1780
Bryan's Station. 1779	Fort Nelson, 1781
Lexington Blockhouse, 1779	Chenoweth Station, 1781
McAfee's Station, 1779	Rogers' Station, 1775
Limestone, 1779	Brashear's Station, 1779
Linn Station, 1779	Low Dutch Station, 1779
Strode's Station, 1779	Goodin's Fort, 1780
Estill's Station, 1780	Pottinger's Station, 1781
Masterson's Station, 1785	Kincheloe's Station, 1781

Remember the Great Kentucky Battles

These were the landmark battles that were fought by Kentuckians and that are properly annotated in historical writings. They are the battles that are easily identified by all of us as the battles that wrestled Kentucky and the Northwest Territory away from the British and the Indians. But be clear on this point: the history so well documented in the great Kentucky battles was acted out anonymously every day at every Kentucky frontier fireside. The fight for survival for every man, woman and child in Kentucky was won and lost on a daily basis in every fort, station and log cabin.

Wabash and Northwest Indian Campaigns of 1789-1794
Boonesborough, 1775-1782, September 1778
Bryan's Station, 1779-1782, August 14-15, 1782
Long Run Creek Massacre, 1781

Logan's Station, 1777	Floyd's Defeat, 1781
Kaskaskia, July 1778	Blue Licks, August 19, 1782
Vincennes, February 1779	Thames, October 5, 1813
Ruddles, 1780	River Raisin, January 22, 1813

The Heroines of Bryan's Station

Up hands, with handkerchiefs awave,
Hearts, thrill with admiration
To-day for women bright and brave
Who lived at Bryan's Station.
Great mother's of the wilderness,
Fair damsels of the forest,
Whose courage grand in men's distress
Relieved when need was sorest.

They came when these in virgin growth
Were seen in wild disorder,
Domain of elk and howling wolf
And Indian marauder;
A land of beauty, Nature's green
By foes held surrounded;
They braved its dangers, cleared its green
And forts and homes were founded.

Their story comes to us adown
The course of many dangers;
Our land has now so far outgrown
It seems the tale of strangers.
The old log forts, the spring and gun
Demand commemoration;
The brave and fair who fought and won
Our cause at Bryan's Station.

When pioneers were close besieged
By savages and Girty,
And Bryan's guard within was hedged,
And scarcely numbered thirty,
The story goes; food almost gone,
No meal was in their pockets,
And worse, they saw at mornings dawn
No water in their buckets.

Men dared not venture out the fort
To reach the spring of water,
So, through the wood, an open court,
Went forth each wife and daughter,
What though the ambushed Indian there
Stood standing back to spear them?

With heads erect and dauntless air,
As though they did not fear them.
No glittering spoil was their reward,
They spurned the foe's condition;
But never knight or plumed lord
More grandly wrought their mission.
The men were few; the fort was lost
If foes saw their prostration;
'Twas life or death at fearful cost---
Thus women saved the station.

They asked not for remembrance when
The scribes at Bryan's Station
Were writing history of the men
Who quashed the Indian nation;
They did not ask a word of praise
For their heroic action,
But nobly passed those war-gloomed days
As God gave them direction.

But pioneers so true at heart,
Thrilled by their dread endeavor,
Told of these angel's part
With gratitude forever.
They left on record their report---
But for those pails of water
All might have perished at the fort
Of famine, thirst, or slaughter.

Note: The poem depicts the heroic effort of the women residing within the fort during the siege of Bryan's Station, Kentucky, that began August 16, 1782. When the water supply was exhausted, the pioneer women heroically carried water from a spring, at a considerable distance from the fort, under the guns of the enemy.

—Mrs. Jennie Chinn Morton

Author's Note: Mary Boone Bryan was the leader of the women carrying the water and is the great grandmother of Col. Michael Masters, seven generations past. The Daughters of the American Revolution erected a stone wall around the spring in 1923. The DAR inscribed the names of the heroines on the stone wall as warriors in the patriotic battle of the Revolutionary War known as the Siege of Bryan's Station.

Kentucky Civil War Monuments

Bardstown	Confederate Monument, St. Joseph's Cemetery
Crab Orchard	Confederate Monument, Crab Orchard Cemetery
Cynthiana	Confederate Monument, Battle Grove Cemetery
Danville	Confederate Soldiers Martyrs Monument, McDowell Park
Eminence	Ky. African Amer. Civil War Veterans, Eminence Cemetery
Fairview	President Jefferson Davis Monument
Frankfort	Confederate Soldier Monument, Green Hill Cemetery
Frankfort	Confederate Monument, Frankfort Cemetery
Georgetown	Confederate Monument, Georgetown Cemetery
Harrodsburg	Civil War Martyrs Monument, Springhill Cemetery
Harrodsburg	Beriah Magoffin Monument, Springhill Cemetery
Jeffersontown	Confederate Memorial, Jeffersontown Cemetery
Lawrenceburg	Ladies' Confederate Mem., Anderson Co. Courthouse
Lexington	Confederate Soldier Monument, Lexington Cemetery
Lexington	General John Hunt Morgan Memorial, Lexington Cemetery
Lexington	General John C. Breckinridge, Old Fayette Co. Courthouse
Lexington	General John Hunt Morgan, Old Fayette County Courthouse
Louisville	General John B. Castleman Monument, Cherokee Road
Louisville	Union Soldiers Monument, Cave Hill Cemetery
Louisville	Cave Hill National Cemetery Confederate and Union Burial
Louisville	General Lovell Rousseau Monument, Cave Hill Cemetery
Louisville	Our Confederate Dead Monument, Third Street at U of L
Midway	Confederate Monument, Midway Cemetery
Mt. Sterling	General Zollicoffer Monument, Maplewood Cemetery
Nicholasville	Confederate Monument, Jessamine County Courthouse
Paris	Unknown Confederate Dead Monument, Paris Cemetery
Perryville	Confederate Monument Battlefield Historic Site
Perryville	Union Monument Battlefield State Historic Site
Pewee Valley	Dutton Hill Monument, Pewee Valley Cemetery
Versailles	Confederate Memorial, Versailles Cemetery

Kentucky Constitution
Ratified on: August 3, 1891;
Revised on September 28, 1891

Preamble

We, the people of the Commonwealth of Kentucky, grateful to Almighty God for the civil, political and religious liberties we enjoy, and invoking the continuance of these blessings, do ordain and establish this Constitution.

Bill of Rights

That the great and essential principles of liberty and free government may be recognized and established, we declare: the rights of life, liberty, worship, pursuit of safety and happiness, free speech, acquiring and protecting property, peaceable assembly, redress of grievances, bearing arms.

All men are, by nature, free and equal, and have certain inalienable rights, among which may be reckoned:

First: The right of enjoying and defending their lives and liberties.

Second: The right of worshipping Almighty God according to the dictates of their consciences.

Third: The right of seeking and pursuing their safety and happiness.

Fourth: The right of freely communicating their thoughts and opinions.

Fifth The right of acquiring and protecting property.

Sixth: The right of assembling together in a peaceable manner for their common good, and of applying to those invested with the power of government for redress of grievances or other proper purposes, by petition, address or remonstrance.

Seventh: The right to bear arms in defense of themselves and of the State, subject to the power of the General Assembly to enact laws to prevent persons from carrying concealed weapons.

Kentucky Fine Foods and Spirits

Kentucky has a worldwide reputation for outstanding hospitality. Each year, the citizens of our commonwealth welcome people from all over the globe to Kentucky to enjoy our horses, our racetracks, our grand hotels, our fabulous parks, our forests and the great wonders of our historical cities and towns. Our visitors come to visit our state shrines at My Old Kentucky Home, Waveland Plantation, Ashland, White Hall, Locust Grove, Boonesborough, Fort Harrod and Isaac Shelby Cemetery. And our guests come to enjoy our fine food and our fine aged Kentucky bourbon whisky.

Kentucky exports hospitality throughout the world. Our distilleries bottle Kentucky hospitality and ask that their patrons enjoy a spirit beverage that has been produced in Kentucky for more than 200 years. This beverage still evokes images of Kentucky Colonels sipping mint juleps with Kentucky ladies under the shade of neo-Grecian columns supporting the elegant verandah. Our racecourses at Churchill Downs and Keeneland embody Kentucky hospitality and are diligent in making their patrons feel that their experience in watching the Thoroughbred horses run is an exceptional day in their life. Our hotels and bed-and-breakfast industry embrace Kentucky hospitality and present an elegant ambience in an atmosphere of courtesy and good manners.

Kentucky has a well-deserved reputation for exceptionally good cooking. Indeed, it would be extremely difficult to discuss Kentucky hospitality without sharing our tradition of simply elegant cooking and entertaining. *Hospitality–Kentucky Style* is a collection of some of the recipes that capture Kentucky's rich culinary history and that contribute to this genre of American cooking.

The Kentucky Gentleman

Gentlemen in Kentucky have often been considered good cooks and hosts. The Kentucky gentleman is a competent cook for the recipes he has embraced, be those recipes for food or libation. The Kentucky gentleman knows how to make guests in his home feel welcome. He knows by tradition that his role is to charm the women and children, to prepare the foods that are associated with him and to tend an excellent bar.

It is a common experience in Kentucky to join your host at breakfast after an overnight stay in the family's home and to be pleasingly surprised that he is baking you his signature breakfast biscuit or baked cheese grits. The family will heap fond praise upon this gentleman as encouragement and to see once again the pride with which he offers his breakfast to those assembled. And you will find, if you have an extended stay, that at every meal, he will prepare one or two of his recipes.

Kentucky gentlemen, polite men of a chivalrous and generous nature, enjoy the privilege of cooking for their family and friends. This is not to say that the foods they prepare are of an intricate nature requiring a great deal of time and forethought. To the contrary, a Kentucky gentleman in the kitchen has recipes that are within his ability to prepare and that, when he presents them at table, bring him rave reviews.

When Margaret Sue and I entertain, many in our extended family prepare the foods that we glowingly acknowledge are their specialties, and they bring them. Everyone looks forward to Margaret Sue's pimiento cheese, Mama Sudie's yeast rolls, Mimi's chocolate sauce, Sue Carol's Benedictine and the Colonel's Beef Masters. On my word I could do it all, but we would miss the convivial spirit of contributed specialties. In my world, praise has an infinite quality.

In the modern day, it is important that we make time for the people with whom we choose to share our lives. We make every attempt to celebrate not only the birthdays and the holidays but also the seasons. In our fast-paced world, all too often, our children, parents, sisters, brothers, cousins and old friends live along every point on the globe.

Kentucky is known worldwide for gracious hospitality. We speak of old friends as being a part of our family, and we hold the out-of-town guests of our friends in the same high regard that we hold the friends they are visiting. On our table is the Kentucky cuisine that our friends and out-of-town guests remember lovingly for the rest of their lives. On our bar is stocked what we consider the finest bourbon.

I have read most of the cookbooks that professional writers have published about Kentucky cuisine. My observation has been that often, the recipes they offer are of a different time. Few people today are going to find attractive any food preparation process that involves intense labor and an extraordinary level of cooking skill to achieve superlative results.

Also, many writers do not entertain in their homes; they therefore tend to report recipes and ways of doing things that were related to them by professional chefs and catering concerns. I have read books about cooking that must have required a dozen staff and multiple layers of editors to bring them to press.

I do not claim to be a chef; this title is reserved for cooks of formal training who possess an academic background in the chemistry and art of food preparation. I rely upon my experience as a host and the training I have received from numerous family and friends, many of whom were exceptionally good Kentucky cooks with great flair in their entertaining. The fact that I was a vice president of a large regional restaurant chain, no doubt, also had considerable influence on me.

You will notice that I accommodate modern sensibilities and, wherever possible, I use food combinations to sweeten and season the foods I cook. When I err from the past, it is usually on the side of olive oil, lemon and ground pepper. In this collection, you will find recipes that are traditional to Kentucky and are easily prepared by anyone who enjoys cooking. I leave the complex recipes to those who have gourmet training.

I have selected the entrées, vegetables, dressings, sauces, breads, salads and desserts that I know are simply great. You do not need many signature recipes to be acknowledged as an excellent cook. The recipes that I enjoy are ones that I can prepare ahead of time or that are simple enough to put together while I socialize with my guests, all of whom crowd into the kitchen, although there are eight other rooms in the house.

In our entertaining at McManus House, our style is to embrace recipes that can be prepared either a few hours or a day before our party. Our way is to enjoy the people in our lives and to welcome them into our home. We have no intention of becoming slaves to the kitchen while the drinks are being poured.

The elegance that characterizes our social occasions is not based upon lavish spending; rather it is in the beautiful presentation of our dining table and bar and the welcoming warmth of our homes. I offer you my recipes and our way of entertaining in the spirit of *Hospitality – Kentucky Style* and wish for you an adventure in *Kentucky Fine Foods and Spirits*.

Entrées

I have dozens of recipes for beef, lamb, chicken, turkey, fish and pork, and during the course of the year, I find time to use a great many of them. My wife has always claimed that at heart I am a grill man, which is true. For family dining, I rarely cook our meat indoors; I cook on the grill in all seasons and all weathers.

But when we entertain, and our guests have traveled great distances to get to us, we want to fix those foods that they have come to remember us by.

The entrée is the centerpiece of our sideboard or buffet table. We choose our entrée based on the climate and the number of guests in our home. All of our recipes are easy to prepare and absolutely delicious. We cook plenty and present the entrée in as grand a fashion as we know how to do.

In our home, the silver serving pieces and crockery do not live to dusty old age in the cabinets. They are brought out at every opportunity to give our entertaining a flair that tells our guests that they are special and important people in our lives.

I feel a great sense of satisfaction when I watch the women of our family hauling out the silver bowls, platters and chafing dishes. There is nary a piece that is similar in style, size or era. Each piece has a history, each a previous owner, or four, all of them known to us, all of them remembered.

Aging Prime and Choice Beef Loin

Kentucky is a cattle state that produces and pastures a very high grade of beef for the world market. In Kentucky, we know that a great steak and proper aging is critical to the process of serving a fork-tender cut of meat. I revel in setting my table with a steak dinner so fine, so tender and so delectable that the meal is talked about for years.

The best steak for aging is graded prime or choice. We like a whole strip, ribeye or tenderloin. The designation of prime or choice is a quality standard defined by the USDA and has to do with meat texture, color and fat marbling. As always, I advocate familiarity with these terms so that you feel competent in seeking the highest possible quality in your meat purchases. Look for fat marbling in the end piece of the whole strip or rib-eye beef loin. For prime, it should be flecked with white fat over about half the surface; for choice, about a quarter of the surface is marbled. The beef you want will appear a light red color with the good marbling characteristic. You will encounter the prime and choice grade often in good meat cases.

I only trust a meat department's grading of beef cuts to the extent that my eyes verify the cut and grade of the meat so labeled. The head of the meat department may have adequate training, but it is almost certain that no one else behind the counter has a whit of knowledge. Verily, however, every employee, from the most recent hire to the butcher, will defend the label demanded by the central office, no matter the rightness of the issue, as if they had a Ph.D. More often these days, I suspect that mislabeling grades of meat upward has more to do with moving excess beef inventories out of Nebraska cold storage lockers than with truth.

The beef you find on sale for impossibly low prices is generally utility grade showing no marbling; in other words, cattle dramatically past their optimal weight, size and age. A lack of marbling usually translates to no taste and tough as strap leather.

To dry age beef, buy the entire loin; wrap in paper toweling. Then wrap in wax paper. Place into the back of the refrigerator. Change the paper toweling each day and change the flat side. Continue this process for 16 days.

To wet age beef, as it is termed, buy the beef loin vacuum pack. Place the beef in the rear area of the refrigerator for 16 days, turning the beef loin each day.

When aged, using either method, remove the loin and slice into 1-1/2-inch steaks. Freeze individually those steaks not consumed for dinner.

Rare Beef Tenderloin

Rare beef tenderloin is always a special dinner. Although I find I cook beef tenderloin on special occasions, I acknowledge a preference for this cut of beef and serve it with little prompting. Cooked to perfection and presented on a silver tray, the beef tenderloin is magnificent.

In our family, we host our holiday dinners on the eve of the actual holiday. This allows our extended family to join us while reserving the holiday for their family and children. Beef tenderloin is our choice for the entrée. The more traditional fare will be served the following afternoon.

We like purchasing a young beef tenderloin that weighs about 4 pounds. When you purchase a beef tenderloin, ask the butcher to trim it for you. If you are in the dark as to what I mean, just let it lay, and take it on faith that the butcher is doing you a favor.

Marinate the beef tenderloin for a day before cooking. We like to use a marinade that consists of equal parts of dry red wine and olive oil. Rest the beef tenderloin in a glass baking dish sized to accommodate the meat. Cover with plastic wrap and place in the refrigerator. Turn the beef tenderloin at least once.

The beef tenderloin I prepare depends on a high roasting temperature; 500 degrees is perfect. I coat the beef tenderloin with butter and place it on a roasting pan or on the cool side of the grill. You will cook the tenderloin for 10 minutes, turning once. You will then cook the beef tenderloin for another 8-10 minutes, depending on your oven or grill, resisting the powerful urge to turn it again. When the beef tenderloin has a hot-red center or is 135 degrees in the thickest part, it is done.

Three minutes before removal, cover the top of the tenderloin with blue cheese and return to the heat, allowing the blue cheese to soften. Grind black pepper generously across the top of the blue cheese.

Slice the tenderloin to a thickness of 1 inch on the diagonal. You will want to serve two or three slices to the plate. Drizzle Masters Steak Sauce sparingly over the tenderloin slices and leave a bowl on the side for those who desire more. I would allow about half a pound of tenderloin per dinner guest, uncooked weight.

Accompany with yeast rolls, asparagus, new potatoes, stuffed eggplant and baked zucchini squash. Vanilla ice cream with chocolate sauce for dessert completes this excellent dinner.

Beef Masters

A good Kentucky cook will have a version of this flavorful stroganoff dish. Do not be lulled into complacency by using inferior cuts of beef. I use strip steak and would use beef tenderloin, nothing less. My dinner guests always come back to the buffet for a second pass. You will have more in the pan after your initial serving, but they will return for more, I promise you. Beef Masters is evening fare and very dignified.

INGREDIENTS

4 oz. wild rice
1 lb. mushrooms, sliced
1 stick butter, cut in half
1 T fine aged Kentucky bourbon whisky
4 8-oz. strip steaks, fat removed, cut into 1-inch pieces
1 C red wine
2 beef-bouillon cubes, dissolved in 2 T hot water
2 T flour, dissolved in 2 T hot water
8 oz. sour cream
2 t seasoning salt
1 t pepper, ground

DIRECTIONS

✔ Cook the wild rice and set aside.
✔ Lightly sauté mushrooms in 1/2 stick of butter and set aside.
✔ Deglaze a skillet with fine aged Kentucky bourbon on a high heat. Add the remaining 1/2 stick of butter and the steak pieces.
✔ Sauté the steak until cooked to a light brown finish.
✔ Turn the heat down to a low setting. Add the wine and the bouillon. Stir in the flour, holding back a little for additional thickening.
✔ Add the mushrooms and stir in the sour cream. It is important that the sour cream be added last, as sour cream breaks down quickly under heat. Stir in the seasoning salt and the pepper.
✔ Simmer for about 5 minutes; add the remaining flour, if necessary. Beef Masters is served thickened. Ladle Beef Masters over the wild rice. Accompany with a large Bibb lettuce salad.
Serves 8.

Bourbon-Glazed Filet of Beef

Your significant other will fall in love with you every time you prepare bourbon-glazed filet of beef. Knowing this always inspires me to cook it on private evenings. I like to cook this dish for two, but it expands nicely to four at dinner, if you cannot find a way to keep company at bay.

When cooking for two, this is an easy dinner to cook while enjoying a fine aged Kentucky bourbon whisky and is further enhanced by a second drink of fine aged Kentucky bourbon whisky while dining. After the dinner and dessert, send the guests home, if you have them—for the evening has just begun!

INGREDIENTS
2 6-oz. filets of beef
1/2 C butter
4 oz. fine aged Kentucky bourbon whisky
pepper, ground

DIRECTIONS
✔ Sauté the filet of beef in the butter on a high heat until medium rare and place the beef tenderloin on the dinner plate.
✔ Deglaze the pan with a fine aged Kentucky bourbon, and using a spoon, make certain you capture the beef-butter
✔ Pour the glaze over the beef tenderloin. Grind black pepper onto the beef tenderloin and serve immediately.
Serves 2. Double to serve 4.

Meat Loaf

I do not care that I am derided for enjoying a good meat loaf. My family says that one of my favorite pastimes is baby-sitting a meat loaf. I make the meat loaf, wrap it to chill overnight in the refrigerator, then pack it securely in my ice chest for a fishing or hunting trip. I have been known to visit the meat loaf in the middle of the night for a taste check.

The next morning, a sharp knife, salt and pepper, sourdough bread and a bottle of Masters Steak Sauce or Henry Bain Sauce completes the assignment. I must admit, when I am ninety years old, I do believe I will enjoy baby-sitting a meat loaf no less.

I experiment with recipes for meat loaf, always looking for a version I might like as well or better than the one I have offered herein. However, this meat loaf is a tried-and-true standard recipe that I have enjoyed for many years.

INGREDIENTS
1-1/2 lbs. ground chuck
1/2 lb. breakfast sausage
1 C bread crumbs
1/2 C green pepper, diced small
1/2 C yellow onion, diced small
1 egg, beaten
1-1/2 t salt
1 t pepper
1 cup diced tomatoes

1/2 C tomato sauce

DIRECTIONS
✔ In a large mixing bowl combine the ground chuck and the sausage by hand. Set aside.
✔ Mix the remaining ingredients, except the tomato sauce. Pour the mixture onto the meat and combine by hand.
✔ Pour into an oiled glass loaf pan and level. Pour the tomato sauce onto the top of the meat loaf and spread evenly.
✔ Bake at 375 degrees for 1 1/2 hours. You will need to pour out the ensuing liquid from the loaf pan at the end of each 30-minute period. When the juices run clear, the meat loaf is ready.
Serves 4-5.

Roasted Prime Rib of Beef Loin
with a Butter Bourbon Sauce

This is the most flavorful cut of beef. We like to cook it a reddish medium rare, which means we absolutely do not allow the internal temperature of the meat to rise above 135 degrees. This means you must use a meat thermometer placed in the middle of the beef loin. Preheat the oven to 500 degrees and bake. Remove the beef loin at 135 degrees and allow it to stand for 10 minutes before serving; it will continue to cook.

The prime rib of beef makes a very attractive presentation on a platter. Cut the beef into 1-inch slices and place the beef slices attractively on a platter. Pour a swath of the bourbon butter sauce down the middle of the beef. Garnish the side of the platter with parsley. Make available the Butter Bourbon Sauce for zest and Masters Steak Sauce or Henry Bain Sauce for taste.

INGREDIENTS
8-10 lbs. whole prime rib loin
olive oil
black pepper
salt

DIRECTIONS
✔ **Rub a whole prime rib with olive oil, then with pepper and salt.**
✔ **Place a meat thermometer in the middle of the loin and roast until the thermometer reads 130 degrees for rare, 135 degrees for a reddish medium rare.**

Butter Bourbon Sauce

In a skillet over medium high heat, brown a quarter cup flour in a half stick of butter. Pour some of the meat drippings into the skillet. Turn heat to medium and blend in a half-cup of sour cream and a quarter-cup of fine aged Kentucky bourbon whisky. Add chives, a pinch of basil, pepper and salt.

Shrimp

For the love of money, by all means, peel and devein your own shrimp. It is simple and, once gotten used to, a task that heralds a good appetizer or a great dinner. We use shrimp as a cocktail and in soups and cream- and tomato-based sauces. Sautéed shrimp on a broiled buttered roll with lettuce and thick slices of purple onion slathered with horseradish sauce is a Southern bayou treat. I advocate the use of imagination with shrimp. It complements so many foods.

Our more Gulf-coastal friends live close to shrimp and wax piquantly about the scintillating qualities and the many wonderful recipes of their shrimp-based cuisine. I have no doubt that there are a thousand things one can do to a shrimp, and I am certain that all of them are terrific. Heaven knows, I have stood my tour of duty listening to the variations on shrimp cuisine.

Let me declare, I too am enthusiastic about shrimp. In New Orleans, I am quick to find a Po' Boy, the wonderful sautéed shrimp sandwich. And I often find where lurks the shrimp in a cream sauce over pasta in the Italian restaurants I frequent. Moreover, I am always thrilled to see the magnificence of oversized shrimp on ice served with a tangy cocktail sauce. The Low Country boil — shrimp, oysters, clams, mussels and corn on the cob all boiled together in a raging water for a few minutes, then dumped on a table covered with a thick layer of newspaper — is a seafood feast I try never to miss.

Let me proclaim that there are only two ways to cook shrimp — briefly or forget it. Shrimp are sensitive to overcooking and deteriorate rapidly in flavor and texture when subjected to prolonged heating. Shrimp boiled or sautéed for 4-5 minutes is about right. The other crime perpetrated against shrimp is allowing it to stand in water when chilling. Ice down the shrimp, by all means, but use a method that allows the melting ice to drain. Mushy shrimp is inedible.

Shrimp Cocktail

Buy shrimp that have a good size, 15-20 count to a pound is about right. You will want to serve 6-8 shrimp for each cocktail. Toss the shrimp into a 2-quart pan of boiling water. Cook for about 4 minutes, then drain in a colander. Rinse under cold water to stop the cooking. Place in the refrigerator for at least 2 hours to chill. If you can, place the colander in a large bowl and pack crushed ice around it placing the ice over the shrimp is even better, though you must not allow the shrimp to stand in the melting water.

When ready to serve, quickly peel and devein the shrimp, taking care not to break off the tails. Place the clean shrimp in a bowl, while discarding the shells. If the shrimp are to be served later in the hour, refrigerate to maintain the chill.

Do have fun in the presentation of the shrimp cocktail. In the summer, we might place a couple dozen shrimp around a large plate with a bowl of cocktail sauce dominating the center of the plate. The shrimp so arranged often fail to make it to a tabletop; they are consumed en route by those bearing a drink in one hand, leaving a free hand for attacking shrimp. For more formal dining, we hang the shrimp on the rim of a wine glass for each guest, with a small bowl of cocktail sauce alongside. Both ways work, for it is the shrimp that is the object of desire.

Southern Shrimp Creole

INGREDIENTS
1 C onion, diced
1 C green pepper, diced
2 stalks celery, diced
2 cloves garlic, sliced thin
1 stick butter
3 lbs. shrimp, peeled and deveined
2 C tomato, diced
1 C tomato juice
4-1/2 t cornstarch
1 bay leaf
4 t Worcestershire sauce
3 t Tabasco sauce or to taste

DIRECTIONS
✔ Sauté the onion, green pepper, celery and garlic in the butter until soft. Pour into a 2-quart pot. Add the remaining ingredients and slow simmer for 30 minutes.
✔ Serve over rice in a bowl or cup. If on a buffet, keep warm in a lighted chafing dish with the rice in a separate bowl alongside.

Oysters

I have several sources for oysters, and when they alert me or when I divine that a fresh supply has hit the Louisville or Lexington receiving docks, I am the first customer. I know the men who empty the truck and have worked assiduously to ingratiate myself with them through the years with a hearty banter and modest tipping. It is my belief, based on anticipation and expectation, that they cull out and reserve the best oysters for me. Margaret Sue swears that I delude myself and act foolishly in regard to my early-morning visits to the fish market, but that is the way I am around these mollusks.

Fried Oysters

When I have a notion to fry oysters, I look for fresh packed oysters that arrive on ice, in pint- and quart-size containers. A pint will produce a meal for two people. Dip each oyster in beaten egg and roll in bread crumbs seasoned with salt and pepper. Fry the oyster in a hot skillet for a minute, turning several times. Drain on paper towels for 30 seconds and serve hot.

A half-dozen oysters fried to a golden brown served with cocktail sauce for dipping is perfection; a dozen fried oysters is even better. The addition of a Bibb lettuce salad with french dressing completes this meal.

Oysters on the Half Shell

For those of us who are rapacious when confronted with a fresh oyster shipment packed in seaweed, eating them live out of the shell with a bottle of Tabasco sauce for liberal dousing is nirvana indeed. But living inland often deprives us of oysters on the half shell in the fresh state we covet.

Oysters on Spinach

Steam cook a big batch of properly deveined spinach, drain, then spread the spinach in a shallow glass pan. Pour melted butter and some half-and-half onto the spinach and mix in. Pour the oysters and then the oyster liquor over the spinach. Grate a sharp white cheddar cheese over the oysters and spinach. Cover and bake at 500 degrees for about 10 minutes. Garnish with paprika and parsley.

Baked Oysters

The Thanksgiving Day dinner and the Christmas Eve repast always feature baked oysters. Not because everyone has a taste for baked oysters, for certainly not everyone does. However, those of us who have the acquired taste for oysters associate the baked oysters with the holiday buffet table.

INGREDIENTS
1 qt. oysters
3 C Ritz crackers, crushed coarse
3/4 C butter
2 T parsley, chopped
3 t salt
1/4 t pepper
2 eggs, beaten
2 T water
1 C half-and-half
1 lemon
pepper

DIRECTIONS
✔ Drain the oysters.
✔ Combine the crackers, butter, parsley salt and pepper in one bowl.
✔ Combine the egg and water in a second bowl.
✔ Roll each oyster in the crackers, then in the egg, then again in the crackers. Place each oyster so breaded in a well-oiled baking dish, one layer only. Pour in any remaining butter or breading.
✔ Pour in the half-and-half.
✔ Bake 15 minutes at 350 degrees.
✔ Grind black pepper and squeeze lemon over the oysters.
✔ Garnish with chives.

Country Ham

I have found that my guests have a real taste and longing for country ham, a ham-curing process revered by all who know it. The best hams have traditionally been those that have been aged between one and two years. These wonderful hams have graced our tables for over 200 years.

That having been said, let me tell you that there is little market demand for these great country hams. The market is in that honey ham that we in Kentucky have always derided as city ham, dripping in a sugary mess, spiral sliced, the only age being the time it took to process it. I hate the way these honeyed hams look; I deplore the way they taste; I detest handling them, but to this generation, they are sweet magnificence.

One of my friends, a researcher with a Kentucky university, performed a demonstration for us at a food trade show. He set out a platter of properly aged country ham, a platter of honey-coated city ham and a platter of the caramelized pieces of the coating on the city ham and asked each of the thirty samplers of the platters which ham they preferred. Twenty-eight of the thirty chose the caramelized coating. My, my.

But if you want the real thing, the noble country ham, then be bold and order it from your meat department, if they stock it; or order from a dependable mail-order purveyor. It is almost certain that it will not have full aging, but it will have some, three to six months being the modern standard. Ask for the cooked center slices, sliced thin.

I will give you the recipe for baking a whole country ham, but most of you will not do it. Our generation is not fascinated with preparing a leg of anything.

Country Ham Breakfast

Country ham served skillet hot with scrambled eggs; baked cheese grits; a chilled, peeled tomato; a bowl of cantaloupe; and breakfast biscuits is a classic.

Lemon Chicken and Country Ham

Take a chicken breast filet and flour it, knocking off all the excess flour. Dip the floured chicken breasts in beaten egg, then dredge them in finely rolled breadcrumbs. Sauté the chicken breast in a small amount of olive oil until done. Squeeze a quarter of a fresh lemon onto the chicken breast. Place a thin slice of peeled tomato on top of the chicken breast and sprinkle with basil. Add 3 thin slices of country ham. Sprinkle blue cheese lightly across the top.

Fruit and Country Ham

Place cantaloupe slices and red seedless grapes on a bed of Bibb lettuce and garnish with slivers of country ham. Cut the country ham slice into medium-size pieces and place the slices over a salad of grapefruit, orange and mandarin orange slices set upon a bed of Bibb lettuce. Drizzle french dressing on the top and grind pepper over all.

Asparagus Wrapped in Country Ham

Cook asparagus. Then fold a thin slice of country ham around 4-5 asparagus and secure with a wooden spear. Drizzle cheese sauce over each bundle and sprinkle with spring onion. Asparagus wrapped in country ham, served with sliced beef and a Bibb lettuce salad, is a beautiful presentation.

Baked Country Ham

Buy a country ham, optimally cured for at least one year. I advise you to purchase a Kentucky country ham, disclosing my bias. Soak the ham in water overnight. Next morning, wash the ham thoroughly on both sides and scrub off any mold that you see. Trim off any hard surfaces on the cut side of the ham.

Fill a large roaster pan about half full of water. Put the ham into the roaster pan skin side down, initially, and cover. Place the ham in the oven at 450 degrees until the water begins to boil rapidly, then reduce the heat to 300 degrees. Cook 30 minutes to the pound and turn the ham every hour. After the proper cooking time has elapsed, turn the heat off and allow the ham to cool in the covered roaster pan for 5 hours.

Upon taking the ham out of the roaster pan, remove the skin and the fat layer, which will peel off easily. Drain the water from the roaster pan. Score the ham lightly in 1-inch squares and pat in cloves where the scored lines intersect. Then pat in cinnamon and black pepper. Put the ham back in the oven, uncovered, and bake for 30 minutes at 400 degrees to brown the ham and seal in the seasonings. Allow to cool and refrigerate.

Chicken Breast Filet and Country Ham

Flatten a chicken breast filet. Place a layer of deveined cooked spinach onto the chicken breast filet along with a thin slice of country ham. Fold the chicken breast filet over itself and secure with a wooden spear. Then bake until the chicken breast filet is done. Pour a few spoonfuls of melted blue cheese over the chicken breast filet before serving to complete a delightful, simple, elegant and flavorful dish.

Pork Tenderloin

Pork tenderloin has virtually no fat and really no moisture. It is a smallish cut of pork; a 1-1/2-pound tenderloin that serves about 4. I find that we cook pork tenderloin in the winter months, but the reason escapes me.

The preparation of our pork tenderloin may seem off center; I make that remark each time I cook it. That said, it is fabulous. My cousin, who manages a big resort hotel, was satisfied that it was the best pork tenderloin he had ever eaten and directed his staff to adopt it. Or so he told me.

Make a sauce of 1/2 C strawberry jam, 2 T white wine, 2 t fine minced garlic and 1 t black pepper.

Spread a coating of the sauce generously across the top of the pork tenderloin. Place a long piece of tin foil on the counter and, with a knife, cut three 1-inch slits at various places in the middle portion of the tin foil to allow the liquid to drain.

Place the pork tenderloin on the tin foil, wrap it tightly and place it on a broiler pan. Bake at 350 degrees for 1 hour, open it, make certain no pink is in evidence; grind black pepper on top and broil for about 5 minutes to give it a good color.

A second way to cook a pork tenderloin is to roast it in a searing hot oven of 500 degrees. The more genteel among us would be inclined toward this method, as the high roasting temperature forms a crust on the tenderloin. I am dauntless when faced with a nose turned skyward.

When roasting at a high temperature, simply rub the tenderloin with olive oil, sprinkle on the dry-rub mixture and grind black pepper across the top. Roast the tenderloin for 25 minutes or until the center is done, showing no pink color.

Slice the pork tenderloin in 2-inch cuts.

Accompany with twice-baked potato, broccoli and cauliflower with lemon butter and a spinach salad.

A pork tenderloin will serve about 4.

Grilled Pork Chops

Ask the butcher to slice a pork loin in T-bone fashion 1/2 inch thick. Marinate the pork chops in Worchestershire sauce, salt and pepper. Place in the refrigerator for a couple of hours.

On a hot grill or under a close broiler, sear the chops on both sides for 1 minute. Move the chops to a less intense heat and cook for about 7-8 minutes, turning once.

Baby Back Ribs

Everyone gets really excited when the hue and cry goes up to cook baby back ribs. I cook them only occasionally, but when I do, I tend to serve them for small groups of intimate family and friends, having never found a way to eat them or watch them being eaten without all being concerned about wearing the meal. I like to cook ribs on the hottest day of the summer and serve them in outdoor fashion on platters with chilled red potato salad and corn on the cob. Serve this meal to your Yankee cousins, and they will, God love 'em, never forget their visit.

There is hot debate on the proper method of cooking baby back ribs, but to my mind, the real issue is to make the ribs fully cooked and tender, almost regardless of the cooking method. Cooking ribs is a suit-yourself procedure.

A generation ago, it was not uncommon for the host, or a hired man, to cook the ribs slowly over a smoking bed of hardwood coals for half a day, basting and turning them every 10 minutes throughout the afternoon. The cooking of the baby back ribs was a warm-weather rite, a ritual laced with rules and secrets. Alas, the romance found in an all-day cooking enterprise at home has gone with the wind for anyone past their college years.

As for choosing not to spend the day sweating over hardwood coals, do as we say in Kentucky, "don't think a thing about it." The taste and glory in baby back ribs is in the sauce. The Masters Steak Sauce I give you is simply great. Put a bowl of the sauce on the table. Your guests will love it.

There are probably as many ways to cook the baby back ribs as there are barbecue cooks. We use a dry-rub procedure that is wonderful.

Concoct the dry-rub mixture. I will give you mine, but I encourage you to add a little something extra that you fancy—and keep it secret. In this way, you will immortalize your barbecue as your own.

Mix a bowl of 2 t each of garlic powder, salt and Cajun seasoning. Rub it into the top of the ribs. A very light amount of the dry rub is used, the idea being to season the ribs, not coat them. Place the ribs, covered, in the refrigerator for 2 hours.

Place the ribs on a broiler pan. Preheat the oven to 500 degrees. When you put the ribs in the oven, lower the heat to 325 degrees. Bake the ribs for 1-1/2 hours. You do not need to turn them. If you grill the ribs outdoors, mound the charcoal on one side and place the ribs on the cool side of the grill.

After the ribs have cooked, coat them on both sides with the Masters Steak Sauce and broil them at a 6-inch height, turning the ribs several times. Watch that you do not burn the sauce. If you finish the ribs over charcoal, place them over the charcoal, turning often. Either way, the ribs will form a nice crust, and you will declare them ready. Supply all at table with damp cloth napkins.

Quiche

The basic quiche is a favorite across the South for early luncheon. It is simple, and with some imagination, different tastes can be achieved. Women, I have found, find the quiche attractive for brunch. Men like the quiche too, as long as it is given a different name.

INGREDIENTS
1 piecrust
1/2 C Swiss cheese, grated
1 C bacon, country ham, lobster or crabmeat, cooked
4 eggs, beaten
2 C heavy cream
3/4 t salt
pinch of cayenne pepper and nutmeg

DIRECTIONS
✔ Layer the piecrust with the cheese and a meat item, if you wish.
✔ Combine the egg, cream, salt, pepper and nutmeg. Pour into piecrust.
✔ Bake at 400 degrees for 15 minutes, then reduce heat to 300 degrees and bake for 30-40 minutes or until the knife inserted withdraws clean.
Serves 4-5.

Kentucky Omelet

The best omelets are made individually for each plate. As eggs complement almost any vegetable, there appears to be no limit to the cook's creativity.

The omelet that I am called to make most often is the cheese, onion, and green pepper combination. Using a nonstick pan, pour in about 1-1/2 T of butter. Sauté a 1 T each of onion and green pepper until soft. Pour in 2 beaten eggs and stir from the middle, allowing all the egg to cook. Pour in a 1 T of grated cheddar cheese and fold 1/2 the omelet over itself.

Garnish with canteloupe and strawberries.

Buttered Lamb Chops

I have a longing for buttered lamb chops as for no other cut of meat. I enjoy a leg of lamb and have a fondness for mutton, but I am passionate in regard to buttered lamb chops. They are perfection, straight out of the broiler or off the grill. This fact mitigates against serving them in quantities appropriate for a huge gathering. I can manage about twenty at a time, which translates into serving them at a seated dinner for eight.

Although in the modern marketplace, there does not appear to be a particular season of lamb availability, we seem to want buttered lamb chops in the cold of winter or the early spring. There is something about the warmth of the fireplaces at McManus House and the ambience of our old home that seems to invite friends for a formal seated repast in our long, narrow, wood-paneled dining room.

A week before your need, order rib lamb chops from your butcher and ask him to delete the long bone; this will allow the lamb chops to better fit the plate. Ask the butcher to cut off any visible fat and to scrape the lamb chops. All this is done more easily by him than by us.

I rub the lamb chops with lemon juice and place them covered in the refrigerator for 2 hours. I then rub the lamb chops in garlic olive oil, seasoned with rosemary and basil.

Grill the lamb chops on a 400-degree grill or 3 inches below the broiler. After searing well on both sides, move the chops to a cooler place on the grill or 5 inches below the broiler. When the lamb chops appear cooked and show a pale pink in the center, they are ready. The cooking will take about 25 minutes for 1-1/2-inch chops and about 15 minutes for 1-inch chops.

As you remove the lamb chops from the heat, spread softened butter across them. If you like, grind black pepper and chives onto the butter.

The buttered lamb chops vary in size, and you will serve 2-3 to the plate, trying for even portions.

Accompany with wild rice, string beans, baked zucchini squash and a McManus House Salad.

Lamb Fries

For many decades we have delighted in serving our out-of-town guests a wonderfully light and tasty appetizer called lamb fries. They are served piping hot with a sharp cocktail sauce for dipping. Lamb fries are passed, with each guest receiving the benefit of tasting one or two. We love 'em, and everyone does who has tried them. However, and I must be candid, lamb fries are mostly for the fun of it all. Lamb testicles are what these fries are all about. I am usually an advocate of full disclosure, but there is comic value in waiting to tell your guests that the culinary substance of their delight is testicles. The reaction of women is especially cute. Make no mistake, lamb fries are absolutely delicious, and you may serve them with confidence.

Have the butcher devein and cut the lamb fries into strips for you, an adventure I am certain you will want to miss. Soak the lamb fries in milk for a few minutes. Roll the lamb fries in beaten egg and then in sifted flour that has been seasoned with salt and pepper. Fry them to a light golden brown in a hot skillet with about 1/2 inch of shortening. Drain them on a paper towel and serve immediately. Allow 2-3 lamb fries per guest.

Fried Chicken

I veer away from frying these days and tend to enjoy chicken baked, broiled or sautéed. But I have been asked to share my recipe for fried chicken on innumerable occasions, and so I have.

For the sake of great fried chicken, use a small chicken, which usually translates into a young, tender chicken. An old rooster or a hen past her prime is not worth the bargain purchase price. Either cut or have the butcher cut the bird into its six pieces and ask him to trim out the back. There is no reason I can think of to fry a piece of chicken devoid of meat.

It is critical that you keep the chicken that you purchase very cool. The good taste of chicken deteriorates rapidly as it warms to room temperature.

There are cooks who advocate double breading, soaking the chicken between breading courses with beaten egg. I find this practice unnecessary. If the chicken is fresh and has been handled properly, the chicken breaded one time will be sufficient.

We like to marinate the chicken in a big bowl of salty water. We use 1-1/2 t salt for each pound of chicken, then place it in the rear of the refrigerator for at least 8 hours. When ready to cook, allow the chicken to drain on paper towels and then pat dry.

Season 1 C flour with salt and pepper for each chicken and pour into a brown paper bag. Place chicken pieces in the bag and shake it, thereby coating the chicken. As you remove the chicken from the bag, knock off any excess flour. Place the chicken pieces on a tray, cover loosely and return to the refrigerator for an hour. This will assist the breading to bond with the chicken so it does not fly off during frying.

I have a cast-iron skillet with high sides that I deem perfect for fried chicken. Bring fresh vegetable shortening to the point of smoking. Then, just before adding the chicken, turn the heat to medium. The idea is to give the chicken a proper scald that will brown the chicken and seal in the flavor. Turn the chicken several times to ensure that the chicken does not burn.

Cook the chicken 8-10 minutes to the side. When removing the chicken pieces, take the wings and legs out first, wait a minute or two, then remove the thighs and breasts.

Drain each piece on paper towels and either serve warm or cover and refrigerate for delectable eating later in the day or the following day.

Chicken Breasts and Baked Broccoli

In a baking dish, place 4 small chicken breast filets in the center of the baked broccoli ingredients. Surround the chicken breast filets with the broccoli (see recipe for Baked Broccoli in "Vegetables" section). Layer the top of the chicken with sliced, peeled red tomato that has been seasoned with Worcestershire sauce and parmesan cheese. Cover and bake at 375 degrees for 1 hour. Serve with brown or wild rice. And by all means, make certain everyone has a slice of the tomato.

Creamed Chicken Louisville

INGREDIENTS
1 C chicken broth
1 lb. mushrooms, sliced
1 green pepper, diced
2 T butter
1/2 C flour
1 C half-and-half
1 T white wine
4 C chicken breast, boiled, cubed
1/2 t salt
1/2 t pepper
1/2 t paprika

DIRECTIONS
✔ Pour the chicken broth into a large pan. Simmer mushrooms and green pepper until just soft.
✔ Add butter and flour; whisk until well dissolved.
✔ Turn heat to very low and add the half-and-half and the wine.
✔ Add the remaining ingredients. Stir until thickened.
Serves 8.

Turkey Hash

INGREDIENTS
1 onion, chopped
1/4 C butter
4 C chicken stock
3 T flour
4 C turkey breast, boiled and diced
2 C potatoes, cooked and diced
salt
pepper

DIRECTIONS
✔ Sauté the onion in the butter until translucent. Transfer the contents of the sauté pan to a larger pan.
✔ Add the remaining ingredients. Stir until thickened.
Serves 8.

Chicken Breast Filet in White Sauce

I have a circle of friends that I cook for. I guess that is the way to say it. Their children are grown and have left the nest. At some point during the month, the prospect of my cooking another intimate dinner for two begins to gnaw at them. They call me with an offer to bring over chicken breasts, with a request that I cook chicken breast filets in white sauce.

I know that they are capable of cooking the dish, but then it would be a night in instead of out for them. Out of meanness, I always allow them the task of scullery after dinner, while I take my ease and keep them company. To date, they have not shown any signs of rebellion.

INGREDIENTS
4 boneless chicken breasts, flattened.
2 T olive oil
salt
pepper
2 T butter
1/2 C half-and-half
1/4 C flour
1 lime, skin grated, then juiced
1/2 t chives, dried
1/2 t dill, dried
salt and ground pepper

DIRECTIONS
✔ Flatten the chicken filets. Sauté the chicken filets in the olive oil until done. Season with salt and pepper and set aside.
✔ In a separate sauté pan, stir in the butter and half-and-half over a medium heat. Add in the flour slowly and stir with a whisk until all is thickened.
✔ Stir in the grated skin and juice of the lime, the chives and the dill.
✔ Allow the sauce to settle for 5 minutes over a very gentle heat before serving.
✔ Season with salt and pepper to taste.
✔ Place chicken filets on a platter and swirl the white sauce around on top.

Chow Mein

This very American dish has been a favorite in the South for more than a century. I have seen hotel menus that have broadcast the superlative quality of their chow mein as far back as 1875. I know of restaurants large and small that have built regional reputations on the presentation of a great chow mein. Like burgoo, the chow mein recipe is variable, according to the peccadilloes of the cook.

In my pursuit of ducks and geese down the Mississippi and Ohio river flyways, I have dined on chow mein from Stuttgart to New Orleans to Louisville. There is no better state of being than that experienced at the end of a successful day of goose hunting.

I am exhausted, tired to the bone. My eyes are dry and swollen with windburn. My throat is raw from the strain of calling geese. Tonight we speak of a frigid day spent on the river's edge in a leaking pit blind, calling geese that are a mile away. Mostly our efforts failed, except for one group, more curious than the others, that responded to our calling and came floating over our decoy spread to investigate the nature of the ruckus we were raisin'. Big mistake.

Start me with a double ration of fine aged Kentucky bourbon whisky. Give me a couple of bottles of the old dry wine from your private stock. Then, bring on the specialty of the house, the chow mein you are famous for, and plenty of it. For tonight, we drink and toast old friends.

You want to boil 2 chickens until done, then strain and reserve the broth. Discard the skin. Pull the meat off of the cooked chicken and hand shred into quarter-size pieces. Set aside.

In a large iron skillet on medium heat, add 2 C chicken broth, 1 stick butter, 4 C diced celery, 1/2 lb. sliced mushrooms, 2 diced yellow onions, 1 diced green pepper and a minced garlic pod. Allow to cook until soft.

Add 2 C bean sprouts, 1 C water chestnuts and 1/4 C soy sauce. Cover skillet and simmer for 20 minutes. Lift the lid toward the end and thicken with some flour. Add the chicken and allow to heat an additional 5 minutes.

Ladle over rice. Sprinkle on the topping, each according to your pleasure. (Traditionally, the toppings are placed in separate bowls surrounding the chow mein: Chinese fried noodles, chopped green onions, coarsely ground almonds and coarsely ground unsalted peanuts.) Serves 6-10.

"The Almighty Smiled"

The Almighty rested when He had
made the world,
but there was a smile upon the face of
God when He created Kentucky

—Anonymous

"Good Kentuckian"

Good Christian I would be,
and bloom
In heaven if I can;
But if I miss it,
on my tomb
Write "Good Kentuckian."

—Oliver Tilford Dargon

Salmon, Tuna and Swordfish

Salmon, tuna and swordfish are easy, but do make certain you are buying fresh fish. Have the butcher present a filet. Poke a finger at it. If the so made finger impression in the flesh immediately recovers, the fish is fresh. If the fish eyes are in evidence, make certain they are clear, not white with age.

Whole-fish presentation at the table is the way I like it, but believe me, there is a knack to doing it attractively. My advice, unless you are experienced with this sort of thing, is to order these fish from the butcher as deboned filet steaks cut about 8 ounces to a portion. At one point or another, I have used every herb I can think of in myriad combinations. Try seasoning fish filet several ways. You will eventually discover flavors that appeal to you. But season lightly. Salmon, tuna and swordfish stand well on their own great taste.

I often sauté the filet steaks, if they are less than an inch thick, in olive oil on a high heat. You will want to keep the pan covered. The filets require no preparation for cooking but receive the spring onion, parsley and ground pepper when placed upon the plate.

To bake, place the filet on an oiled pan, skin side down, if it comes that way. Squeeze lemon or lime over the fish filets and spread olive oil or mayonnaise over the surface. Sprinkle dill and ground pepper over the olive oil or mayonnaise. Bake at 500 degrees until the meat separates easily with a fork and is "flaky." Sprinkle some chopped spring onion and parsley over each filet before serving.

Salmon, tuna and swordfish are good broiled at about a 6-inch height. Prepare as discussed. Preheat the oven to 500 degrees, then switch to broil for cooking the filets. You should not need to turn the filets. Again the filets are done when they exhibit that flaky texture. And again, spring onion and parsley are a good garnish.

I grant no apology. My more cosmopolitan friends enjoy, what is to them, the fine eating quality of chilled raw fish. And even though I relish oysters on the half shell, I call fish filets properly cooked when my eyes say the meat is flaky. Others like fish filets more moist than my description, and if so, and I know about their preference, I heed not. I do as I please at my house.

Fried Fish Filets

Truly great foods are all about great taste, absolutely. But there is more. Truly great foods have a way of conjuring up pleasant memories of times shared with the people in our life. But this is not all. Truly great foods also have a mystical quality that satisfies and comforts us. And some foods are held in such high esteem that they bring together families, communities and regions. Fried catfish is one of those truly great foods.

In my warrior past I remember setting up an overnight camp on a tree-canopied riverbank on a hot, sweltering Kentucky summer Saturday. We would haul in small boats, and a truckload of trot lines fishing lines and cane bank poles. The older men, toò stiff with age to manage the boats along the slippery mud riverbank, supervised the young boys who gathered firewood and prepared the campsite. The more limber of the troop then maneuvered the boats along the river edge setting trot line at the narrow ripples, pushing bank poles into the river edge and tying limb lines on low hanging tree branches. Each hook received a perch minnow for bait.

The fishermen would set the lines at dark and then would run the river throughout the night, checking the lines, re-baiting the hooks and harvesting the fish. Our quarry was catfish, white of meat and succulent as to flavor. A good night of fishing would yield a hundred pounds of catfish. We would clean the catfish, placing them on ice.

I find that frying catfish in the great outdoors is one of life's imperatives, though I now often purchase fish at the market. We host our fish fry on Sunday afternoons accepting gifts of chilled beer, iced tea, green beans, corn pudding, hush puppies, corn bread, pies and cobblers from friends and neighbors. The afternoon is spent in the shade, in the satisfaction associated with having consumed a fine fried fish dinner. No question, there is a primeval need that is met when participating in a fish fry. Simply articulated, I find great pleasure in the company of the people in my life, who have responded to my invitation to come to McManus House for fried catfish, to sit with me under the maple and poplar trees that grace my lawn.

The first decision when frying fish is to select the proper size. I favor fish filets at about three to four ounces apiece. If you purchase the fish at the market, have the butcher slice the fish filet to the proper size for you if you wish. Tell him that you are hosting a fish fry. He will feel like he has a role in this special human event.

When I purchase whole filets, I slice the fish filets into 1/2-inch thick pieces about 6 inches long. I like to cook fried fish outdoors under propane heat.

My favorite fish to fry is catfish, farm raised or steam caught. However, perch, cod, bass and trout fry nicely. It is important to keep fish in a chilled state from the moment of cleaning or purchase. Keep the fish filets on ice up to the very moment of cooking. The great flavor of fresh fish is lost as the fish warms to room temperature.

Into a bowl, sift together a cup of yellow cornmeal and a cup of flour. Season with salt and cayenne pepper. In a separate bowl, pour in 6 beaten eggs that have been combined with a cup of evaporated milk. Dredge the fish filets in the egg and milk, then dredge into the seasoned cornmeal and flour mixture.

Into a cast iron skillet, pour in your favorite cooking oil enough to float the fish filets. When the oil is hot enough to sizzle flour, cook the fish filets. It is extremely important that you do not crowd the fish filets in the skillet and important that you do not allow the cooking oil to get smoking hot. The fried fish will be properly cooked in just a few minutes. Drain the fish on paper towels. Serve within 10 minutes of cooking with quartered lemons on the side.

After every batch use a hand held strainer to extricate the cornmeal and flour crumblins in the skillet, so they do not burn up, thereby, adversely affecting the cooking quality of the oil.

A good sauce for catfish can be prepared quickly by combining Hellmann's mayonnaise with lemon pepper, seasoned salt and tabasco sauce.

Trout with Lemon Butter

When I can, I serve trout. The small trout, white of meat and flaky when cooked, cannot be beat. We are blessed in Kentucky with more miles of streams and rivers than any state in the Union, except Alaska. And many of these streams have trout.

Fresh-from-the-stream trout are the berry patch. In the woods, we savor trout on the grill, opened and rubbed inside and outside with olive oil and cooked over the coals. I am weak in the knees just thinking about the fine times we have spent camping in the woods and catching trout for breakfast.

As my children have grown older and left home, I have lost my fishing buddies. Now, increasingly, I seek out fresh young trout in the fish markets. However, minus the nostalgia, the store-bought variety, if young and fresh, is delectable. I will recommend that you seek out the trout that is so young that it has white flesh not yet turned pink.

Regardless of the means by which trout comes to your kitchen, it is good and works well for a dinner of two or eight. I have friends who remember decades later their dinner of trout shared with us.

If the trout still possess their heads and tails, cut them off. Or, if the task will distress the womenfolk, have the butcher do it before taking it to the house. The trout should already be split open; rub the trout inside and outside with lemon butter. Place lemon slices in row fashion along the length of the cavity; three slices should be sufficient. Broil or grill the trout at a 6-inch height on one side, then the other, until the flesh is flaky and firm; guard against cooking the trout too dry.

Serve one trout per person, placing them on a platter in a row. Squeeze lemon across the top of the trout. Sprinkle slivered almonds, fresh parsley and chives for appearance and taste.

Accompany with wild rice, cold marinated asparagus, orange bourbon carrots and a Bibb lettuce salad. Lemon squares are for dessert.

Southern Gumbo over Wild Rice

INGREDIENTS
3 lbs. shrimp, cooked

9 T flour
8 T butter

9 C chicken broth
3 chicken breasts, skinned, deboned, diced
1 lb. polish sausage, diced

3 onions, diced
3 C celery, diced
2 cloves garlic, minced
1 green pepper, diced

42 oz. diced tomatoes (2 28-oz. cans)
12 oz. tomato sauce

4-1/2 t parsley flakes
4-1/2 t salt
1-1/2 t Worcestershire sauce
2 t Creole seasoning
1-1/2 t pepper

1-1/2 lbs. okra, cut

DIRECTIONS
✔ In a pan, boil the shrimp; drain and set aside. Boil the chicken and sausage in the chicken broth; dice and set aside.
✔ In a 4-quart pot, blend the flour and the butter over a low heat and stir for about 20 minutes or until brown. Add the onion, celery, garlic and green pepper—sauté 5 minutes. Add the remaining ingredients and the chicken broth but withhold the shrimp, chicken, sausage and okra. Simmer for 1 hour, then add the shrimp, chicken, sausage and okra. Simmer for another 30 minutes.
✔ Serve over wild rice. Accompany with a Bibb lettuce salad and corn bread.

Vegetables

My way of presenting a luncheon or dinner is to serve the entrée, a vegetable or two, a salad, bread and a dessert. I make certain that I have plenty. Whatever is left over is Sunday lunch.

In a former day, this notion of plenty was greatly expanded. There would be two or three meats, heaping bowls of soufflés and casseroles, every manner of cooked vegetables, compotes of fruit and numerous salads, breads and desserts.

In these modern times, we find ourselves more moderate, finding longevity a virtue. The vegetables I present to you are recipes I use throughout the year. I have always fled from casseroles, and I run smartly away from soufflés. But I find myself drawn to certain vegetable recipes that I can prepare quickly, that have a good appearance and that my guests are wild about.

Baked Sour Cream Potatoes

INGREDIENTS
6 C potato, skinned, grated
2 C cheddar cheese, grated
2 C sour cream
1 C chicken broth
1/2 C butter
1/2 C onion, chopped

DIRECTIONS
✔ Combine all of the ingredients and pour into an oiled baking dish.
✔ Bake at 350 degrees for 45 minutes.
Serves 6-8.

Scalloped Potatoes

INGREDIENTS
4 Idaho potatoes, large, peeled and sliced 1/4-inch thick
2 yellow onions, peeled and sliced thin
1 C butter
2 C half-and-half
1-1/2 t salt
3/4 t pepper
1 bunch spring onion white bulbs, sliced for garnish
paprika

DIRECTIONS
✔ In a well-oiled glass baking dish, alternately layer the potatoes
and onion. Dot each layer of potato with butter and season with
salt and pepper. Pour in the half-and-half.
✔ Cover and bake at 375 degrees for 1-1/2 hours. If after an hour of
cooking, you think more half-and-half is needed, add some to keep
the potatoes moist.
✔ Sprinkle paprika for color and cover the top of the scalloped
potatoes with the spring onion.
Serves 6-8.

New Potatoes

When I am serving rare beef tenderloin, new potatoes are present. I have a decided preference for the smaller new potato and find myself judiciously culling through the new potato selection to find them. I have not decided that these smaller new potatoes have superior taste qualities, but they present a fine appearance on the plate.

Collect four new potatoes per guest. Simply pare a strip around the potato about 1 inch wide, while lifting out any unseemly potato blemishes. Place them in a boiling pan of water and cook them until fork tender. It is essential that the new potatoes not be overcooked.

Drain the new potatoes in a colander. Pour enough melted butter over them to give good coverage. Sprinkle fresh chopped parsley generously upon the new potatoes. Add salt to taste and add paprika for color. Toss the new potatoes gently, so as not to break them, and add more parsley and paprika. Serve immediately.

Elegant Mashed Potatoes

This mashed-potato dish is so good that I find I must make a larger quantity than the usual allotment of one potato per guest. The key to great mashed potatoes is in the tasting of them after you add the ingredients. When they taste right, they are ready to serve.

Peel 8 medium-size Idaho potatoes and quarter them. Place them in boiling water and cook until fork tender. When they are tender enough, place the potatoes in a colander and allow them to drain.

Place the potatoes in a mixing bowl and mix them on slow speed until they are of a coarse consistency, then mix on medium speed for half a minute.

Return the mixer to slow speed and put in 1 C sour cream and 4 T butter. When thoroughly blended, add 1 T green onion chives and 1 T salt.

At this point you must taste the mashed potatoes for correct seasoning. Add salt if your taste requires more. If the desire strikes to add additional sour cream, resist it.

Place the mashed potatoes in an oven-proof serving dish and sprinkle the top with chopped spring onion. Sprinkle with paprika, lightly. Cover the serving dish tightly and place in a 275-degree oven until ready to serve. The mashed potatoes will dry out quickly, and therefore, I try to serve them within 20 minutes. Serves 6 and doubles easily.

Twice-Baked Potato

Serve this potato whenever you have grilled meat. It is special. If you find it convenient, the potato mixture can be made up the morning of. Allow it to cool, then cover and refrigerate. Add 10 minutes to the baking time, if refrigerated before heating.

INGREDIENTS
4 potatoes, large and baked
olive oil
1/2 C onion, finely chopped
2 T butter
1 C sharp cheddar cheese, grated
1 C sour cream
1 t salt
1/2 t pepper

DIRECTIONS
✔ Wash and dry the potatoes, then coat the skins with vegetable oil. Pierce each potato 4 times with a fork to allow steam to escape. Bake the potatoes at 375 degrees for about an hour or until a fork slides into them easily.
✔ Cut each potato in half, lengthwise. Pick up each potato half with a toweled hand and scoop out the flesh, leaving a potato shell. Be careful not to tear the potato shell.
✔ Sauté the onion in the butter until soft and set aside.
✔ Place potato flesh into a mixing bowl. Add the onion and sour cream and season with the salt and pepper. Add the cheddar cheese but with 2 T of cheddar cheese held back. Mix at slow speed until the potato flesh is smooth.
✔ Place the potato shells into a baking dish. Then, using a spoon, place potato flesh back into the shells until big and heaping, being careful not to make them lopsided.
✔ Sprinkle the potato tops with the held-back cheddar cheese.
✔ Bake at 350 degrees for 15 minutes, then broil the top until the cheese is brown.

Broiled Browned Potatoes

You will be astounded at the good taste of broiled browned potatoes. In our quest to divorce our cooking from the heavy oils of the deep fryer and the skillet, we have migrated to the broiler to achieve even better results. All at table will heap praise upon this very simple hash brown.

At McManus House, these potatoes are as popular for dinner with grilled T-bone as they are at breakfast with country ham and eggs. You will love the way they puff up.

INGREDIENTS
4 Idaho potatoes, skinned
1 T butter
2 t seasoning salt
2 t garlic powder
pepper, ground

DIRECTIONS
✔ Cut the potatoes lengthwise into 1-inch-wide slices.
✔ Boil the potato slices until fork tender, then drain in a colander. When dry, drizzle on the butter, sprinkle on the seasoning salt and garlic powder and grind pepper onto the potatoes.
✔ Tumble the potatoes in the colander until all of the potato slices are coated.
✔ Place the potatoes in a single layer on a baking sheet that has been sprayed with cooking oil and broil until brown, turning one or two times until all of the potato slices are golden.
Serves 6.

Bourbon Sweet Potatoes

Sweet potatoes are an odd potato, queer to look at and unseemly to handle. However, let me tell you in all honesty, you will rarely cook a vegetable this good. I have sampled dozens of recipes from every corner of the South, and I consider this recipe for bourbon sweet potatoes the standard to which all other sweet potato dishes must rise. In simpler words, bourbon sweet potatoes are excellent.

For many years, I did not prepare bourbon sweet potatoes, deferring to Mimi of Elmwood, who always volunteered to bring them to our larger social functions and sent them home with us when we visited with her—admonishing us, invariably, to return the bowl. I have always adopted, shamelessly I admit, the good recipes perfected by Mimi at the Elmwood mansion. Bourbon sweet potatoes is her recipe, as far as she knows and as far as any of the rest of us care to know.

Those who partake of bourbon sweet potatoes for the first time will notice some alacrity, as they place a speck upon their plate out of courtesy to their host. You can tell by their comments that for them, the sweet potato is an anomaly of Southern cuisine, certainly to be tasted but not to be overenjoyed. After sampling, however, they return for a more substantial helping with exclamations of delight. This recipe travels well; like Mimi, we have sent it home with our guests on innumerable occasions.

INGREDIENTS
3 C sweet potatoes, cooked and mashed
1 C butter, melted
1/2 C sugar
1/2 C heavy cream
2 eggs, beaten
1/4 C fine aged Kentucky bourbon whisky
1/4 t salt
1/8 t cinnamon
1/16 t allspice

DIRECTIONS
✔ In a large mixing bowl, combine all the ingredients.
✔ Place in an oiled baking dish.
✔ Spread topping evenly.
✔ Bake at 350 degrees for 30 minutes.

Topping

INGREDIENTS
1/2 C butter, melted
1 C brown sugar
1 C pecans, chopped
1/4 C flour

DIRECTIONS
✔ Blend all ingredients together with a wooden spoon.

Stuffed Eggplant

Stuffed eggplant has been served in Kentucky for many generations. It has been a signature dish at many of the great hotels and inns. It is a very elegant dish that is easy to prepare and offers an outstanding presentation. We serve stuffed eggplant in all seasons, though we like it best served in wintertime formal dining.

INGREDIENTS
1 large eggplant
1-1/2 C water
1 C onion, chopped
1 T butter
1 T parsley, chopped
1 can cream of mushroom soup, undiluted
1 C mushrooms, sliced thin
1 t Worcestershire sauce
1 C Ritz cracker crumbs (24 crackers)
1/2 t salt
1-1/2 C water
1 T butter, melted

DIRECTIONS
✔ Slice around the top of eggplant, leaving a bowl of the eggplant. Scoop out the eggplant flesh to within 1/2 inch of skin, taking care not to tear skin. In a pan, simmer the eggplant flesh in the 1-1/2 C of water about 10 minutes and, when done, drain thoroughly and set aside.
✔ Sauté the onion in the butter until clear and set aside.
✔ Then in a large bowl, combine eggplant flesh, parsley, mushroom soup, mushrooms and Worcestershire sauce, salt and all but 3 T of the crackers and mix gently with a wooden spoon.
✔ Pour 1-1/2 C of water into a baking dish. Place the eggplant into the baking dish, making certain they do not become lopsided. Drizzle the melted butter on the top of the eggplant and top with the remaining crackers.
✔ Cover and bake at 375 degrees for 1 hour.
Serves 6.

Asparagus

The queen of vegetables is the asparagus. When we can find the long, slender young asparagus, we serve it at the next meal. At Elmwood, Mimi peels the asparagus with a paring knife, a practice that makes eating the asparagus a transcendental experience. As much as I love peeled asparagus, I don't peel 'em; I don't have the patience for it, but have mercy on me, it is good.

The meal period does not dictate our use of asparagus, just the availability of the younger stalks.

The best way to store asparagus, if purchased for cooking a day or two later, is to clip the base about 1/2-inch and stand it, tips upright, in a glass or measuring bowl, anything with high sides, fill the container with water and refrigerate. You will be pleased with the result.

When time for cooking, remove the asparagus from the refrigerator and cut or snap off the bottom third of the asparagus stalk. You are trying to sever the hard part of the stalk from the tender part, which you will cook.

To cook asparagus, steam or boil in water that just covers the stalks for about 10 minutes. The asparagus is ready when the base is just this side of fork tender. We like to use a shallow baking pan or a steaming grate that allows the asparagus to stay above water.

Asparagus and Country Ham

It is worth mentioning asparagus and country ham a second time. Cook the asparagus. Wrap 4-5 asparagus in country ham, secure with a wooden spear and drizzle cheese sauce over them. If you feel the need to do more of something, sprinkle chopped fresh spring onion on top after placing in a serving dish. A bit of spring onion works with almost everything.

Asparagus and Cheese Sauce, Sour Cream Dressing or Lemon Butter

Cook the asparagus. Place in a serving bowl and drizzle cheese sauce, sour cream dressing or lemon butter over them. Grind pepper on top.

Cold Marinated Asparagus

Cook the asparagus. Marinate in vinaigrette with pimentos as a garnish and refrigerate for 2 hours before serving. We enjoy cold marinated asparagus for breakfast, lunch and dinner.

Orange Bourbon Carrots

A cooked carrot has always been tough for me. I find myself wanting to do more with it than simply putting carrots to a boil. The solution is orange bourbon sauce. We have always found a way to cook with bourbon, enjoying its ability to impart its own magnificent flavor while also bringing out the flavor of the food it is paired with.

Carrots glazed with orange bourbon sauce solve my cooked carrot problem. I love to serve orange bourbon carrots, and my guests love to eat them. The cooked carrot is rarely a standout, but orange bourbon sauce transforms this bland tuber into a dish that prompts requests for the recipe.

After scraping the carrot, cut into marble-size pieces. Boil in salted water for about 10 minutes, no more. Drain the carrots, place in a baking dish with about 1/4 inch of water, drizzle orange bourbon sauce over the carrots, cover and bake at 325 degrees for 30 minutes. Delightful.

Wild Rice

I cannot imagine a better-tasting food than wild rice. The nut-like flavor seems to complement every entrée. The tendency to mix wild rice with either white or brown rice is unfortunate. The fine taste of wild rice stands on its own. I often serve wild rice instead of a potato.

Turnips

Turnips are an old-fashioned vegetable that are absolutely delicious steam-cooked and cubed. You will want to pare away the hard outer shell of the turnip.

We like turnips best when placed upon a bed of cooked greens, like spinach or kale. Turnip and mustard greens find favor throughout the South as a delicacy of our cuisine, though I find them coarse.

Cook these greens in the same manner as you would my recipe for kale greens.

Peeled Tomatoes

W hen I serve tomatoes, I serve them peeled. My nutrition-obsessed friends berate me, for it seems to them that I have violated some code of conduct, but believe me when I tell you that they, and all others at table rave about my peeled tomatoes. I serve them in several different ways, according to my mood. I only peel locally grown, vine-ripened tomatoes. I may cook with tomatoes that are not vine-ripened in the wintertime, but I do not like them, never have and never will.

Peeling and Serving Tomato

Y ou will need to have ready a pan of boiling water and a bowl of ice water. Boil the tomato for 10 seconds. Recover the tomato with a slotted spoon and place it into the bowl of ice water for about a minute. The tomato skin can now be removed easily with a small paring knife. Refrigerate for use within the hour.

Breakfast
Cut thick and sprinkle with chopped basil, ground pepper and a pinch of salt.

Luncheon
Slice medium onto a bed of Bibb lettuce with pecan chicken salad centered in the tomatoes. Garnish around the outside of the plate with fresh fruit of the season. My favorite fruits are blueberry, strawberry, cantaloupe and honeydew.

Dinner
Slice about 1 inch thick and place on a bed of Bibb lettuce on a salad plate. Top with a generous spoonful of smearcase. Garnish with chives and ground pepper.

Snack
Cut two pieces of fresh bread and spread smearcase or Hellmann's mayonnaise on each slice. Place 3 slices of tomato and 3 slices of crisp bacon. Salt and pepper to taste.

Baked Cheese Grits

Grits. Nobody ever seems to know what to do with 'em. To the uninitiated, espying them in a bowl or on a plate only intensifies the mystery. Most encounters with grits are resolved by not eating them and then reporting that, "I just don't like 'em." Not to be obstreperous—but grits are great. I know the odds are against me gaining converts to grits. I love 'em, but I have grown up with 'em morning, noon and night.

Grits are at their best as baked cheese grits. I wish I could tell you I use regular grits, cooking them for an hour, then preparing the recipe. Regular grits taste better. However, I use quick grits, heresy to those who were my teachers.

And yet my Yankee friends are crazy about this dish; they feel very Kentucky when they eat it. They proclaim the mystery of grits upon viewing them, but they are soon relieved to smell and taste ingredients familiar to them. They are one of those foods that guests tend to remember you by. So many times I have heard our guests from the northern regions exclaim, years later, how impressed they were with our hospitality and their experience with—grits.

INGREDIENTS
2 C quick grits, cooked
2 C sharp cheddar cheese, grated
1 C half-and-half
1/2 C butter, melted
1 T garlic powder
1 t salt
1/2 t pepper
4 egg yolks, beaten
1-1/2 t parsley, chopped fine
6 spring onions chopped fine

DIRECTIONS
✔ Cook the grits according to the instructions.
✔ Add in the remaining ingredients, except the parsley and the spring onions, stirring briskly with a whisk. Pour the grits into a well-oiled baking dish.
✔ Bake at 360 degrees for 30 minutes.
✔ Then garnish the top with the parsley and spring onion.
Serves 6-8.

Broiled Zucchini Squash

Zucchini squash is good almost any way you fix it. My crowd always bellows for this recipe. The appearance of this squash, sliced lengthwise next to a beef rib-eye is electric. It is as though nobody ever thought of doing it this way. Of coarse, the idea did not originate with me; it is the way we have always done it.

Serve 2 halves to a plate. Make as many as you have guests.

INGREDIENTS
4 small zucchini squash
1 T butter, melted
1/2 C slivered almonds
1 t salt
1 t pepper
paprika
lemon

DIRECTIONS
✔ Slice the ends off the squash, then slice in half lengthwise. Place the squash skin side down in a baking dish, taking care they do not become lopsided.
✔ Cut a shallow slice down the middle of each squash. Drizzle the butter across the top of the squash and season with salt and pepper.
✔ Broil until brown and fork tender.
✔ Place on a serving dish. Sprinkle the slivered almonds, then add the paprika for color. Squeeze some fresh lemon across the top if you have a fancy to. Lemon is good on almost everything.

Broccoli and Cauliflower

Things always appear right with the world when we see florets of broccoli and cauliflower in a bowl, steaming at the end of the sideboard. We like to have them share the same bowl, feeling good about their combined presence.

We like to steam the florets of broccoli and cauliflower, briefly, just to the point of fork tender. Then we flavor with the cheese sauce, sour cream dressing or lemon butter. Carefully drizzle one of the sauces over the broccoli and cauliflower. The idea is to enhance the flavor of these vegetables, not to saturate. Grind pepper over the florets. Wow!

In the summertime, we like to add zucchini and yellow squash. We sauté the vegetables separately, as they soften quickly. We prefer our vegetables fork tender, not mushy.

Green Beans, Central Kentucky Style

I know green beans. Like squash and tomatoes, green beans are a staple in the Kentucky garden. I guess if there is a cooking procedure, we do it for green beans. We pickle, sauté, boil, bake, poach, blanche and stir-fry green beans.

But my favorite is the simply boiled, wonderful taste of green beans. Buy them young, long and slender, and by all means, buy a stringless variety. I cannot stand stringing green beans, though the elder members of my family find my distaste for stringing green beans indolent. Begging your pardon, I am just not going to do it.

INGREDIENTS
2 lbs. green beans
3 T olive oil
2 t Tabasco sauce
1-1/2 t seasoning salt
1/4 C almonds, slivered
juice of 1 lemon, freshly squeezed

DIRECTIONS
✔ Clip the ends off the stringless green beans.
✔ Place in a pan of boiling water to cover. Pour the olive oil, Tabasco sauce and seasoning salt on top of the green beans. Turn the beans over one time. Do not stir the green beans again. This is very important. Reduce heat to a simmer, just a bare bubble, and cover with a tight-fitting lid.
✔ Cook for 40 minutes, never stirring, as stirring will break the olive oil glaze on the green beans.
✔ Drain. Add the slivered almonds, a squeeze of lemon and pepper. Toss gently and serve.
Serves 6-8.

Baked Broccoli

For goodness sake, use fresh broccoli. I know as well as any that this adds a prep step, but fresh broccoli is so fine. I like to experiment with different cheeses and different combinations of cheese. Grated cheese is good if ground onto the baked broccoli just before serving.

Cut broccoli into bite-size pieces. Place into a well-oiled baking dish enough to cover the entire dish about 3/4 up to the rim.

Crumple 20-25 Ritz crackers and 2 C of sharp cheddar cheese over the top of the broccoli.

In a separate pan over very low heat, cream 2 C half-and-half, 1 stick butter, 1/2 C sugar, 1 t salt and 1 egg yolk. Pour over the broccoli and cheese.

Cover and bake at 325 degrees for 1 hour. Sprinkle paprika and grind pepper over the broccoli as it comes out of the oven.

Baked Onion

The onion—chopped, diced, sliced and ground—rarely gets an opportunity to share center stage with other vegetables as a main coarse. As acrid and pungent as a raw onion is, baked, the onion is sweet and mild.

You will use medium white onions on the small size. Cut off the ends of the onion so that it will stand up on end. Strip the onion of the outer skin and the first layer. Cut several shallow slices in the top of the onion, being careful not to pierce the outside layer. Rub the entire onion with a light coating of butter, and press some of the butter into the slices you made in one of the ends.

Wrap each onion in tin foil and place in a baking dish, standing upright, so that the butter you forced into the end slices will work itself down.

Bake at 350 degrees for 1 hour.

Remove tin foil; place onions in a serving bowl, squeeze fresh lemon onto the onions and garnish with paprika. Grind pepper to taste. Provide one onion to each plate.

Succotash

I am fond of dinner served outside late on a summer evening, after the searing heat of the day has subsided, under the maple trees. I like a grilled ground-steak sandwich with melted blue cheese, topped with Masters Steak Sauce. Next to the sandwich are thick-sliced peeled tomatoes with smearcase as a dressing and several spoonfuls of succotash, all of it occupying the same dinner plate. A big salad in a big bowl on the side completes the meal. Couple this dinner with a gigantic glass of iced tea, and I am content.

Margaret Sue maintains I am a simpler man than the world allows me to be. I do not resist. I know she is right and squarely on the mark.

The classic Southern succotash is the kernels of four ears of corn cut from the cob, with a pound of lima beans. The vegetables making up the succotash are always boiled together. Drain the succotash and add a small amount of cream and butter. Season with salt and pepper. Serve immediately.

We often combine cut corn with our green bean recipe and call that succotash. And so as not to leave zucchini squash out of the picture, we will mix cut corn with the zucchini and call that succotash.

And last, corn, lima beans and young okra cooked with ripe, peeled tomatoes and slices of turnip is the succotash of late summer, as we bend mightily to use the bounty from the garden.

Diced yellow onion is placed on the table for a topper.

Fried Corn

The best fried corn is made by lightly cooking several strips of bacon in a skillet, tossing off the drippings and chopping the bacon fine. Add 3 T butter to the skillet and add the kernels from 6 ears of corn. Use a spatula to keep the skillet bottom clear. Simmer the corn for 1 minute. Then add 1 cup of half-and-half, salt and pepper. Simmer 5 minutes more. Add a little flour dissolved in cold water at the end to stiffen the cream, if you feel it is necessary.

Corn Pudding

C orn pudding is a delicacy that is as old as the South. It is an unusual preparation procedure for the modern cook, as it requires the inner kernel of the corn to be used, not the whole seed kernel, we are all used to.

The Kentucky cook that cares about corn pudding has a way of preparing the dish and defends it stoutly. I have my recipe, and while I recognize that my way is not the only way, I will not cook it any other way.

INGREDIENTS
8 ears corn, husked
1/4 C yellow onion, chopped fine
1-1/2 C half-and-half
1/2 C sugar
1 stick butter
2 egg yolks
1 T flour
salt
ground pepper
paprika
parsley, chopped

DIRECTIONS

✔ Using a sharp knife, slice down each row of corn as it resides on the cob. With the dull side of a dinner knife, scrape down the length of the corn cob to extract the inner kernel, leaving the outer husk on the cob. Allow the corn scrapings to fall into a well-oiled glass baking dish.

✔ In a separate pan, cream and blend together the remaining ingredients, except the pepper, paprika, and parsley. Pour the creamed mixture over the corn. Grind black pepper generously over the corn pudding.

✔ Bake at 350 degrees for about 45 minutes. Remove from oven when still a little loose. Allow to cool somewhat before serving. Sprinkle with paprika and chopped parsley.
Serves 6-8.

Kale Greens

It has been a belief of mine for many years that women only need men to love them, help them, protect them and reach items in high places for them. I can easily add preparing kale greens for the stockpot. It appears that this task is my job, exclusively.

Fight the lassitude that comes from the notion of having to prepare an enormous amount of kale greens to set a moderate amount on the table. Keep faith with me and work with fresh kale greens. It is the best of cooked leafy vegetables. It is also the most tedious to prepare. A great mound, two big bunches, are just about right to feed four or five.

I like to trim the kale under a big shade tree on a lazy weekend afternoon by removing the leaves from the primary, secondary and tertiary stems. I find the stems, regardless of size, inedible. My family finds my obsession with stem removal overly fastidious and fussy. They mock my labor. Therefore, I remove myself from their company to the solitude of my shade tree and do it my way, to my satisfaction. The end result is magnificent kale greens.

In days gone by, my grandmother would reserve the liquid in the stockpot after the kale was removed for the children, who called it "pot likker." A big country ham bone laden with meat flavoring the kale greens was a prize to be fought over.

I use olive oil instead of a country ham bone, unless one is readily at hand. I reserve the pot likker for vegetable soup the next day, as it makes a good stock for the rest of the orphaned vegetables I toss in from my garden.

After you have trimmed the kale greens in the way that pleases you, rinse them in several salted cold waters. This will remove any grit and critters that may cling to the leaves.

Fill a big stockpot about halfway with cold water. Salt the water liberally and pour in 1/2 cup of olive oil. Stuff the kale greens into the pot, tightly if you must; they are going to render down quickly. Cover the pot, bring to a boil, then lower heat to a slow simmer and cook the kale greens for 2 hours. Taste for salt and add Tabasco sauce.

Spinach Greens

Spinach greens do not have the tough stems indigenous to kale greens. Simply strip the spinach leaves from the more primary stems. Wash in several cold waters. Stuff the spinach greens into a 2-quart saucepan with a 1/4 C olive oil. Steam cook for 20 minutes. Chop boiled egg or onion over the top of the spinach greens as they are served, according to your preference.

Pick-Up Foods

Informal dining in Kentucky means only that to sit or not to sit is the choice of the guest and that the meal to be shared will be casual. We have often presented an entire dinner or luncheon at McManus House with only wooden spears for eating utensils. The idea for this kind of service is to allow the guests to eat, drink and socialize, either standing or sitting, without their having to carve an item on their plate.

In the heat and humidity of a hot Kentucky summer, we often present a bountiful table of pick-up foods. This kind of food presentation also works well for social occasions where people come and go, as at Christmas or before an event.

The pick-up food idea is also useful when you find yourself having to throw something together quickly for an occasion that will not fit into your dining room, and you are completely in the dark as to the number of people that will descend upon your property. We threw a party for the daughter of our dear friends a few years back. Announced only a week earlier, the wedding ceremony was to be performed later in the month. The invitations went out by passing the word, pigeon and telephone. It appeared that time was of the essence. We received compliments on our table for years, and we were far from gussied up.

The social occasion may be casual and the dinner informal, but the foods presented will be from outstanding recipes honored by time. The table so prepared usually has ten to fifteen food choices, inviting the guests to place upon their plates as little or as much as they wish. I present the pick-up recipes I seem to gravitate toward and that I find are respected and appreciated throughout Kentucky.

You will find that Benedictine and pimiento cheese, if used on an informal buffet table, are usually spread on white sandwich bread and the sandwich then diagonally quartered. You will need to cover the plate of sandwiches with plastic wrap until served, as the bread so quartered dries out quickly. However, if used as an appetizer, crackers are provided.

Pimiento Cheese

When you prepare pimiento cheese, you will be amazed to find the many ways in which your guests will choose to use it. Those who are familiar with this spread will use it as contemplated but will also combine it with other finger sandwiches, leaving off the bread tops. The clandestine operation I often see executed is the Benedictine-pimiento cheese combination, performed as often as not with an accomplice, who watches your back, knowing you will return the favor. Margaret Sue has always growled at me for the practice, although I find her accepting of others who engage in it.

I have often seen pimiento cheese heaped onto a winter's afternoon chili and have seen it added to a club sandwich, all surreptitiously taken from the confines of the bowl in which it resides.

INGREDIENTS
1/2 lb. sharp cheddar cheese, shredded
1/2 lb. mild cheddar cheese, shredded
1/2 C Hellmann's mayonnaise
1/4 C pimientos, diced
1 t pepper, cayenne
sugar, pinch

DIRECTIONS
✔ Mix all ingredients at slow speed until blended but cheese is still coarse.
✔ Place in a covered container and place in refrigerator overnight to blend the flavors.
Serves 12, if served with crackers. Serves 10, if spread on thin bread, then quartered diagonally. Serves 6, if layered onto whole slices of sandwich bread. Serves 1, if attacked with a spoon standing in front of the refrigerator door.

Benedictine

In the Bluegrass region of Kentucky, we have enjoyed Benedictine throughout the twentieth century. Created by a restaurateur of that name, it has graced the finest Kentucky tables. It is served either as an appetizer on crackers or as a finger sandwich. The next day, after the social occasion has passed, friend and foe alike will consume whatever remains, if they know you have it in the refrigerator.

I have always heard that it is a tricky recipe to make and even trickier to describe, as there is a fine line between just right and too runny. I find Benedictine easy to make, but I have made a mess of it if I felt rushed. Just add the cucumber juice slowly and watch the consistency, because you will want Benedictine creamy. If you feel the need to add some small amount of cucumber and onion pulp, then add it. I do not, but others do. If you add it, add it sparingly. There is no substitute for Philadelphia cream cheese.

INGREDIENTS
2 large cucumbers, peeled
1 medium white onion, peeled
2 8-oz. packages Philadelphia cream cheese
food coloring, green

DIRECTIONS
✔ In a blender, separately grind the cucumber and the onion into pulp. Separately, place the pulp of each into a handheld fine-mesh strainer. Gently press the pulp into small bowls until you have accumulated most of the juice. You now have a bowl of cucumber juice and a bowl of onion juice. I discard the pulp.
✔ Place the cream cheese into a mixer at slow speed.
✔ Gradually, add juice from the cucumber. When you are satisfied that the Benedictine is nice and creamy, add about half the juice from the onion.
✔ Then add 2 drops of green food coloring. If your eye says add more, then add 1 more. If your eye tells you to add 1 more after that, don't do it. The ideal color is peeled cucumber green.
Serves 12-15 as an appetizer.

Pecan Chicken Salad

You will never make enough of this salad. I have served pecan chicken salad on toast as a sandwich, over lettuce and peeled tomatoes as a luncheon salad, in the summertime as the dinner entrée and as an appetizer with crackers.

I have watched polite company scooping it bulk fashion onto their plates from the appetizer plate, leaving the crackers as refugees, and eating it with a fork.

I have watched this same polite company making clandestine raids into the kitchen to find the bowl it was made in, attacking the pecan chicken salad with a spoon.

Similarly, I have watched them study the lay of the land, decide upon a point of interception and ambush the serving help attempting to cart the pecan chicken salad appetizer from kitchen to table.

Shameless behavior, I admit. However, it is not new to my generation; my mother and grandmother have witnessed a similar reaction to pecan chicken salad.

Sweet pickle juice is used in the pecan chicken salad. It sounds bizarre, but take it from me, it works. Mama Sudie and Sue Carol, always with an eye to making a great recipe better, introduced sweet pickle juice to me many years ago, and I adopted it as my own.

There is no substitute for fresh boiled chicken breast.

INGREDIENTS
4 chicken breasts, boiled, skinned, deboned and cubed
1 C Hellmann's mayonnaise
1/2 C pecans, chopped
1/2 C seedless white grapes, cut in half
1/2 C celery, chopped
3 T sweet pickle juice
juice of 1 lemon, freshly squeezed
pepper, ground
salt

DIRECTIONS
✔ Place all ingredients in a bowl and mix with a wooden spoon.
✔ Add a touch more mayonnaise, if that is your preference. Grind pepper and salt to taste.
Serves 12-15, if an appetizer. Serves 6, if sandwiches. Serves 4, if a salad for luncheon or dinner.

Bourbon Cheese

Sunday afternoon in the cold of winter is a special time for our household. The evening comes early. The fireplaces are ablaze and glowing candles are on the table. Neighbors drop in, and the drinking lamp is lit. A fine aged Kentucky bourbon whisky is poured, and the bourbon cheese and crackers are placed on the end tables.

INGREDIENTS
8 oz. sharp cheddar cheese
8 oz. cream cheese
1/4 C fine aged Kentucky bourbon whisky
1/2 C pecans, chopped fine
1/4 C parsley, chopped
3 T onion, grated
1 t Worcestershire sauce
1/4 t salt
1/4 t pepper, white
4 dashes Tabasco sauce

DIRECTIONS
✔ Combine all ingredients in a mixer on slow speed. When the cheese appears to be thoroughly blended, form into a ball and place in a covered container. Refrigerate overnight.

Country Ham or Turkey Breast Biscuit

There are many ways to enjoy country ham. The Kentucky way is to place two slices on a beaten biscuit or an angel biscuit. We like the country ham plain, but we often place a bowl of Hellmann's mayonnaise or Durkee's dressing next to the country ham for those who require something extra.

Arranged on a platter, this is the quintessential pick-up entrée, and I do love it. When securing a good country ham is impossible, use slices of turkey breast. Not nearly as outstanding but good, and after all, "one does what one can."

When I entertain a large group, I almost always serve a platter of both country ham and turkey breast on beaten biscuit or angel biscuits.

Bourbon Balls

T he bourbon ball is a piece of the fabric that forms the Kentucky hospitality tapestry. Bourbon balls are presented at times as an appetizer, occasionally as a dessert and often on coffee tables when the drinks are being poured.

When I am sipping fine aged Kentucky bourbon whisky and our company is graced by the presence of a number of women on a warm, breezy day, I try to make the passing of bourbon balls a studied ritual. Women seem to adore bourbon balls, and after all is said, I do seem to spend much of my life striving to make the women happy.

Your guests will go crazy when they taste bourbon balls. Keep the recipe handy; they will ask you for it.

INGREDIENTS
1/4 C butter, softened
2 lbs. powdered sugar
3/4 C fine aged Kentucky bourbon whisky
1 C pecans, chopped

4 oz. semisweet chocolate
1-inch square of paraffin

pecan halves, optional

DIRECTIONS
✔ Blend butter and half of sugar, blend bourbon and the other half of sugar, then combine the two sugars and the pecans. Refrigerate for at least 4 hours.
✔ Shape into small balls and return to refrigerator.
✔ Melt the chocolate and paraffin in a double boiler over medium heat.
✔ Retrieve the bourbon balls from the refrigerator and dip each bourbon ball in the chocolate with a fork and place on wax paper to cool. If you want the optional pecan half on top of the bourbon ball, place it securely on the hot chocolate as you place the bourbon ball on the wax paper.
✔ Place the cooled bourbon balls in a tin, each layer separated by wax paper, and cover tightly. Keep the bourbon balls in the refrigerator, and they will keep well.

Stuffed Mushrooms

Stuffed mushrooms are a standard on the serving tables of Kentucky homes. I have served them most often in the summer for large gatherings on the lawn. However, I have seen stuffed mushrooms on the sideboards of many homes in all seasons.

INGREDIENTS
12 oz. hot breakfast sausage
1 C sharp cheddar cheese, shredded
1/2 C bread crumbs, finely rolled
2 T parsley, chopped fine
1/4 t pepper, red flakes
24-30 medium to large mushrooms, stems removed

DIRECTIONS
✔ Blend all of the ingredients, except the mushrooms, by hand. When ingredients are completely blended, stuff each mushroom with a heaping amount of stuffing and place on a well-oiled baking sheet in such a way that they do not become lopsided.
✔ Bake at 375 degrees for 45 minutes and serve immediately. Serves 8-10.

Salted Walnuts

I enjoy salted peanuts as much as the next man; dry roasted and red-skins are my favorite. If, however, you decide to salt your own nuts, walnuts are a fine choice.

INGREDIENTS
4 C walnuts, shelled and left whole
1 T butter
1 T salt

DIRECTIONS
✔ Place walnuts in a bowl. Drizzle the butter over the walnuts and swoosh around until completely covered. Mix in the salt, making certain that all the walnuts have equal coverage. Arrange walnuts on a dry baking sheet so that there is no overlapping.
✔ Bake at 275 degrees for 30 minutes.

Sausage Balls

I have never seen a sausage ball outside of Kentucky, which probably means I do not get away from the house as much as I should. They are simple and delicious. Be patient and persistent in working the mixture. Mixing the ingredients together always takes longer than I think it should.

INGREDIENTS
1 lb. hot breakfast sausage
1/2 lb. mild breakfast sausage
1 C sharp cheddar cheese, shredded
6 C Bisquick

DIRECTIONS
✔ Mix the cheese and the sausage by hand. Add the flour a cup at a time, again working the mixture by hand. Form into balls about the size of large marbles. After forming into balls, the sausage balls may be frozen for later use.
✔ Bake at 350 degrees until golden brown, about 45 minutes, watching that they do not overcook, as they will get hard. If previously frozen, add about 10 minutes to the cooking time.
Yields 75 sausage balls.

Cheese Straws

INGREDIENTS
2 C sharp cheddar cheese
6 T butter, melted
1 C flour, sifted
2 t baking powder
1 t pepper cayenne

DIRECTIONS
✔ Cream the cheese and butter in a mixer at slow speed. Mix in the remaining ingredients. Place on a cutting board, pat down more or less flat and cut into 4-inch-long straws.
✔ Place on a well-oiled baking sheet so they are not touching. Bake at 325 degrees for about 25 minutes or until they are crisp and dry.
   Again, your guests will eat as many as you bake.

Fried Green Tomatoes

I have been asked innumerable times for my recipe for fried green tomatoes. It is one of those foods that people are aggressively partisan about. Really, there are many ways to prepare the tomato for the skillet, and all of them are correct. Make up your own way of coating the tomato and defend it vigorously. It does everyone good to take a principled stand on fried green tomatoes. And besides, fried green tomatoes are ever so good almost any way you fix them. Serve hot with a bottle of Worcestershire sauce in one hand and a fork in the other.

I like the tomato that is just about to show color (red). I peel the green tomatoes, core them and slice them medium thick. Set aside.

Put vegetable shortening in a skillet about 1/4 inch deep and bring up to a medium-high heat.

Mix up a bowl of fine cornmeal, salt, pepper and some sugar. Beat some egg in a separate bowl.

Drag each slice of tomato on both sides through the egg; then coat the tomato with cornmeal, knocking off the excess. Fry each tomato in the skillet until golden brown on each side. Drain on paper towels.

Deviled Eggs

There are certain foods that ensnare me and certain cooks of those foods that I gravitate toward. Deviled eggs is one of those foods that trap me, and believe me, I have identified the cooks in my world that make them in an especially delicious way. It would appear simple enough to make a good deviled egg, but not so; deviled eggs take on the personality of the cook. My sisters claim that it has a lot to do with tongue placement between the teeth. I have read a dozen recipes for deviled eggs utilizing myriad ingredients. I like my recipe, but there are others equally as good. Deviled eggs must be served chilled.

INGREDIENTS
8 eggs, hard-boiled, sliced in half lengthwise, yolk removed
1 T vinegar
3 T Hellmann's mayonnaise
1 T vinegar
1 t salt
1/2 t powdered mustard
1/2 t sugar
1/8 t cayenne pepper
paprika
parsley

DIRECTIONS
✔ Be careful not to tear the egg as you scoop out the yolk.
✔ In a bowl, mash the yolk and combine all the other ingredients, except the paprika.
✔ Refill the egg hollows with the deviled egg mixture. Sprinkle with paprika and a slight leaf piece of parsley for accent and color.
✔ Arrange the deviled eggs attractively on a platter. Cover with plastic wrap and refrigerate for at least 2 hours.

Country Ham Salad

This is a spread that is sought whenever a visit is made to a member of our extended family. By heaven's grace, I speak the truth: Country ham salad on a cracker has no peer. Life appears sweet when the fine aged Kentucky bourbon whisky is being poured and bowls of country ham salad, Benedictine and pimento cheese, all surrounded by crackers and cocktail breads, are presented.

Have the butcher grind half a pound of country ham very fine for the country ham salad. Take the half-pound of ground country ham and moisten with Hellmann's mayonnaise. Add 1/4 C grated onion, 2 T sweet pickle relish and 1 T brown sugar. Stir together all the ingredients. Refrigerate for a day before use.

Artichoke Dip

INGREDIENTS
2 14-oz. cans of artichokes, drained, mashed
2 C parmesan cheese, shredded
2 C mozzarella cheese, shredded
1-1/2 C Hellmann's mayonnaise

DIRECTIONS
✔ Bake at 350 degrees for 40 minutes, covered. Broil until brown and crust forms.

Black Bean Dip

INGREDIENTS
16 oz. can black beans
2 C tomato, peeled, chopped
1 C purple onion
1 bunch green onions, bulbs only
juice of 1 lime
2 T olive oil
1 T red wine vinegar
1 t salt
1 t pepper

DIRECTIONS
✔ Combine the ingredients. Cover and place in refrigerator for at least half a day to blend the flavors. Serve chilled.

The Conquered Banner

Furl that Banner, for 'tis weary;
Round its staff 'tis drooping dreary;
Furl it, fold it, it is best;
For there's not a man to wave it,
And there's not a sword to save it,
And there's no one left to lave it,
In the blood that heroes gave it;
And its foes now scorn and brave it;
Furl it, fold it—let it rest!

—Father Abram Joseph Ryan (1838-1886),
a stanza from his monumental poem

Father Ryan, from Irish stock and born in Virginia, made his home throughout the South and lived his last years in Louisville. This great and noble priest joined the Confederate army as a chaplain at large, as a minister to the great suffering being endured by the combatants. Father Ryan was the editor of several religious newspapers, *The Star* in New Orleans and *The Banner of the South* in Augusta, Georgia.

Father Ryan's great work, *Poems, Patriotic, Religious and Miscellaneous,* had many printings after the Civil War. His poem "The Conquered Banner," written at the close of the war, endeared him to millions of Southern survivors of "the lost cause."

Breads

I have spent a lifetime making friends with the baking arts. Just as I think I have learned something, it disappears on my next attempt. Maybe it is my heavy hand or a lack of sensitivity or that the planets are aligned against me.

I decided many years ago to bake four great breads: breakfast biscuits, yeast rolls, angel biscuits and beaten biscuits. When people light at McManus House, they will be served one of these breads; if they stay the weekend, they will probably sample all four.

Yeast rolls are my favorite bread to bake. They are easy to prepare, once you have experience with them. I often make the dough the night before and place it in the refrigerator. The trick is to learn what I mean by bubbly yeast.

When you prepare yeast rolls, you will lose your last days of peace upon this earth. You will be expected to bake these yeast rolls when company travels to your house. That same company will invite you to their home, and when you ask, "What can I bring?" they will tell you yeast rolls.

Yeast rolls are a Kentucky thing. I find them on good Kentucky tables but rarely outside of Kentucky. I have surmised that our distilling industry, practiced by many in the back shed, afforded us a continuous supply of yeast and an active interest in the fine bread it produced. The cook who can master these rolls can build a career on the applause. I have neighbors who would fall out with me if I made yeast rolls without sending some over.

I am telling you straight, if you would allow it, folk high and low will make a meal out of yeast rolls. They are that good.

Baking times will vary according to the size of the roll you are baking and the accuracy of the oven. When Margaret Sue and I purchased a new oven, my old times needed adjustment. Just attend to the rolls. Golden brown is the color my eye is seeking.

Breakfast Biscuits

This recipe delivers an excellent baking powder biscuit. The recipe calls for cream of tartar, a very old method used to enhance the rise. Be gentle with these biscuits. My family laughed at my first attempts many years ago, attributing my lackluster results to my heavy hand, which is the size of a bear paw. A grandmotherly friend told me to handle the dough as if holding a baby's hand. Since having that as a mental image, I have been successful with the breakfast biscuit.

This piece of advice is experience, not science: cut the biscuit straight down and do not twist the biscuit cutter, otherwise the biscuit will tend to become lopsided. These biscuits are very easy to make, but be kind to yourself: make them in private the first time out so you can get the feel of them.

If some are left over, cover them with tin foil the next morning, halve them, put a small pat of butter on each half and broil. Heaven.

INGREDIENTS
3 C flour
3/4 t salt
3/4 t cream of tartar
4-1/2 t baking powder
2 t sugar
3/4 C shortening
3/4 C milk
1 egg, beaten

DIRECTIONS
✔ In a large bowl, sift together the flour, salt, cream of tartar, baking powder and sugar.
✔ Add the shortening, cutting it in with a pastry knife until the texture is pebbly and coarse.
✔ Mix the milk and egg together with a whisk. Pour onto the flour mixture and quickly but gently stir into the dough with the wooden spoon.
✔ The dough is ready when it follows the spoon around the bowl.
✔ Turn out the dough onto a lightly, and I do mean lightly, floured table. Knead 6-8 times, lightly and gently, folding the dough over itself. Roll to a 1-inch thickness and cut into 2-inch biscuits. Place on a dry baking sheet.
✔ Bake at 450 degrees for 15 minutes or until tops are browned.

Yeast Rolls

INGREDIENTS
5-1/2 C flour, sifted,
1/2 C flour, sifted at the ready for dusting
2 C milk or sour cream
1/4 C water (lukewarm, 110 degrees)
2 T sugar
2 t salt
2 T butter
1 egg, beaten
1 package dry yeast

DIRECTIONS

✔ Heat the milk in a pan until it comes almost to a boil, then cut off the heat.

✔ Add the sugar, salt and butter and let the mixture cool until lukewarm. This will take about 10 minutes. When lukewarm, add in the egg. Set aside.

✔ Warm a mixing bowl by running warm water over the inside and outside, then dry with a cloth. Place the yeast into the bowl, add the water and stir until you are convinced that the yeast is dissolved. Let stand until bubbly, about 20 minutes.

✔ Pour the milk or sour cream, sugar, salt, butter and egg into the mixing bowl and combine with the yeast.

✔ Add 1/2 C of flour in the mixing bowl and beat the dough for 3-4 minutes with a wooden spoon, making certain you include the sides and bottom of the bowl. Add the remaining flour and beat for 3-4 minutes.

✔ Cover the bowl with a damp cloth and allow dough to rise in a warm place, about 80-85 degrees, until doubled in bulk, which will take about an hour and a half.

✔ If the dough is to be used the following day, cover the bowl and place in the refrigerator. If it is to be used the same day, release the dough upon a table, which has been dusted lightly.

✔ Knead the dough with flour-dusted hands by bringing the far edge of the dough toward the center and pressing in the center of the dough gently with the heel of your hand. The idea is to knead the dough without pressing out the gases generated by the active yeast. Turn the dough and repeat the kneading procedure. If you need to dust the table again to prevent sticking, then do so. Knead the dough until the underside is smooth and silky.

✔ Then place the dough on a lightly dusted table. With your hands, press the dough from the center in all four directions. Then, using a lightly dusted rolling pin, gently but quickly roll out the dough from the center in all directions. Be careful not to roll past the edge of the dough. Lightly dust the top and the bottom of the dough as needed to prevent sticking.

Yield: 25-30 rolls

Dinner Rolls

DIRECTIONS

✔ Roll the yeast dough 1/2-inch thick. Cut with a 2-inch biscuit cutter or a tumbler. Crease the dough across the middle and fold over for effect. Brush the tops of the rolls with butter. Place the rolls in an oiled baking pan.

✔ Cover the pan with a damp cloth and allow the rolls to rise in a warm place until doubled in bulk, about 30 minutes.

✔ Bake at 400 degrees for 12-20 minutes, or until golden brown.

Clover Leaf Rolls

DIRECTIONS

✔ Roll the yeast dough 1/2-inch thick. Pinch off a piece and roll it into a marble-size ball. Dip each ball in melted butter and place three in an oiled muffin pan.

✔ Cover the pan with a damp cloth and allow the rolls to rise in a warm place until doubled in bulk, about 30 minutes.

✔ Bake at 400 degrees for 12-20 minutes, or until golden brown.

Butterscotch Breakfast Sweet Rolls

DIRECTIONS

✔ Roll the yeast dough 1/4-inch thick, brush the dough with softened butter and sprinkle 1/2 C brown sugar on the buttered dough. Roll the dough up from the long side. Brush the top and the sides of the rolled-up dough with butter. Cut into 3/4-inch pieces.

✔ Melt 4 T of butter in an oiled baking pan and cover the butter with 3/4 C brown sugar. Sprinkle mixture with chopped pecans. Place rolls close together, face down in the butter.

✔ Cover the pan with a damp cloth and allow the rolls to rise in a warm place until doubled in bulk, about 30 minutes.

✔ Bake at 400 degrees for 12-20 minutes, or until golden brown.

✔ After baking, upend the pan onto a plate and allow the butter-brown sugar-pecan mixture to seep down into the roll for a minute and liberate rolls.

Cinnamon Rolls

I have attended many a feeding frenzy when cinnamon rolls are on the breakfast table. Young people seem to like these rolls with more sugar than I have offered in this recipe. When more sugar seems to be good politics, dissolve 1/2 C of brown sugar to 1/2 stick butter and spread upon the rolled-out dough.

DIRECTIONS
✔ Roll dough to 1/4-inch thick and brush the top of the dough with softened butter.
✔ Prepare a mixture of 1/4 C sugar and 2 t cinnamon and sprinkle it evenly across the top of the dough.
✔ Roll the dough up from the long side and pinch the edge so as to seal in the cinnamon and sugar.
✔ Cut the roll into 3/4-inch pieces.
✔ Place the rolls into an oiled baking pan with their sides lightly touching.
✔ Cover the pan with a damp cloth and allow the rolls to rise in a warm place until doubled in bulk, about 30 minutes.
✔ Bake at 400 degrees for 12-20 minutes, or until golden brown.

Cinnamon Rolls Icing

DIRECTIONS
✔ Bring 4 T half-and-half or milk almost to a boil and add in enough powdered sugar to make a good spreading consistency.
✔ Stir with a wooden spoon until the sugar is dissolved.
✔ Flavor with 1/2 t vanilla.
✔ Spread the icing over the tops of the cinnamon rolls as they come out of the oven.

Angel Biscuits

When the prospect of making beaten biscuit leaves you cold and the baker never seems to have a truly great small roll for the sliced ham and turkey, angel biscuits are the answer. They are easy to make and wonderful.

The rolls can be made a day ahead of time if you place them in the refrigerator, covered with a cloth. When you are ready to use them, remove from the refrigerator and let stand for 10 minutes. Keep an eye on them; you do not want them to rise.

INGREDIENTS
5 C flour
2 C buttermilk
3/4 C vegetable shortening
1/2 C water (lukewarm, 110 degrees)
3 T sugar
1 T baking powder
1 t salt
1 t baking soda
1 pkg. yeast

DIRECTIONS
✔ Dissolve yeast in the water with 1 T of the sugar and set aside.
✔ In a large bowl, combine flour, sugar, salt, baking powder and baking soda and stir gently with a wooden spoon. Cut in shortening with a pastry knife until dough is coarse and pebbly. Add yeast and buttermilk and stir gently with the wooden spoon.
✔ Take a second large bowl and coat the inside of the bowl with shortening. Transfer the dough to this second bowl and turn the dough around the inside of the bowl until the outside of the dough is lightly coated. This will keep a crust from forming.
✔ Roll the dough to 1/2 inch and cut with a small-diameter biscuit cutter. In the absence of a small-diameter biscuit cutter, a whiskey jigger will suffice.
✔ Bake at 400 degrees for 12 minutes.

Beaten Biscuits

I have fond memories of my grandparents and my father and mother making these biscuits in large quantities for an upcoming party. The beaten biscuit is a roll that brings out the best flavor of ham and turkey. I usually make the beaten biscuit on the Thursday night before a Saturday party. Make plenty; if you have some left over, they make delicious buttered toast for Sunday breakfast. The old way is to use lard for the shortening; I use vegetable shortening for reasons that are obvious to me.

The making of beaten biscuits calls for them to be rolled through the rollers of a biscuit brake. If you know the biscuit brake and would like to obtain one, write to me. I will see if I can find one or give you the name of a company that can make one for you.

Alternately, you can make beaten biscuit by rolling the dough out with a rolling pin. The dough should be rolled out to 1 inch, then folded north to south, rolled again to 1 inch thick and then repeated continuously until the dough pops. The old way — when without a biscuit break — was to beat the dough with a rolling pin hundreds of times for your family and hundreds more for company. Sounds charming, but I am not inclined to that work. I have experimented with rolling the dough with success in my effort to imitate the biscuit break.

I realize that only the most flinty-eyed cook will go to the trouble of rolling dough until it blisters, but it is worth it and, to my mind, very satisfying. Hopefully, you will discover the charm and grace of making a biscuit that has been enjoyed in Kentucky for hundreds of years. Pour a fine aged Kentucky bourbon whisky about halfway through the dough rolling enterprise. If your courage fails, you can always bake angel biscuits to put up with your ham and turkey. But as for beaten biscuit, here you have it.

INGREDIENTS
3 C flour, sifted twice with the baking powder and salt
1 t salt
1 t baking powder
1/4 C vegetable shortening
1/2 C whole milk

DIRECTIONS
✔ **Blend all of the ingredients.**
✔ **Roll out until the dough blisters and pops.**
✔ **Cut small biscuits and bake at 350 degrees for 30 minutes.**

Sourdough Bread

INGREDIENTS
2 C flour
1-3/4 C water (lukewarm, 110 degrees)
2 T dry yeast
2 T honey
2-1/2 C flour

Starter

✔ Warm a mixing bowl by running warm water over the inside and outside, then dry with a cloth. Place the yeast in the bowl along with the water and honey. Let stand until it is bubbly, about 20 minutes.
✔ Add the 2 C flour and stir well.
✔ Cover the bowl with a damp cloth and allow starter dough to rise in a warm place, about 80-85 degrees, until doubled in bulk, which will take about an hour and a half. The starter is now ready to use. If you wish to store the starter, place it in an earthenware pot, cover it and keep it at room temperature. It should keep for about a week.
✔ I use my starter up within the week, preferring to make a new batch as I need it. Some like the challenge of keeping the starter active for months on end. Not me. Most of the bourbon distilleries like a new batch of "donna" for each still run, and that is good enough for me.

Sour Dough

✔ The night before you bake, take 1 C starter and sift in 2-1/2 C flour. This will be your sourdough bread.
✔ Add 2 C water and beat well with a wooden spoon. Cover and set in a warm place for 12-15 hours.
When time to ready the dough for baking, return 1 C of the dough to the starter for future use or use it all up with the next batch, according to your preference.
✔ Add enough flour to make dough elastic. Turn out onto a floured board and knead for 10 minutes.
✔ Return the dough to a well-oiled bowl and turn the dough several times to receive a coating of the oil so a crust will not form. Cover the dough and let it rest for 30 minutes.
✔ Divide and form into bread loaves. Cover and let rise until doubled, about 1-1/2 hours.
✔ Bake at 400 degrees for 25 minutes.
Yields 2 loaves.

Buttermilk Pancakes

INGREDIENTS
2 C flour
1 t sugar
1 t salt
1 t baking soda
2 C buttermilk
3 egg yolks, reserve the egg whites in a separate bowl
2 T butter, melted
1 C blueberries, if so inclined, added to the batter

✔ Sift together the flour, sugar, salt and baking soda.
✔ First, combine buttermilk, egg yolk and butter. Then, fold in the egg whites gently.
✔ Pour the flour mixture into the buttermilk mixture and blend together with a whisk gently and briefly. You will want the buttermilk pancake batter lumpy and coarse.
✔ Using a tablespoon drop two spoonfuls onto a hot pan that has just received a teaspoon of vegetable shortening.
✔ When the top of the pancake is about half bubbles, turn it.
✔ When a prick with the edge of the spatula is dry, the pancake is done.
Serves 4-5.

Wheat Loaf Bread

INGREDIENTS
2 C milk
1 pkg. yeast
2 T sugar
2 T butter
2 t salt
3 C whole-wheat flour
2 C white flour

DIRECTIONS
✔ Scald milk by bringing to boiling point for several seconds. Add in the sugar, butter and salt.
✔ Allow to cool to about 110-115 degrees and add yeast, stirring with a whisk until dissolved.
✔ Sift flour into an oiled bowl and add milk gradually. Stir with a wooden spoon until a soft dough is formed. Take care not to make the dough overly moist.
✔ Cover and let rise until doubled in bulk. Shape into loaves. Place loaves onto an oiled pan and allow to rise until doubled.
✔ Bake at 375 degrees for about an hour.

Carrot Zucchini Muffins

These muffins come to me by way of the University of Kentucky Extension Homemakers. They are simply great. I use a small-size muffin pan. If you need a simple muffin that tastes great, this is your deal.

INGREDIENTS
1-3/4 C flour
3/4 C brown sugar
1/2 C wheat germ
3/4 t salt
1-1/2 t soda

1-1/2 t cinnamon
3/4 C buttermilk
1/4 C canola oil
1/4 C applesauce
1 egg, beaten
2 t vanilla

1-1/2 C zucchini, shredded
1/2 C carrot, shredded
1/2 C raisins
1/2 C pecans, rolled coarsely

DIRECTIONS
✔ Use three separate bowls.
✔ In the first bowl mix together the dry ingredients. In the second bowl beat the buttermilk ingredients lightly with a whisk. In the third bowl mix together the zucchini, carrots, raisins and pecans.
✔ Combine the contents of all three bowls in the largest bowl and stir with a wooden spoon until the batter is thoroughly blended.
✔ Bake in a well-oiled muffin tin using paper liners at 350 degrees for 25 minutes.

Hushpuppies

INGREDIENTS
2-1/4 C cornmeal
1 C milk
3 T self-rising flour
1 T onion, finely chopped
1 egg, beaten

DIRECTIONS
✔ Combine the ingredients. Roll into desired size. In a skillet, bring shortening to a hot point and fry the hushpuppies to a golden brown.

Buttermilk Corn Bread

There are so many corn bread recipes. I have received well-deserved criticism over the years for deviating from historic corn breads that were the staple diet of the brave families who originally settled Kentucky. Many of these early corn bread recipes were born of hardship and seasoned with strife. I have read many an account of our pioneer families sitting down to a meal of a corn bread made up of cracked corn, mixed with a mashing of pulverized corn and then rolled into the available lard and either baked or fried. This meal basic was then flavored with the proceeds of hunting that day, if any luck had prevailed. Praise be to them; the tribulations they endured for the sake of future generations have my complete respect and admiration.

When I catch trout and cook over an open fire, I enjoy cooking some of our frontier foods under what I imagine to be a similar condition. Otherwise, I have felt no necessity to use the bland coarse food of privation, siege and survival, just for the sake of it.

However, I like the tradition of baking corn bread. The texture and aroma of cornmeal flour is appealing. Depending on the entrée, we will bake corn bread in iron muffin or iron corn pans. If you want to cook corn bread the old-fashioned way, pour the batter into a cast-iron skillet and bake it. Truth be known, this is the way I like it. However, I am encouraged by the women who surround my life to present corn bread with a pleasing appearance, which for them is not associated with a big slice of crumbling corn bread scooped out of the skillet and placed onto my plate with a dab of melting butter on top.

Fill the irons or the skillet about 3/4 to the rim. The corn bread will rise.

INGREDIENTS
2 C cornmeal
1 t salt
1-1/2 t baking powder
1/2 t baking soda

3 T shortening, melted

1-1/2 C buttermilk
3 eggs, beaten

DIRECTIONS
✔ Place corn bread irons or the skillet into a 400-degree oven.
✔ Mix the dry ingredients together. Add the shortening to the cornmeal mixture. Add the buttermilk and the eggs. Stir all of the ingredients together with a wooden spoon.
✔ Retrieve the corn bread irons from the oven and pour the batter into the irons. Bake at 400 degrees until golden brown. If using a skillet, test the middle.

Banana Nut Bread

INGREDIENTS
2/3 C sugar
1/3 C shortening
3 T buttermilk
2 eggs, beaten

2 C flour, sifted
1/2 t soda
1/2 t salt

1 C ripe bananas, mashed
1/2 C pecans, finely chopped

DIRECTIONS
✔ In a mixing bowl, cream the sugar, shortening, buttermilk and eggs. Over the mixing bowl, sift in the combined flour, soda and salt. Blend with a wooden spoon. Fold in the banana, pecans and buttermilk.
✔Make certain your loaf pan is well oiled. Bake at 350 degrees for 50-60 minutes.

Kentucky Spoon Bread

INGREDIENTS
1 C boiling water
1/2 C cornmeal

1 T baking powder
1/2 t salt
1/4 C milk

3 eggs, whites only, beat until stiff

DIRECTIONS
✔ Pour the boiling water over the cornmeal, then mix in the baking powder and salt. Pour in the milk and beat briskly.
✔ Fold in the egg whites.
✔ Pour into an oiled glass baking pan. Bake at 350 degrees for about 30 minutes. Spoon the bread onto each plate.

Meat/Vegetable Sauces and Salad Dressings

I have a dozen good meat/vegetable sauces and salad dressings that dominate my cooking. I use them frequently and often. My wife, Margaret Sue, and I have a feud that started with our marriage and has lasted to this day over sauces. Margaret Sue feels I should increase the range and scope of my sauces and dressings. I defer to her judgment in most matters relating to style but fight her fearlessly on sauces and dressings. I find pleasure in preparing certain sauces and dressings and, therefore, stand my turf.

It is a cooking imperative that you taste any sauce or dressing that you prepare. When you have completed your sauce or dressing, by all means, taste it. This is an area of cooking where your opinion really matters. The addition of some salt or pepper or a little more thickening can make a world of difference to the final outcome.

I have a decided preference for using sauces and dressings lightly. When you purchase the best-quality meats and produce, you have the essential ingredients for an outstanding dining experience. The sauces and dressings are presented to enhance the great tastes of those foods. Therefore, I tend to place the amount I think is correct upon the food and leave a bowl on the side for those that prefer more.

Masters Steak Sauce

If you do not have a steak sauce that you can claim, use this sauce. I have been making up sauce recipes for years, and I love this one. What is the secret ingredient? Somebody, somewhere, told me to try ginger in my sauce. I did and the rest is history. Masters Steak Sauce will keep indefinitely when refrigerated, although at my gatherings it is inhaled, the bowl scraped clean.

Masters Steak Sauce is used on all premium steak cuts but reaches majesty on rare beef: prime rib and tenderloin. It is the reason we cook baby back ribs. As a dressing for grilled or broiled ground meats, it is divine. We have also drizzled it on Bibb lettuce salads and used it to flavor green beans with great success. That tells me folks will take Masters Steak Sauce any way they can get it.

Many a time I have been standing at the grill at McManus House with a gallery of folk around me when the question came, "May I taste your sauce?" Long ago I learned to place Benedictine, pimento cheese and crackers in close proximity to the grill. That way a fellow can dip a cracker, and I do not have to suffer a finger dragged around the bowl wherein dwells my Masters Steak Sauce.

I have seen many a man taste Masters Steak Sauce on a cracker. His next foray into the sauce is with a cracker loaded down with Benedictine and pimento cheese. Makes sense to me. Done it myself.

I almost always double the recipe for Masters Steak Sauce. This sauce disappears quickly at McManus House.

INGREDIENTS
2-1/2 C tomato sauce
1 C brown sugar
1/2 C red wine vinegar
4 T dry mustard
2 T powdered ginger
2 t pepper
2 t salt
2 t garlic powder

2 T fine aged Kentucky bourbon whisky
1 T lemon juice

DIRECTIONS
✔ Combine all ingredients except the olive oil, lemon and bourbon. Simmer for 20 minutes, stirring with a whisk.
✔ Turn off the heat and stir in the olive oil, lemon and bourbon.
Let Masters Steak Sauce cool in the pan for about 30 minutes. This will allow the vinegar and bourbon to settle. Cover and refrigerate overnight to blend the flavors. I find the sauce especially good on the third day.

Bourbon Cheese Sauce

We have served our bourbon cheese sauce over asparagus, broccoli and cauliflower for many years. I often steer around hollandaise sauce, mainly because I find this too delicate for entertaining a large group when I am doing the cooking, drinking a fine aged Kentucky bourbon whisky, enjoying my friends and not having a precise dinner schedule.

INGREDIENTS
1 C sharp cheddar cheese, grated
1/2 C half-and-half
1/4 C butter
2 t fresh lemon juice
parsley, chopped
4 dashes fine aged Kentucky bourbon whisky
pepper, ground

DIRECTIONS
✔ Place the cheese in a pan. Add the half-and-half and the butter. Stir the sauce on a low heat with a whisk until it is creamy.
✔ Add the lemon juice, parsley and bourbon whisky. Grind pepper onto the sauce.

Hollandaise Sauce

INGREDIENTS
1/2 C butter
2 egg yolks, beaten
1 T lemon juice, fresh
1/4 C water, in the lower pan
1/4 t salt
pepper, ground

DIRECTIONS
✔ Using a double boiler, bring water in lower pan to a simmer.
✔ In upper pan, melt one-half of the butter; add the eggs and the lemon juice. Stir constantly with a whisk. When the sauce begins to thicken, add the remaining butter. As this thickens, add the boiling water. When the mixture is thickened once again, season with the salt and pepper.
✔ If the sauce separates, add boiling water drop by drop, stirring with the whisk.

Lobster Sauce

A dd to hollandaise 1/2 C finely chopped lobster. It is a wonderful sauce on broccoli, cauliflower and asparagus. We love to serve it on premier cuts of filet of fish such as swordfish or salmon.

Horseradish Sauce

A dd to hollandaise 4 T grated horseradish and 2 T heavy cream as it is removed from the heat. Stir briskly with the whisk until the sauce has stiffened. A real good complement to buttered lamb chops and rare filet of beef.

Béarnaise Sauce

A dd to hollandaise 1 t each of fine chopped parsley and tarragon. It is a classic with rare beef. We like it best on strip steak that has been grilled with the upper side heavily coated with coarse black pepper.

Chives Sauce

A dd to hollandaise chives or finely chopped spring onion (bulb and upper leaves). Pour over new potatoes.

Mushroom Sauce

A dd sautéed mushrooms to the basic cream sauce for use on filet of beef or chicken breast.

Sour Cream Dressing

The sour cream dressing is a favorite of Margaret Sue's, and this is a recipe she favors. I have always found that egg-based sauces tax my patience. Margaret Sue prepares sour cream dressing for asparagus, and when she does, I am her most enthusiastic supporter. Like hollandaise sauce, it is a trick to make it in quantities required for a large group; therefore, its making lends itself to a dinner of two or three couples, making sour cream sauce a product of Margaret Sue's domain.

INGREDIENTS
2 egg yolks, beaten
1 C sour cream
1 T lemon juice
1 t salt
1/4 t dry mustard
1/4 t sugar
Tabasco sauce to taste

DIRECTIONS
✔ In a mixing bowl and using a whisk, blend the egg yolks and the sour cream.
✔ Add the remaining ingredients and stir them into the mixture.
✔ Using a double boiler on a simmering boil, heat the sauce very gently, stirring continuously with the whisk. The dressing will curdle if it gets too much heat.

Blue Cheese Dressing

INGREDIENTS
1/4 lb. blue cheese, crumpled

1/4 C evaporated milk
1/2 C Hellmann's mayonnaise

1/4 C olive oil
1/4 C red wine vinegar
1/2 t Worcestershire sauce
1/4 t ground pepper
1/4 t salt
1 clove garlic, minced

DIRECTIONS
✔ Beat milk and mayonnaise until light.
✔ Combine the remaining ingredients and stir.

Basic Cream Sauce

If there is a sauce that can be used a hundred different ways, it would have to be cream sauce. There are chefs around the world that spend a lifetime perfecting their cream sauces. I advocate the learning of the basic cream sauce, and in this sauce is the foundation for dozens of interesting flavors. Let your imagination lead you to a couple of cream sauces you enjoy, and by all means, name one after yourself.

I enjoy the taste and visual appeal of herbs, especially on sauces. I often sprinkle parsley and basil on top of the sauce and do not hesitate to use chives and spring onion.

Be creative. Your guests will love it.

There is a simple elegance I admire that is inherent in the basic cream sauce. I use this sauce on fowl of any kind, filet of fish and numerous pasta and vegetable dishes. As it might suit your purpose, flavor the sauce with fresh lemon, lime or paprika. Tabasco sauce finds a place on occasion.

Prepare lima beans, boiled or baked onions, green peas, zucchini squash or cauliflower. Pour basic cream sauce over your vegetable of choice and toss gently. Serve immediately.

The basic cream sauce is a wedding of butter, cream and flour. Remembering that milk products deteriorate under heat; be kind to the sauce and just simmer it.

The basic cream sauce is: 1 C half-and-half, 3 T butter, 3 T flour, 1/4 t salt and ground pepper.

DIRECTIONS
✔ **Place the half-and-half in a pan, add the butter and stir with a whisk over a low heat. Stir in the flour. When you are satisfied that the cream sauce is well blended, if thickening is deemed desirable, add a small amount of cornstarch dissolved in a small amount of cold water, gradually. Stir the cream sauce with a whisk over a low simmering heat until it is of the consistency you require. Add the salt and ground pepper.**

Egg Sauce

Add a lightly beaten egg yolk to the basic cream sauce and stir in with a whisk over a low heat. Serve over broccoli and cauliflower. Sprinkle the top with paprika.

Cheese Sauce

Add grated mild cheddar cheese to the basic cream sauce and add fresh lemon or lime juice, if you like. The combination is good on all manner of steamed vegetables.

We like this sauce on open-faced club sandwiches. To toast, add a thick, peeled tomato slice, lettuce and four strips of cooked bacon, and give the sandwich a good covering of cheese sauce. Pour on Masters Steak Sauce for a powerfully great Sunday breakfast treat.

Clam Sauce

Add clam liquor to the basic cream sauce to create a wonderful sauce over pasta noodles or filet of fish. Add anchovy paste for accent. If you enjoy clams, if or when they are cooked, mince them and stir them into the sauce.

Shrimp Sauce

Add a good quantity of cooked and cleaned whole shrimp to the basic cream sauce. Pour the sauce over egg noodles. Sprinkle poppy seed and grind black pepper over the sauce.

Scallop Sauce

Steam scallops and place in a serving bowl. Squeeze half a lemon over the scallops. Pour the basic cream sauce over the scallops. Pour the sauce over egg noodles. Sprinkle the sauce liberally with fresh chopped parsley and spring onion. Grind black pepper onto the sauce.

Almond Sauce

Sauté slivered almonds and add to the basic cream sauce to complement fish and fowl.

Wine-Flavored Vinaigrette

INGREDIENTS
3/4 C olive oil
3 T red wine, port or sherry
3 T red wine vinegar
1 T Coleman's mustard powder
1-1/2 t Worcestershire sauce
pepper
salt
pinch sugar

DIRECTIONS
✔ Process in a blender.
Yields 1 cup.

French Dressing

We use french dressing on Bibb lettuce and spinach salads. We also enjoy it on grapefruit and orange slices. Refrigerate overnight to blend the flavors. Some like to retain a portion of the onion; I do not.

INGREDIENTS
1/2 C olive oil
juice of 1/2 orange
juice of 1/2 lemon
1 T parsley, finely chopped
1 T onion, finely chopped
1 t Worcestershire sauce
1 t onion salt
1/4 t mustard powder
1/4 t paprika

DIRECTIONS
✔ Combine all of the ingredients and mix well with a whisk.
✔ Cover and refrigerate one day to blend the flavors. Pour the dressing through a handheld fine-mesh strainer into a bowl to capture the onion, which you will discard.

Vinaigrette

You will use this simple-to-make, basic dressing for lettuce-based salads and cold marinated asparagus. We include crumbled blue cheese, feta and other dry cheeses when it suits our fancy, making the vinaigrette a good foundation salad and vegetable dressing.

Sliced cucumbers, tomatoes and red onion, marinated for an hour in vinaigrette, are terrific. We love this salad in the heat of summer. It can be made in large quantity for a barbecue or picnic.

I often find myself amazed that vinaigrette is such a fine marinade for meats, and over the years I have made multiple and various use of it.

INGREDIENTS
2 T lemon juice, freshly squeezed
2 cloves garlic, minced
1 C olive oil
1 T white vinegar
2 t salt
1 t pepper, ground

DIRECTIONS
✔ Place the lemon juice in a bowl; scrape the lemon pulp into the bowl. Add the garlic. Let stand for about an hour.
✔ Pour the mixture through a handheld fine-mesh strainer into a mixing bowl.
✔ Then, using a whisk, mix in the olive oil, vinegar, salt and ground pepper. Cover and refrigerate until ready to serve.

Thousand Island Dressing

INGREDIENTS
1 C Hellmann's mayonnaise
1/4 C chili sauce
2 hard-boiled eggs, chopped fine
2 T spring onion, chopped fine
2 T green pepper, chopped fine
2 T half-and-half
1 t Worcestershire sauce

DIRECTIONS
✔ Blend the mayonnaise and the chili sauce with a whisk.
✔ Then, one at a time, stir in the eggs, onion and green pepper.
✔ Add the half-and-half and the Worcestershire sauce and stir for several minutes with the whisk.
✔ Refrigerate and serve chilled.

Creamy Cocktail Sauce

INGREDIENTS
1 C tomato sauce
2 T horseradish
juice of 1/2 lemon
1/2 C sour cream
1/2 t ginger
salt
pepper
Worcestershire sauce to taste

Cocktail Sauce

INGREDIENTS
1 C ketchup
1 T horseradish
juice of 1 lemon

Henry Bain Sauce

I have encountered several recipes for this sauce, which originated with the headwaiter at the Pendennis Club in Louisville early in the twentieth century. This is the one I use.

INGREDIENTS
7-oz. bottle tomato ketchup
6-oz. bottle chili sauce
5-oz. bottle Worcestershire sauce
5-1/2-oz. bottle A-1 steak sauce
1 lb. chutney, chopped fine

Mornay Sauce

Pour 3 C béchamel sauce into a double boiler. Add 3 egg yolks, 3/4 C parmesan cheese and 1 T butter. Stir with a whisk over medium heat until blended.

Béchamel Sauce

INGREDIENTS
3 C half-and-half
1/2 C flour
1/2 C butter
1/2 C onion, diced finely
1 t salt
1 t red pepper flakes

DIRECTIONS
✔ In a pan, blend the half-and-half and the flour.
✔ In a separate pan, sauté the onion in the butter and then combine with the half-and-half. Stir with a whisk over a low heat. Season with the salt and red pepper.

Mayonnaise

Refrigerate all of the ingredients in their containers before making the mayonnaise, thereby keeping the temperature of the ingredients uniform. Two hours of refrigeration should be sufficient. There is no substitute for fresh-squeezed lemon.

INGREDIENTS
1 egg, beaten
2 egg yolks, beaten
1 C olive oil
1/2 t salt
1/2 t mustard powder
juice of 1 lemon, squeezed and strained
1/2 C whipping cream, optional
1 T onion juice, strained, optional

DIRECTIONS
✔ Mix the eggs in a bowl at slow speed for a minute and add the olive oil a teaspoon at a time.
✔ Add the salt, mustard and lemon juice.
✔ Mix mayonnaise until thickened.
✔ Optional: If a creamy mayonnaise is desired, add the whipping cream.
Yields 1-1/2 cups.

Brown Mushroom Sauce

I use the brown mushroom sauce for buttered lamb chops and roasts of beef.

INGREDIENTS
basic cream sauce
butter
mushrooms, sliced thin
red wine or sherry
1 T onion, finely chopped
drippings or beef bouillon

DIRECTIONS
✔ Prepare the basic cream sauce and set aside.
✔ In a pan, sauté thinly sliced mushrooms in butter and a small amount of red wine or sherry until the mushrooms are tender.
✔ In another pan, sauté butter and a tablespoon of finely chopped onion over medium-high heat until the butter and the onion are a good brown color.
✔ Use some of the drippings from a prepared red meat or use a dissolved beef bouillon cube and add to the cream mixture. Stir in with a whisk.
✔ Add the mushrooms and the onion and allow the brown mushroom sauce to slowly simmer, all the while stirring with the whisk.

Horseradish Sauce

McManus House likes horseradish sauce. It is a versatile sauce that is good on rare beef and, with the addition of some Hellmann's mayonnaise, is a fine vegetable dip. Experiment with other herbs, like basil, dill, chives and mustard.

INGREDIENTS
2 C sour cream
3/4 C prepared horseradish
1/2 C spring onion, chopped
1 T lemon juice, freshly squeezed
salt

DIRECTIONS
✔ In a mixing bowl combine the ingredients.
✔ Refrigerate for several hours to blend the flavors.

Salads

Every meal, in my opinion, benefits from a salad. I like to serve mixtures of fruits at any meal in a big bowl or on a bed of Bibb lettuce or spinach leaves. I combine Bibb lettuce and spinach with fruit for luncheon and dinner.

Several slices of pineapple cut fresh with a dab of smearcase is elegant. Melons and fresh blueberries are wonderful. Strawberries and blackberries are an early-summer treat. The trick is to use fresh fruit and avoid the syrupy mess that canned fruit is immersed in. My one exception is mandarin oranges; I buy them in the can.

One of the more irritating vexations in life, as far as I am concerned, is a warm salad, intentional or otherwise. I like chilled salads. I have not tasted a warm salad that ever appealed to me. To the extent that I can, I make my salads ahead of time so they may cool in the refrigerator. I even go so far as to place my lettuce in a colander, setting the colander in a bowl and layering ice cubes across the top to achieve maximum chilling effect. I withhold the dressing until serving time.

Mixed Green Salad

The mixed green salad used in our entertaining is a meal unto itself. I serve it in all seasons but find it especially attractive as an early Sunday dinner.

When we are entertaining people we know from central Kentucky, we use a cheese made by the cloistered friars of Gethsemani Abbey that they call Trappist Cheese and that we affectionately call Monk's Cheese. The cheese is absolutely strong as to taste and absolutely pungent and sour in aroma. Those of us who have grown up around the Gethsemani Abbey, just south of Bardstown, have an appreciation for their cheeses and bourbon-soaked fruitcakes. The bourbon-soaked fruitcakes have found a loyal clientele and are exported all over the world as the best of their kind. Monk's Cheese, however, I fear, is an acquired affinity, and therefore, I offer feta cheese as an acceptable substitute.

Margaret Sue likes tarragon as an additional spice; I like basil and chives. McManus House is an American household, and we tend to accommodate both of our preferences and use all three, thereby circumventing a challenge. The herb garden, outside the back door, is kept well clipped by our usage of it.

Use 8 ounces of beef tenderloin or 2 chicken breasts. Sauté one or the other in butter until the beef tenderloin is medium rare or the chicken breast is cooked throughout. Slice the beef or the chicken on the diagonal, thin, keeping the pieces as long as you can.

INGREDIENTS
5 C mixed young lettuce
5 eggs, hard-boiled, chopped
1 C red onion, diced
6 oz. feta cheese
2 tomatoes, peeled and quartered
tarragon
basil
chives
pepper, ground
vinaigrette dressing
8 oz. beef tenderloin or 2 chicken breast fillets

DIRECTIONS
✔ Combine the lettuce and the hard-boiled eggs and divide the lettuce among four dinner plates.
✔ Sprinkle the lettuce on each plate with the red onion and the feta cheese.
✔ Garnish the sides of each plate with the quartered tomatoes.
✔ Season with tarragon, basil, chives and pepper to taste.
✔ Place 3-4 beef tenderloin or chicken breast strips on top of the salad.
✔ Pour the vinaigrette dressing over the salad.

McManus House Salad

There are times when only the most delicious salad I know of will suffice. McManus House salad is one I enjoy grazing upon. I always regret finding my bowl empty. This salad is strictly hammers back and ready.

The McManus House salad works well with a light entrée such as buttered lamb chops or a small cut of filet of beef. It can be made in good quantity for a seated dinner or a luncheon of eight guests.

INGREDIENTS
2 C chicken breast, diced
2 heads Bibb lettuce
1 head iceberg lettuce
1 stalk of romaine lettuce, inner leaves
1 C Thousand Island dressing
3/4 C blue cheese, crumbled
2 T white wine vinegar
tarragon
parsley
basil
ground black pepper
16 bacon slices, cooked

DIRECTIONS
✔ Shred the lettuce into bite-size pieces. Mix all of the ingredients together.
✔ Season with the tarragon, parsley, basil and ground pepper.
✔ Place the McManus House salad into eight bowls.
✔ Place two strips of shredded bacon on the top of each salad.

Field Salad

The field salad is an elegant salad, wonderful in appearance, exceptionally good in taste. This is a salad that uses a collection of lettuces, such as romaine, mesclun, Bibb and iceberg. To the lettuce mixture, add crumpled feta cheese, diced green onion and half a smartly seasoned sautéed chicken breast that has been cut into quarter-size pieces.

After the field salad has been portioned to each salad plate, garnish the top of the salad with purple onion and surround the lettuce with slices of hard-boiled egg and peeled cucumber. The dressing we like to use is a flavored vinaigrette, such as a raspberry vinaigrette. Grind black pepper liberally across the salad as it resides on each plate.

Spinach Salad

INGREDIENTS
8 oz. spinach leaves
1 medium red onion, sliced thin
8 bacon strips, cooked crisp and chopped fine
1 can mandarin oranges, drained
4 medium-size mushrooms, fresh and sliced thin
1/4 C almonds, slivered
pepper, ground
french dressing

DIRECTIONS
✔ Devein spinach leaves, wash in several cold waters, drain and dry thoroughly. Shred the spinach into reasonable pieces.
✔ In a mixing bowl combine all the ingredients with the spinach leaves. Cover and refrigerate until time to serve.
✔ Just before serving, mix in french dressing and toss until spinach leaves are moist. Grind pepper onto salad. This salad performs best when the dressing is used lightly.

Bibb Lettuce Salad

INGREDIENTS
3 heads Bibb lettuce
1 grapefruit, peeled, sections removed
1 can mandarin oranges, drained
1 bunch spring onion, chopped up to the green leaves
french dressing
pepper, ground

DIRECTIONS
✔ Place 6-8 Bibb lettuce leaves on each dinner plate or salad plate.
✔ Arrange grapefruit and mandarin oranges on top of lettuce.
✔ Sprinkle on the spring onion.
✔ Pour on the french dressing, sparingly. Grind pepper onto salad.

Red Potato Salad

INGREDIENTS
12 red potatoes, boiled
2 C sour cream
1 bunch green onion, onion bulb and green leaves, chopped
1 C celery, diced
1 T seasoning salt
2 t pepper

DIRECTIONS
✔ Allow the potatoes to cool, and when cool, quarter them.
✔ Coat the potatoes with the sour cream, tossing gently.
✔ Distribute the spring onion, celery, seasoning salt and pepper throughout the bowl and again, toss gently.
✔ Refrigerate the red potato salad overnight to blend flavors.

Apple Salad

We often use fruit in our salads as a counterpoint to the meat we serve. I have always favored lemon and the natural sweet taste of fruit. Apple salad is another fine example of this tendency. Apple salad is used as a summer salad, but we also like to place a nice spoonful next to roasted pork tenderloin and any of the wild birds we harvest in the fall and winter, such as dove, duck and goose.

INGREDIENTS
6 Granny Smith apples, cut in slices and then cut in half
4 bananas, sliced medium thin
1 C dried cranberries
1 C walnuts, chopped coarse
1/2 C Hellmann's mayonnaise
juice of 1 lemon, freshly squeezed
pepper, ground

DIRECTIONS
✔ Combine all the ingredients and toss, making certain that all the fruit is coated with the mayonnaise.
✔ Cover and refrigerate for 8 hours to blend the flavors.

Wild Rice Salad.

This is a wildly popular salad for those that know it. Mimi served it so often at Elmwood that she developed a regular following that included a number of the best Southern cooks in Louisville. For those of us that cook wild game, it is a standard, and for others, it is a wonderful accoutrement to baked chicken and turkey. But really, it is good anytime and can be made in good quantity the day before.

You will want to cook a cup of wild rice in 4 cups of water and allow it to cool. To the wild rice add 1/2 C each of white raisins, dried cranberries, mandarin oranges, diced celery and spring onions. Scrape the zest from one orange.

The dressing is 1/2 C of fresh orange juice and 1/2 C of olive oil. I like to squeeze lemon over the salad just before serving.

Smearcase

I have never seen smearcase outside of the Bluegrass region of Kentucky. It is a very elegant tomato topping. A bed of Bibb lettuce with thick-sliced peeled tomatoes and smearcase is a great salad.

Margaret Sue and I enjoy smearcase as a sandwich dressing. Peel chilled cucumbers. Run the tines of a fork down the length of a cucumber to create an attractive appearance. Slice the cucumbers, as if for a salad. Dress slices of party or loaf bread with smearcase and place slices of cucumber on each piece of bread. Season with salt and pepper and garnish with paprika.

INGREDIENTS
1 qt. cottage cheese, large curd
1/4 C Hellmann's mayonnaise
2 bunches spring onions, bulb only, diced
ground pepper

DIRECTIONS
✔ Combine the cottage cheese and the mayonnaise in a mixing bowl and blend at a slow speed. You will need to turn off the mixer several times and use a wooden spoon to bring the cottage cheese to the top.
✔ When blended, add the spring onion.
✔ Cover and refrigerate for eight hours.
✔ When ready to serve, grind black pepper across the top of the smearcase.

Sandwiches, Soups and Stews

My grandfather made his meal into a sandwich, no matter the part of day, no matter that which occupied his plate. My best friend from the day of my birth transforms his repast into soup, calling upon copious quantities of gravies, sauces, dressings and melting ice cream to perform his despicable work. My duck-hunting partner makes every breakfast, lunch and dinner into a stew. These aberrant dining practices have no respect for the clans or the classes. So it is with sandwiches, soups and stews; what one man desires the other disdains. The eye of the beholder defines the nature of the meal and asks not the opinion of another.

So many sandwiches, soups and stews start with the bounty harvested from our vegetable gardens. In the days before refrigeration, the potatoes, carrots, onions and turnips were spread upon racks in dry, dark, cool rooms to await their need, sometimes as much as a year from their pickin'. Elmwood had such a room, even though the modern household of my youth had several refrigerators upon the premises and a grocery store just minutes away. Papa enjoyed the ambience of the vegetable storeroom, though all of us knew he could afford cold storage.

I remember fondly working the vegetable garden with Papa, sharing my father's pleasure of growing vegetables in a garden, straining and sweating under a Kentucky August sun. I remember Papa requiring all of his brood to join him if they evidenced time upon their hands. I remember the smell of the earth turned by file-sharpened hoes, the dust filling the pores of our skin. I remember the feeling that I was my father's companion in the garden. And I remember the delight and approval of my mother and my sisters as they received the baskets of produce from our hands to be made by their skilled hands into sandwiches, soups and stews.

Kentucky Hot Brown

The revered Hot Brown received its legendary beginning in the kitchen of the Brown Hotel in Louisville in the late 1920s. It is a rarebit whose reputation transcends the boundaries of the commonwealth. When people learn that I am an author of a cookbook, I am often asked if I have the recipe for the Kentucky Hot Brown. The Kentucky Hot Brown is so well regarded in the hospitality culture of Kentucky that it finds high appreciation, even when it has not been served. The mint julep and bourbon ball are of the same elevation.

Sadly, the original recipe for the sauce is conjecture, as the original recipe appears to have been lost. No matter, a great Kentucky Hot Brown is all about a good-tasting sauce, regardless of the recipe. Cissy Gregg, the great food editor of the *Courier Journal,* reported that she had known the Kentucky Hot Brown as prepared by the Brown Hotel and asked her readers to combine Mornay and béchamel sauces. I love the Kentucky Hot Brown with this blend of sauces, labor intensive as it may be.

I do not for a minute believe that the original Kentucky Hot Brown utilized a cheese sauce, but so what. If you feel trepidation by making the Hot Brown, simply make a cream sauce of 3 C milk, 6 T flour and a stick of butter. Add two egg yolks and then salt and cayenne pepper to taste. To this add a cup of grated cheddar cheese and 2 T parmesan.

There are many good sauces for the Kentucky Hot Brown, and you can take it on account that when I hear of a restaurant that is reported to have a good Kentucky Hot Brown, I am at the next seating. The imperative in the Kentucky Hot Brown is the use of fresh turkey or chicken.

Make each Kentucky Hot Brown as an individual serving, broiled and served in its own ovenproof dish.

INGREDIENTS
white bread, toasted, 2 slices per dish
chicken or turkey, 4 slices per dish
bacon, crisp, 6 slices per dish
tomatoes, peeled and sliced medium, 2 per dish
paprika

Mornay, béchamel or cheese sauce

DIRECTIONS
✔ **Using a double boiler on low heat, stir and blend the sauce or sauces continuously until the sauce is creamy.**
✔ **Toast two slices of bread and diagonally slice the bread; place in the bottom of the ovenproof dish. In layering fashion, add the tomato, turkey and bacon. Pour the sauce generously over the Kentucky Hot Brown and sprinkle with paprika.**
✔ **Place under the broiler until it is bubbly and browned.**

The Club Sandwich

Have mercy on me, I do love a club sandwich. They are just as easily made in a group of four sandwiches, as once you have hauled out the ingredients, you may as well start an assembly line. The recipe is for one club sandwich, the better to see how the three-deck sandwich is constructed.

I have seen the club made with city ham and pressed meats of every description. Forget it. Leave the ham out and make the club sandwich with fresh sliced turkey breast, and you will experience a monumentally great sandwich.

INGREDIENTS
3 white or potato bread slices, toasted
8 turkey breast slices, thin
6 strips bacon, crisp
4 tomato slices, thin
Bibb or iceberg lettuce
Hellmann's mayonnaise
salt
pepper

4 wooden spears
Durkee's dressing

DIRECTIONS
✔ Spread a generous portion of Hellmann's mayonnaise on a piece of toast and season with salt and pepper. Place lettuce leaves enough to cover the bread. Add 4 slices turkey breast, 3 strips bacon and 2 tomato slices. Top with a second piece of toast.
✔ Build the sandwich again in reverse order, ending with the lettuce. Close the sandwich with the third piece of toast, which has received Hellmann's mayonnaise, salt and pepper.
✔ Slice the club sandwich diagonally twice, and you will end up with 4 quartered sandwiches. Place a wooden spear in each quarter to hold it together. As you gain experience making the club sandwich, you will find that you center the wooden spears in each quarter of the bread before cutting.
✔ Durkee's dressing on the side of the plate for dipping is magnificent.

Bacon, Lettuce and Tomato

Use the classic BLT to act as a foundation for any one of a dozen sandwiches. We always have a half-dozen varieties of tomato in our summer garden, all begging to be a part of one of the BLT derivatives.

Classic BLT

We like the old standard of bacon, lettuce and tomato on toast with Hellmann's mayonnaise, salt and pepper. It would not be a stretch to say we plant some tomato varieties with the classic BLT in mind.

Open-Faced BLT

Top one slice of toast with lettuce, tomato, yellow onion, bacon and sharp cheddar cheese. Grill under the broiler until bubbly. Top with a good dousing of Worcestershire sauce. Two open-faced sandwiches for Sunday brunch with a large glass of iced tea works well for me.

Benedictine BLT

Spread Benedictine on each piece of toast. Add bacon, lettuce, tomato and a thin slice of purple onion.

Corned Beef BLT

Corned beef sliced cold and thin and piled high is a beautiful sight to behold. Adding bacon, lettuce and tomato makes a corned beef sandwich as good as it gets. Some use hot mustard as a dressing. I use Thousand Island, with a good lick of prepared horseradish stirred in for accent.

Garden BLT

To the classic BLT add chopped spring onion, sliced cucumber and sliced yellow squash. Top with smearcase and garnish with chopped pecans or walnuts.

Ground Steak BLT

When you order ground beef, select the cut of meat that is your pleasure. Have the butcher grind it for you fresh. As far as I am concerned, packaged ground beef is mystery meat, and I will not abide it. I select a piece of sirloin from the meat case and request it ground to my specifications. Sounds a little priggish, I know, but that is the way I do it.

Grill an 8-ounce ground-sirloin steak patty medium-well-done, place between two toasted and buttered English muffin halves, then add bacon, lettuce, tomato and a big slice of purple onion. Sprinkle on blue cheese as a topping. We use Masters Steak Sauce as a dressing. Grind black pepper generously across the top of the sandwich.

Dressed Country Ham Sandwich

Cut a yeast roll or a soft egg roll in half. Spread both sides thinly with Hellmann's mayonnaise or smearcase. Cover one side of the roll with Bibb lettuce. Cut a peeled tomato thin and place on the bed of lettuce. Place 4 thin slices of country ham on top of the peeled tomato. Grind pepper onto the country ham. Serve with red potato salad. It is the best-dressed sandwich I know of.

Tuna Salad

Tuna salad is made by eye and by taste. Use only the best, the premium, white fancy albacore tuna. To a can of tuna, add enough Hellmann's mayonnaise to cover. Squeeze half a lemon over the tuna. Add some sweet pickle relish and diced celery. Salt and pepper to taste. Add Tabasco sauce for accent.

Toast bread. Add Bibb lettuce leaves and a smallish slice of onion. Magnificent!

Country Ham Reuben

The Reuben sandwich originated in New York at a restaurant of the same name. It is a remarkable sandwich that finds a following in many cultures. The Irish taverns I frequent in Chicago and St. Louis both prepare an outstanding Reuben that I accompany with a frothy Guinness beer, tapped from a keg and served at room temperature. My favorite Jewish deli in Cincinnati uses a marbled rye bread with a hard crust for their Reuben and it is wonderful. In Louisville I am drawn to a watering hole and restaurant in the Germantown section where the Reuben is made with an oversized dark rye bread.

The ingredients for the classic Reuben sandwich in my view is: Russian dressing spread evenly on rye bread, six ounces of pastrami sliced paper thin, a thin layer of drained sauerkraut and several slices of Swiss cheese. The Reuben is then closed and toasted on both sides in a pan with butter. A good bread and a premium pastrami is the foundation for a great Reuben.

I am a Kentucky boy and it was just a matter of time before I would receive a recipe for the Reuben made with Country ham. The version I like uses: Thousand Island dressing spread evenly on sourdough bread, three ounces of center cut Country ham sliced paper-thin, a thin layer of drained sauerkraut and several slices of Swiss cheese. The Country ham Reuben is then closed and grilled on both sides in a pan with butter. Several chilled dill pickles and chilled peeled tomatoes with smearcase complete the plate.

The Colonel's Gumbo

The Grand Provider knows I try to waste few resources, am attentive to tradition and seek the highest level of quality that I am allowed to grasp. All of these lofty aspirations, I assure you, are self-imposed and at times not at all consistent with the time constraints that seem to dominate my life. Knowing that a modern life has robbed our food preparation time, modern food manufacturing will tell us, and we will agree, increasingly, that a canned or frozen product is better than homemade. Perhaps, but I am here to testify that a homespun gumbo suits me just fine, and I do love it so. I never make it the same way twice. I engineer my gumbo around ingredients that I fancy, fresh young okra being the only sentinel that is required to guard the integrity of this wonderful bayou burgoo.

INGREDIENTS
1/2 C olive oil
1 clove garlic, minced
1/2 C celery, chopped
1/2 C green pepper, chopped
1/2 C onion, chopped

3 C chicken broth, strained
2 C tomato sauce
2 C water

2 C okra
2 bay leaves
1 t red pepper flakes

1 small chicken, boiled cooked, deboned, skinned, broth reserved
1 lb. summer sausage, cooked and chopped
1 lb. shrimp, cooked, shelled

1 T tapioca

DIRECTIONS
✔ Prepare the chicken, sausage and shrimp; set aside.
✔ Reserve and strain 3 cups of the chicken broth.
✔ Sauté the garlic, celery, green pepper and onion.
✔ In a gallon soup pan, pour in the chicken stock, tomato sauce, water, vegetable and seasoning ingredients. Simmer for 1 hour. Then add the chicken, sausage and shrimp and simmer for 20 minutes.
✔ Thicken with tapioca. Serve with corn bread.

Cream Soup Base

The great thing about working from a cream soup base is that you can invent many different kinds of cream soups. Almost any vegetable in the summer garden can be incorporated into a cream soup. The folks in our neck of the woods like mushroom, clam, oyster and mussel soups. Many in the South like to bake cod or a similar white fish and put it in a cream soup of its own or as an additional flavor in mushroom soup. Find your preference. The one or two that you like you will cook for a lifetime.

I have a confession to make. I have often greeted the arrival of fresh clams, oysters or mussels with a quick wash, a quick shuck and a quick dispatch to a simmering pan of cream, a dollop of butter and a dash of salt and pepper thrown in. Two minutes later, the soup is in the bowl with yours truly on the north end of the spoon. Mercy me, I do love it so.

Do as I say, not as I do. The proper way to make a cream soup is as follows: use two 2-quart sauce pans, one to prepare the cream soup base and the other to prepare the soup ingredients.

Bring 3 C half-and-half to a bare simmer. Mix in 1/2 C butter with a whisk. Gradually add 3 T flour, dissolved in cold water, continually stirring the cream soup base with the whisk.

Mushroom Soup

INGREDIENTS
2 C chicken broth
1/2 lb. mushrooms, chopped fine
1/2 lb. mushrooms, sliced thin
1 T celery, chopped fine
3 C cream soup base, by recipe
2 T flour, dissolved in cold water
salt
juice of 1/2 lemon, strained
ground black pepper
parsley

DIRECTIONS
✔ In a 2-quart saucepan combine the soup ingredients. Simmer lightly for 20 minutes.
✔ Combine the cream soup base and the soup ingredients. Thicken with the flour, stirring in with a whisk. Check the need for more salt.
✔ Remove from the heat and cover for 3 minutes to allow the cream soup base and the soup ingredients to become acquainted.
✔ Stir in the lemon, and serve soup in bowls. Grind black pepper over the soup and add a little chopped parsley for garnish.
Serves 6-10.

Clam Chowder
Oyster Stew
Mussel Melange

INGREDIENTS
3 C chicken broth
2 C potatoes, skinned and diced
1/4 C yellow onion, diced
1/4 C celery, diced
1 C clams, oysters or mussels, cooked and chopped
1 C clams, oysters or mussels, cooked and whole
3 T flour, dissolved in cold water
salt
ground pepper
spring onion, chopped
basil

DIRECTIONS
✔ In a 2-quart saucepan combine the chicken broth, potatoes, onion and celery. Simmer lightly for 20 minutes. Then add the mollusk of choice.
✔ Combine the cream soup base and the soup ingredients. Thicken with the flour. Check the need for more salt.
✔ Remove from the heat and cover for 3 minutes to allow the cream soup base and the soup ingredients to become acquainted.
✔ Grind black pepper over the soup. Sprinkle with chopped onion and basil.
Serves 6-10.

Potato Pudding

Potato pudding is considered either a vegetable or a soup. Peel and grate 6-8 potatoes and set aside.

Sauté 1 onion, grated fine, in 1/4 C butter. In a separate bowl, combine 4 beaten eggs, 1 C evaporated milk, and 1/2 T each of salt and pepper.

Combine all the ingredients in an oiled glass baking dish.

Bake at 360 degrees for 1 hour, then turn the oven to broil to brown the potato pudding. Garnish with paprika and whole spring onion.

Black-Eyed Pea Soup

Black-eyed peas have been served in the South for as long as we have had agriculture. They have the same mystery as grits to our more Northern friends, who decry black-eyed peas as an acquired taste or a vagary of a New Year's Day celebration.

I must admit, black-eyed peas are a little old-fashioned, but I am very fond of them. The old way and the best way to cook black-eyed peas for use as a side vegetable is to simmer them for 2 hours with country ham pieces. Chopped onion and Tabasco sauce are passed with the black-eyed peas as a topping, and believe me, both are used liberally.

This is a version of the black-eyed pea soup that we know and love.

INGREDIENTS
1 lb. black-eyed peas, soaked overnight
1/2 yellow onion, chopped
1 green pepper, diced
1 celery stalk, diced
1 T olive oil
6 C water
4 C tomatoes, diced
3 C chicken broth
2 chicken bouillon cubes
1 T salt
ground pepper
yellow onion, diced

DIRECTIONS
✔ Soak the black-eyed peas overnight. Discard the water. Simmer the black-eyed peas for an hour in enough water to cover.
✔ Drain and set aside.
✔ In a sauté pan, cook the onion, celery and green pepper with the olive oil until tender. Add these and the remaining soup ingredients to the pan with the black-eyed peas and cook at a slow simmer for 1 hour.
✔ Pour into bowls, grind black pepper generously across the top of the soup and sprinkle with diced onion.

Beef Vegetable Soup

Beef vegetable soup belongs to the same class of affection as we hold apple pie and the American flag. It is a comfort food that is easily prepared.

There is no strict standard as to recipe. The only imperative in my opinion is the wonderfully great taste of fresh vegetables simmered together throughout an afternoon.

The soup should not be allowed to come to a boil but should just simmer. Season to taste with salt and pepper just before serving.

INGREDIENTS
2-3 lbs. shoulder roast, cut into medium-size pieces, visible fat removed
1/2 C olive oil

1 quart water
2 cans tomatoes, diced, juice added
1 12-oz. can tomato sauce
6 carrots, chopped medium
4 celery stalks, chopped medium
4 potatoes, skinned, quartered and halved
1 yellow onion, chopped fine
1 green pepper, chopped fine
1 lb. mushrooms, sliced medium
1 cabbage, small, chopped medium

1-1/2 t salt
1 t pepper

DIRECTIONS
✔ Pour olive oil into a 2-gallon pot and, on a high heat, brown the shoulder roast pieces.
✔ Then add the water and turn the heat to low.
✔ Add the remaining ingredients. Cover the soup and allow the soup to simmer lightly for 3 hours. Do not allow the soup to come to a boil, just to a slow simmer. Stir each hour.
✔ Taste for additional salt and pepper seasoning.
Serves 6-10.

Beef Stew

It is very Southern to serve beef stew over breakfast biscuits or in a bowl with corn bread. It also works well over egg noodles and rice. I take my beef stew very seriously. I worry about it and take great pride in the final outcome. I am fastidious about adjusting the seasoning and thickness of the gravy toward the end of the cooking cycle. When I serve beef stew, it is an outstanding culinary experience.

The making of really terrific beef stew is a matter of time and low temperature. Beef stew is invariably made up with beef shoulder meat, brisket or chuck roast. Beef shoulder meat benefits from slow, moist, low-heat cooking, the better to tenderize this flavorful yet tough cut of beef. The rise of crock-pot cookery was based on this principle. Axiomatic is that shoulder meat subjected to high heat or a hard boil toughens quickly.

This is a good dish to experiment with tapioca, that derives from the cassava, also known as the yucca plant. I keep a box of tapioca in the cupboard, as it makes very creamy puddings and is a nice thickener in place of flour or cornstarch.

My preference is to use a good cut of boneless shoulder roast, about 3 inches thick. Place the roast in a roasting pan. Pour in 2 cups of water and a cup of red wine. Flavor the top of the roast with seasoning salt and pepper. Add a dash of soy sauce and Kitchen Bouquet for color. Cover and cook at 250 degrees for 3 hours. Then remove the roast from the oven and cut meat into small pieces, removing any visible fat.

Return the meat to the pan. Toss in 6 skinned carrots, 6 peeled potatoes and 2 quartered onions. Add a cup of water if necessary. Cook an additional 2 hours.

Stir in 2 T of tapioca for thickening and return the roast to the oven for about 20 minutes. Remove the roast and the cover. If additional thickening is required, add 1 T of tapioca and stir until it is dissolved. Just before serving, cut the carrots and potatoes to a size that pleases you.

Navy Bean Soup

This soup is a meal when served with fresh-baked corn bread. We serve navy bean soup anytime for family, but it is also well regarded on the buffet table, served piping hot on a wind-chilled night.

Soak 1/2 C of navy beans overnight. To 4 C water, add a 1/2 lb. diced country ham; a ham bone, if you have one; a finely diced carrot; three diced celery stalks with leaves included; and half an onion, diced. Season with 1 bay leaf, 3 whole cloves, 4 peppercorns and salt to taste. Simmer for 2 hours. When ready to remove from heat, add about 1 C of mashed potato to thicken. Garnish with chives when presented at table.

Burgoo

In the Kentucky heart dwells a place for burgoo. It is neither a soup, nor a stew, nor an entrée. It is so good that when we plan a day at Churchill Downs or Keeneland Race Course, our interest in finding the burgoo competes with our desire to play the horses.

The magnificence of burgoo is best appreciated in the outdoors with the wind in your hair. A glance at the recipe for burgoo is intimidating at first glance. Nonetheless, look it over several times, and you will note that it is harmless, a wedding between fresh meat and vegetables. The trick to making a good burgoo is to add the vegetables in the second half of the cooking.

I have read many burgoo recipes, some dating back one hundred years and more. I am certain that in our frontier past, many an elk, buffalo and wild boar found a place in burgoo. Burgoo is an ever-changing landscape. This recipe is a late-twentieth-century version; therefore, you will have no trouble recognizing the ingredients.

Accompany burgoo with a fine aged Kentucky bourbon whisky for your drink. Burgoo and bourbon have always been the best of friends. If you must cook the burgoo in your kitchen, take it outside to serve and eat. The spring and fall seasons work well for the presentation of burgoo, for it is a sporting dish that feeds the hunter and the returning warrior.

Place 2 chickens and 5 pounds each of beef shoulder and pork loin into a 5-gallon pot and cover with water and a lid. Simmer for 3 hours, then skin, debone and dice the meat.

Cut a bunch of celery and carrots, 5 bell peppers, 5 potatoes, 5 onions and a cabbage. Add a quart each of peas, corn, tomatoes and okra, the tomatoes and the okra diced. Add a quart of water and a quart of tomato sauce. Simmer for an additional hour. Flavor with Worcestershire and Tabasco sauces. Salt to taste. Just before serving, thicken with a small amount of flour.

Pot Roast

I will ask that you take care when you decide to prepare pot roast. The term "pot roast" is the nomenclature we use to describe the meal we are preparing, not a cut of meat, as our grocer meat department would have us believe. Our pioneer forebears often said, "All's meat that goes into the pot." Let me tell you, our brave frontier ancestors set the table with many a crow and called it partridge so as to maintain a good sense of humor under trying circumstances. The grocer meat department has no similar hardship to endure. The flagrant mislabeling of meat in our grocery stores today is an outrage. So much for my bully pulpit.

Tell the butcher you want a nice looking shoulder roast. Tell him you do not want an excessively gristled, unsightly and otherwise unmarketable chuck or brisket from old utility-grade cattle, labeled generically as pot roast. That should do it.

INGREDIENTS
4 lbs. shoulder roast
1 T olive oil
black pepper
2 C water
2 dissolved beef bouillon cubes
8 carrots, whole, skinned
4 potatoes, whole, skinned
4 onions, small, whole, skinned
2 celery stalks, cut in half
1/2 C flour

DIRECTIONS
✔ Pour the olive oil into a roasting pan on high heat. Pepper the pot roast and then brown the meat on both sides. Add the water and the bouillon and allow the water to come almost to a boil; turn down the heat to low.
✔ Place all the vegetables on top of the roast and cover the roasting pan tightly. Allow the pot roast to simmer. By no means should you ever allow the roast to boil, as it will toughen.
✔ Check the pot roast after an hour to make certain the water level is at least 1-inch in the pan. Add a cup of water if necessary. You will cook the pot roast about 30 minutes to the pound or about 2 hours.
✔ When ready to serve, place the pot roast on a platter and surround the roast with the vegetables.
✔ Dissolve the flour in cold water and add to the pot roast juices. Turn up the heat and stir the pot roast liquid until a gravy is formed. Pour the gravy into a bowl or a gravy pitcher and serve alongside the pot roast platter.
Serves 4-5.

Dessert

Dessert to the modern mind has become an extra; a part of dining that is loaded with forbidden sugars. I can only tell you that to forgo a taste treat that signals the last bite of a wonderfully prepared meal appears silly. Eat less dessert–smaller portions appear justified–but take a few dessert recipes, make them your own and serve them with pride.

The era of a table overflowing with pies, cakes and cookies belongs to a bygone era. The older people in my family would bake cakes, pies and cookies for all of life's events. If a friend passed away, a cake would always be sent to the house; if family, two cakes. If celebrating a birthday for children, cookies; if for an adult, fruit pies. There were New Year's cakes, Fourth of July pies, Jefferson Davis birthday pies and at Christmas every article of their baking art.

I know from my entertaining that a great dessert is appreciated. But as in all of my cooking, I have taken care to perfect certain recipes that appeal to me, that my guests clammer for and that have been enjoyed in Kentucky for many generations. I choose to offer you desserts that I prepare and leave the full range of dessert recipes to others.

Brandy Cake

INGREDIENTS
1 box chocolate cake mix
1 small box instant pudding
3/4 C strong coffee
3/4 C brandy and Kahlua, mixed
1/2 C canola oil
4 eggs

Brandy Cake Glaze

INGREDIENTS
1 C powdered sugar
2 T coffee
2 T brandy
2 T Kahlua

DIRECTIONS
✔ Combine the cake ingredients in a mixer at medium speed.
✔ Pour into an oiled and floured Bundt pan. Bake at 350 degrees for 30-40 minutes or until the center shows a clean straw.
✔ Allow the cake to cool. Poke holes in the cooled cake and glaze.

Blackberry Cobbler

I remember the blackberry cobbler as the glorious end to an afternoon laboring in the blackberry patch. I have always prepared my cobbler in the same way as my mother and grandmother. A number of years ago, I was invited to judge a blackberry cobbler contest at a county fair. To my astonishment, there were 40 cobblers awaiting my judgement, with 40 cobbler cooks standing in judgement of me. Each cobbler was different as to sight and taste, and each cook with eyes piercing a hole through me made certain I noticed the qualitative difference in their cobbler.

I offer you my blackberry cobbler and ask that you judge for yourself.

Clean and cap 2 C of blackberries. Melt a stick of butter in a glass baking dish. In a bowl, mix 1 C each of flour, sugar and milk. Stir briskly with a wooden spoon until the batter is moist but still lumpy. Mix in the blackberrries and pour into the glass baking dish. Bake at 360 degrees for 40-50 minutes.

Kentucky Jam Cake

INGREDIENTS
1-1/2 C sugar
3 eggs
1/2 t salt
2 C flour
1 C corn oil
1 C buttermilk
1 t baking soda
1 t baking powder
1 t allspice
1 t cinnamon
1 t ground cloves
1 C pecans, finely chopped
1 C blackberry jam, seedless
caramel frosting

DIRECTIONS
✔ In a saucepan, cream the sugar, eggs and salt.
✔ In a bowl, combine all of the cake ingredients, reserving the pecans and blackberry jam until the batter has been beaten well and thoroughly blended, Then add the pecans and blackberry jam.
✔ Bake at 350 degrees for 25 minutes.
✔ Allow the jam cake to cool and then spread the caramel frosting across the top of the cake.
Serves 8.

Caramel Frosting

INGREDIENTS
3 C powdered sugar
1 C milk
2 T butter
1 t vanilla
pinch salt

DIRECTIONS
✔ Place 2 C of the sugar and the milk in a saucepan and boil hard for 1 minute.
✔ Place the remaining sugar and the butter into another saucepan and caramelize by a rapid simmer, watching that it does not burn and constantly stirring with the whisk.

Old South Lemon Custard Cake

INGREDIENTS
6 T flour
6 T butter, melted
2 C sugar, divided in half
4 eggs, yolks beaten, whites reserved
1-1/2 C milk
1 lemon peel, grated
2 T lemon juice
powdered sugar
nutmeg

DIRECTIONS
✔ In a large bowl, combine flour, butter and 1-1/2 C sugar. Add egg yolks, milk, lemon juice and lemon peel and mix completely.
✔ Beat egg whites stiff and fold into cake batter, adding the remaining 1/2 C sugar as you go.
✔ Pour into a well-oiled 2-quart baking dish or individual ramekins. Either way, place the baking dishes into a shallow pan of hot water and bake for about 1 hour until brown and bubbly.
✔ Sprinkle powdered sugar across the top and serve warm. Accent with nutmeg.

Brownie Two-Layer Cake

INGREDIENTS
brownie mixture, by recipe, divided

4 T sugar
2 T butter, melted
1 egg
1 egg yolk
1/2 t vanilla
6 oz. Philadelphia cream cheese, softened

DIRECTIONS
✔ Prepare the brownie mixture.
✔ Mix together the sugar, butter, egg and vanilla. Add the cream cheese and blend completely.
✔ In a well-oiled baking dish, pour in one-half of the brownie mixture. Then pour in all of the cream cheese mixture. Pour the remaining brownie mixture on top of the cream cheese mixture.
✔ Bake at 350 degrees for 45-50 minutes. Do not allow top to harden.

Coffee Cake

INGREDIENTS
3 C flour
1-1/2 C milk
1-1/2 C sugar
2 eggs, beaten
3-1/2 T butter, melted
4 t baking powder
3/4 t salt
1/2 t cinnamon

Coffee Cake Icing

INGREDIENTS
2 T flour
3 T butter, melted
5 T brown sugar
1 T crushed pecans
1 C blueberries, if desired

DIRECTIONS
✔ Combine cake ingredients. In a separate bowl, combine icing ingredients.
✔ Pour cake mixture into an oiled and floured glass baking pan.
✔ Bake at 350 degrees for 35 minutes.
✔ Spread the icing onto the warm cake. Let stand for about 10 minutes.
Serves 8.

Two-Egg Cake

INGREDIENTS
2-1/2 t baking powder
1/4 t salt
2-1/4 C flour, sifted
1 C sugar
1 stick butter
2 eggs, beaten
3/4 C milk

DIRECTIONS
✔ Sift the flour and the baking powder and salt together, twice.
✔ In a mixing bowl on slow speed, cream the sugar and the butter.
✔ Add the eggs and the milk to the creamed mixture. Pour the flour into the mixing bowl, still set on a slow speed, a small amount at a time, making certain that the batter is well blended.
✔ Pour the batter into a baking pan. Bake at 375 degrees for 25 minutes or until the interior of the cake is dry.

Strawberry Shortcake

In the late spring just as southern winds warm the Kentucky soil, strawberries ripen, and the competition to harvest this luscious fruit begins with a passion and a fury. From mid-May to mid-June, the outcome is decided on a daily basis. Birds love red, ripe strawberries. I can usually beat my avian adversary to the berry patch, as they do not roust from their slumbers until just before dawn. To the consternation of Margaret Sue, I am in the spring garden before first light.

I like a strawberry in any form it is presented to me. Strawberry shortcake is a capital way to enjoy this fruit. The amount of sugar used in this dessert is strictly personal. If I thought I could avert a riot, I would delete the powdered sugar, as I find the strawberries sweet enough. Whipped cream is mandatory.

INGREDIENTS
1/2 C sugar
2 C cake flour, sifted
4 t baking powder
1/2 t salt
2 T sugar
6 T shortening
1 egg, beaten
1/2 C whole milk
2 T butter, softened
powdered sugar
whipped cream, chilled
4 C strawberries, crushed then chilled

DIRECTIONS
✔ Make the shortcake. In a mixing bowl, sift all of the dry ingredients together.
✔ Cut in the shortening with pastry knives until it is pebbly. Then cut in the egg and milk.
✔ Turn the dough out onto a floured table and knead 10 times, turning the dough into itself each time.
✔ Roll out the dough to 1/2-inch, spread on the butter and fold the dough in half, pressing the edges together with the rolling pin.
✔ Cut the dough with a 3-inch biscuit cutter and place the shortcake rounds on a greased baking sheet.
✔ Bake at 450 degrees for about 12 minutes or until a light brown. When cool, place a single shortcake round on a dessert plate.
✔ In a mixing bowl crush the strawberries with a fork and set in the refrigerator to cool.
✔ Open the shortcake round and ladle in the crushed strawberries, then ladle some on top.
✔ Place whole strawberries next to the shortcake. Sprinkle the strawberries with powdered sugar and spoon on whipped cream.

Pineapple Upside-Down Cake

W e will use pineapple upside-down cake for any occasion. It is a traditional cake for weddings and anniversary celebrations. By all means, use fresh pineapple. I know the modern way is to use that syrupy version in the can. I simply cannot force myself to use fruit packed that way.

INGREDIENTS
1 stick butter, melted
1 C brown sugar
6 pineapple slices, medium thick
2-egg cake batter

DIRECTIONS
✔ Use a black cast-iron skillet. Pour the butter into the skillet. Coat the side of the pan with the butter up to the rim. Sprinkle the brown sugar on top of the butter that is in the bottom of the skillet. Layer the pineapple slices on top of the brown sugar.
✔ Pour in the batter for the 2-egg cake.
✔ Bake at 375 degrees for 45-50 minutes.
✔ When you remove the pineapple upside-down cake from the oven, turn the pan over onto a serving plate, using a knife around the skillet sides to extricate the cake.

Sour Cream Cheesecake

INGREDIENTS
1 graham cracker crust, by recipe
8 oz. sour cream
1/2 C sugar
3 8-oz. pkgs. Philadelphia cream cheese
1 C sugar
4 eggs, beaten
1 t vanilla
strawberry, raspberry or blueberry glaze

DIRECTIONS
✔ Press a graham cracker crust into the bottom of a springform pan and set aside.
✔ In a separate bowl combine the sour cream and the sugar for the topping and set aside.
✔ In a mixing bowl, on slow speed, combine the cheesecake ingredients for 5 minutes. Pour cheesecake filling into crust. Bake at 350 degrees for 30 minutes. Remove from oven to spread on topping and bake an additional 5 minutes.
✔ Allow cheesecake to cool. Refrigerate for 8 hours. Extricate from the springform pan. Drizzle strawberry, raspberry or blueberry glaze over the sour cream topping in a pattern that is appealing to you. Serves 8-10.

Blackberry Bourbon Sauce Cake

Mimi celebrates everyone's birthday, regardless of age, regardless of family surname. If you come to Elmwood for dinner and she either knows or discovers you are in your birthday week, she makes a blackberry bourbon sauce cake. In all of my years, I never, ever heard anyone who wanted any other birthday cake. Good thing: Mimi never offered any other.

In Kentucky, blackberries are everywhere. Before the thornless variety came into our agriculture, we endured the sharp painful scratches associated with pickin' blackberries. To encourage efficient effort, a string was attached to a coffee can, which was hung from our necks so that we could have the use of both hands while pickin' blackberries. No one above the age of six escaped the chore. And except for an occasional yelp or cussin' attack, there were few complaints, though I must say the occasional snake making its presence known elicited colorful and vociferous language with a simultaneous leap out of the blackberry bush. We endured, for we knew at the end of the pickin' torture, there would be gallons of blackberry jam, jelly and syrup.

Now, instead of finding the blackberry harvest along the fencerows and abandoned roadways, I grow a thornless variety in my arbor. My sisters declare that I have grown soft as I advance in years.

INGREDIENTS
1/2 C buttermilk
1 t soda
1 C flour, sifted
1 t cinnamon
1 C sugar
1/2 C butter
3 eggs, beaten
1 C blackberry jam (1 C blackberries and
1 C sugar blended at medium speed)
2 C bourbon sauce, by recipe

DIRECTIONS
✔ Dissolve the soda into the buttermilk and set aside. Sift the flour with the cinnamon and set aside.
✔ Using a whisk, blend the butter and sugar in a large mixing bowl. Add the eggs and buttermilk and blend until smooth. Add the flour and blackberry jam and stir well.
✔ Pour into an oiled, shallow 12-inch baking dish.
✔ Bake at 325 degrees for 40 minutes. Cut into squares and serve with bourbon sauce.

Apple Pie

I do not know of any food in American life that is as important as apple pie. We speak of apple pie in the same breath that we pronounce our love for our country and the mother that gave us life. I promise you, if you cook a good apple pie and are willing to prepare it often, you will be revered among your family and friends.

There are many good recipes for apple pie, and it seems that each region of the country has a version of apple pie that is dear to them. The common element in every great apple-pie recipe is a great-tasting piecrust. I am adamant about using a homemade piecrust pastry in the making of an apple pie. I never take an apple pie seriously that uses a store-bought piecrust. A homemade piecrust has dramatically more flavor and aroma than a commercially prepared piecrust. And besides, anything that is as emotionally powerful as an apple pie needs to be done right.

INGREDIENTS
2 piecrusts
1 C sugar
1/4 C brown sugar
2 T flour
1 t cinnamon
1 t nutmeg
6 apples, cored, peeled and sliced
1/2 C orange juice
1/2 C butter, softened

DIRECTIONS
✔ Roll out the two piecrusts. Place one piecrust in the pie pan, leaving about a 1/2-inch overhang.
✔ Mix together the dry ingredients and sprinkle about a third of the mixture onto the piecrust that is in the pie pan.
✔ Pour in the apples, which have been quartered and cut 3 times.
✔ Mix together the orange juice and butter and pour over the apples. Sprinkle the rest of the dry ingredients over the apples.
✔ Cover the pie with the other piecrust. Cut 3-4 slits in the middle of the crust. Then press the two crusts together by pinching them along the rim.
✔ Bake at 375 degrees for 1 hour.

Bourbon Butter Cream Pie

INGREDIENTS
1 C heavy whipping cream
1 stick plus 6 T butter
4 eggs, beaten lightly
2-1/4 C sugar
2-1/2 T flour
1 t salt
2 T fine aged Kentucky bourbon whisky
1 t vanilla
1 piecrust

DIRECTIONS
✔ Blend the butter and the cream in the top of a double boiler, stirring with the whisk. Then add the eggs.
✔ Add in the remaining ingredients gradually, stirring constantly.
✔ Pour into the unbaked piecrust.
✔ Bake at 325 degrees for 1 hour, shaking the pie gently twice during the hour. Allow the pie to cool, and the pie will firm up.

Chess Pie

Many years ago at dinner, after a cocktail hour, a wine course at dinner, a sampling of brandies, then Irish whiskey coffee, I was informed by my host that the secret to a great chess pie was finely chopped chestnuts. All of us were summarily informed by an incredulous hostess that there are no chestnuts to be found in chess pie.

INGREDIENTS
2 C sugar
3 T cornmeal
1 C half-and-half
6 eggs, yolks only
1/2 C butter
1/2 T vinegar
1 t vanilla
1 9-inch piecrust

DIRECTIONS
✔ Mix together the sugar and the cornmeal.
✔ In a separate bowl, using a whisk, blend together the remaining ingredients. Then blend together the sugar and the cream.
✔ Pour into a 9-inch piecrust. Bake at 425 degrees for 15-18 minutes.

Brownie Mixture

INGREDIENTS
1 stick butter
1 C sugar
1-1/2 C flour
4 eggs, beaten
16 oz. chocolate syrup
3 t vanilla

DIRECTIONS
✔ Cream the butter and sugar.
✔ Stir in the remaining ingredients with a whisk.
✔ Pour into a well-oiled baking dish. Bake at 350 degrees for about 20 minutes. Remove from the oven while the center is still slightly loose and allow to firm up and cool in the baking dish.

Brownie-Bottom Bourbon Pie

INGREDIENTS
brownie mixture to make a 1/4-inch crust
in a 10-inch pie pan, by recipe
1/2 C bourbon
5 egg yolks
1/4 C sugar
1/4 C cold water
1 envelope unflavored gelatin
4 C heavy cream
shaved chocolate

DIRECTIONS
✔ Pour the made-up brownie mixture into a 10-inch pie pan to form a 1/4-inch piecrust and bake at 350 degrees for 5 minutes.
✔ In one bowl, beat the egg yolks until thick and stiff and then slowly beat in the sugar. In a second bowl, soften the gelatin in the cold water and add the remaining bourbon.
✔ Place the contents of both bowls in a double boiler over a low simmering heat. Constantly stir with the whisk until the eggs thicken, about 8-10 minutes.
✔ Remove from heat and stir in the remaining bourbon. Allow to cool.
✔ Whip the cream and fold one half into the mixture. Pour the pie filling into the pie pan and chill at least 4 hours.
✔ When ready to serve, top the pie with the remaining whipped cream and sprinkle with the shaved chocolate.
Serves 6-8.

Brown Sugar Cream Pie

INGREDIENTS
1/2 C brown sugar
1/2 C butter, melted
3/4 C heavy cream
4 eggs, beaten
1/2 t vanilla
1/4 t cinnamon
1/4 t nutmeg
1 piecrust, baked 10 minutes

DIRECTIONS
✔ Have the piecrust ready.
✔ In a saucepan over low heat, blend the sugar, butter and cream. Then stir in the eggs and vanilla.
✔ Pour the pie filling into the pie pan and sprinkle with the cinnamon and nutmeg.
✔ Bake at 350 degrees until firm but still a little loose. If cooked too long, the pie filling will harden.
Serves 6-8.

Buttermilk Pie

INGREDIENTS
1-1/2 C buttermilk
3/4 C sugar
3 eggs, beaten
3 T flour
3 T butter, melted
3 T lemon juice
3/4 t vanilla
grated lemon rind, yellow only
cinnamon
1 piecrust, baked

DIRECTIONS
✔ Have the piecrust ready.
✔ Briskly blend the buttermilk, sugar and eggs.
✔ Add the remaining ingredients and stir together with a whisk.
✔ Pour into the baked piecrust and sprinkle the cinnamon on the top.
✔ Bake at 375 degrees for about 20 minutes or until custard just sets.
✔ Remove from oven and allow to cool before serving.
Serves 6.

Outrageous Pumpkin Pie

INGREDIENTS
2 C pumpkin
1 C half-and-half
1 C brown sugar
3 T fine aged Kentucky bourbon whisky
2 T butter, melted
2 T flour
1 T lemon juice
2 eggs, beaten
1 t cinnamon
1 t ginger
1/4 t allspice
1/4 t cloves
1/4 t mace
1/4 t nutmeg
pinch salt
1 piecrust, uncooked

DIRECTIONS
✔ Combine all of the ingredients and pour into a piecrust.
✔ Bake at 450 degrees for 15 minutes to set the pumpkin custard.
✔ Then reduce heat to 375 degrees for 30 minutes.
Serves 6-8.

Kentucky Pie

This pie is enjoyed throughout the South and is a Kentucky standard dessert. It is traditionally served sliced, in a small wedge, partnered with vanilla ice cream.

Kentucky pie is a custard dessert, and therefore, it does not require a piecrust cover.

INGREDIENTS
1 C pecans, chopped
1/4 C pecans, whole
3 eggs, beaten
6 oz. brown sugar
2 oz. butter, melted
1 T vanilla
1/4 t salt
1 piecrust

DIRECTIONS
✔ Beat eggs in a large bowl. Add in the chopped pecans, brown sugar, butter, vanilla and salt. Stir with a whisk until blended.
✔ Pour the ingredients into the piecrust.
✔ Dot the top of the pie with the whole pecans.
✔ Bake at 350 degrees for 55 minutes. Allow the Kentucky pie to cool before serving.

Chocolate Bourbon Pie

I have had the privilege of eating nearly as many versions of chocolate bourbon pie as there are Kentucky cooks who prepare pies. This recipe has been widely used in central Kentucky and has been a favorite in my family for many generations. I am certain that each of us has made the pie to suit our taste, but the essence of the pie has always been pecans, bourbon and bittersweet chocolate.

We will make chocolate bourbon pie for any occasion and serve it for dessert at luncheon or dinner. At these mealtimes, it is served warm. The midnight snackers can be counted upon to make a clean sweep of the pie pan, at which time it is consumed at room temperature.

Chocolate bourbon pie is an exceedingly rich dessert. We serve it as a small wedge with strong coffee.

INGREDIENTS
1 piecrust
4 eggs, beaten
1 C corn syrup
3/4 C light brown sugar
1/3 C butter
3 T fine aged Kentucky bourbon whisky
1 T vanilla
1 T flour
6 oz. bittersweet baker's chocolate,
chopped into morsel-size pieces
1 C pecans, coarsely chopped

DIRECTIONS
✔ Place the piecrust into a 9-inch pie plate and fold edges over, pinching the dough around the rim.
✔ In a mixing bowl, using a whisk, blend together the eggs, syrup, sugar and butter.
✔ Add the bourbon, vanilla and flour.
✔ When the mixture is smooth, add the chocolate and the pecans.
✔ Pour the contents of the mixing bowl into the piecrust.
✔ Bake at 350 degrees for 1 hour.

Chilled Chocolate Pie

This pie seems to delight the young enormously. But I stand amazed that the popularity of chilled chocolate pie does not appear to diminish with age. It is so simple, and yet it has the power to trigger fond memories of our days gone by. Thin slices of fresh strawberries mixed with some powdered sugar, spooned on next to each slice on the dessert plate, complete the visual appeal of chilled chocolate pie.

INGREDIENTS
1 graham cracker crust, by recipe
4 oz. baker's sweet chocolate
2 T sugar
1 T milk
16 oz. whipping cream
4 oz. Philadelphia cream cheese.
strawberries, thinly sliced
powdered sugar

DIRECTIONS
✔ Press a graham cracker crust into the bottom of a pie pan and set aside.
✔ In a double boiler, stirring constantly, melt the chocolate, sugar and milk. Remove from heat and set aside.
✔ In a mixer, whip the cream at high speed and pour it into a separate bowl and set aside.
✔ In a mixer, beat the cream cheese at medium speed. Add the chocolate. Add three-quarters of the whipping cream.
✔ Pour the chocolate pie filling into the graham cracker crust. Smooth out the remaining whipped cream as a topping for the chocolate pie.
✔ Refrigerate for 8 hours.
Serves 6.

Fruit Pies

There are plenty of ways to make a good fruit pie. Some use more or less lemon, fruit, sugar or salt. My advice is to experiment. Fruit pies are delicious almost any way you fix them. I highly recommend that you use a homemade piecrust. The fruit pie will end up looking a bit irregular and imperfect, but for me, therein is the charm. I often use a commercially purchased piecrust for fruit pies, choosing not to use the same reverence for fruit pies. Although I stand my ground on apple pie. The truth be known, few will point out the expediency.

INGREDIENTS
2 piecrusts
1 C sugar
4 T flour
1/4 t salt
4 C fruit, washed, hulled or stoned
3 T butter
1 T lemon juice

DIRECTIONS
✔ Line the pie pan with a piecrust pastry.
✔ Mix together the sugar, flour and salt and sprinkle about a third onto the piecrust pastry. Pour the fruit into the pie shell. Sprinkle the remainder of the sugar, flour and salt onto the fruit. Dot the fruit with the butter and the lemon juice.
✔ Crisscross the top of the pie or cover the pie with the extra piecrust.
✔ Bake at 425 degrees for 45-55 minutes. Allow to cool before serving.

Baked Chocolate Pie

INGREDIENTS
1 9-inch piecrust pastry
2 C half-and-half
1 C sugar
1/2 C cocoa
1/4 C flour
3 egg yolks
1 t vanilla
3 egg whites
6 T sugar

DIRECTIONS
✔ In a double boiler combine the half-and-half, sugar, cocoa, flour and egg yolks. Heat until thickened. Then remove from heat and stir in the vanilla. Pour into the piecrust pastry.
✔ Make the meringue topping by beating the egg whites and the sugar until the mixture peaks. Spread onto pie.
✔ Bake at 350 degrees for 15 minutes. Allow to cool and then place in refrigerator to chill for 6 hours.

Brownies with Bourbon Chocolate Sauce

INGREDIENTS
brownie mixture, by recipe
1/4 C fine aged Kentucky bourbon whisky

chocolate sauce, by recipe
1 T fine aged Kentucky bourbon whisky
powdered sugar

DIRECTIONS
✔ Bake the brownies according to directions in a well-oiled and floured baking dish.
✔ While the brownies are cooling, brush on 1/4 C bourbon.
✔ Stir together the tablespoon of bourbon and the chocolate sauce.
✔ Spread the bourbon chocolate sauce over the brownie. Sprinkle powdered sugar over the top of the brownie for accent.

White Chocolate Brownies

INGREDIENTS
4 oz. white chocolate
8 T butter
1 C sugar
2 eggs
1/2 t salt
1 C flour

DIRECTIONS
✔ In a double boiler, melt the butter and add the white chocolate until all is melted.
✔ In a mixing bowl at medium speed, beat the eggs, adding the sugar and salt for about 1 minute.
✔ Turn the mixing speed to low and add the white chocolate. Then mix in the flour until blended.
✔ Pour the brownie batter into a well-oiled baking dish. Bake at 350 degrees for about 45 minutes.
Yields 6-8.

Crescent Wedding Cookies

INGREDIENTS
1 C butter
1/2 C sugar
2 C flour
2 C pecans, chopped
1 t vanilla
2 t water, if needed
powdered sugar

DIRECTIONS
✔ Cream butter and sugar.
✔ Add the flour, pecans and vanilla. Mix until blended, and if too stiff, add the water. Form into crescent shapes.
✔ Bake at 300 degrees for 25 minutes. Do not let the cookies brown.
✔ Remove from the oven and gently pat in the powdered sugar.
Yields 24-30.

Oatmeal Cookies

INGREDIENTS
3 C quick oats, uncooked
1-1/4 C brown sugar
1 C butter
1 C flour
1 C raisins
1/2 C milk
1/2 C pecans
2 eggs, beaten
3/4 t ground cloves
1/4 t salt
1/4 t cinnamon
1/8 t nutmeg

DIRECTIONS
✔ Combine all of the ingredients.
✔ Drop by tablespoons on a well-oiled and floured baking sheet.
✔ Bake at 350 degrees for about 5-6 minutes, and while still soft, remove and allow to cool on the baking pan for a few minutes, then remove to a cooling rack.

Orange Bourbon Sauce

Be extra careful around this sauce. It is good. Seriously, this is really delicious. It is interesting that I do not find this sauce outside of central Kentucky. We have made orange bourbon sauce for years. My guests absolutely love it, and we continue to find new ways to use it.

I have used it for years on pumpkin pie with great effect. And as previously reported, this sauce works great with cooked carrots.

Pour it over chocolate ice cream or on the top of a cheesecake. On puff-filled dessert pastry it is terrific.

If you cook ducks, geese and pheasants during the holiday season, glaze the birds when they are placed upon the table and leave a serving dish filled with orange bourbon sauce.

INGREDIENTS
1/2 C brown sugar
1/4 C water
1/4 C fine aged Kentucky bourbon whisky
1/4 C pecans, chopped medium
1/4 C strawberry preserves
1 orange, peeled, seeds removed, squeezed and diced
1 lemon, peeled, seeds removed, squeezed and diced
2 t cornstarch

DIRECTIONS
✔ Simmer the brown sugar, and water until dissolved.
✔ Then, add the bourbon whisky, pecans and strawberry preserves; simmer about 2 minutes, stirring with a whisk.
✔ Add the orange, the lemon and the cornstarch and simmer until it is syrup thick. If you feel the sauce needs a little more cornstarch, add a teaspoon or two.
✔ Cover and store in refrigerator overnight to blend the flavors. It is generally served warm, but room temperature is fine by me.

Bourbon Sauce

This sauce is world-class. A good bourbon sauce is in every reputable Kentucky kitchen, and all knowledgeable Kentucky cooks have a version they lay claim to. We use it on every manner of cake and puff pastry. The 2-egg cake with bourbon sauce is perfect. It is also delicious over strawberry and cantaloupe. On blackberry cake it is magnificent.

The bourbon sauce I give you, like the chocolate sauce, came from Mimi, a woman under constant siege. Her family and friends have asked her to reproduce her version of this recipe so often that she finally had it printed and kept a supply in her kitchen office drawer. This dessert topping is a Kentucky classic.

There will never be enough bourbon sauce, for if there is a portion left behind, I assure you, it will go home with somebody. You will get so many requests for it that only in the making of it will you achieve peace.

It has been years since I have seen anyone cook with a double boiler that was specifically manufactured for that purpose. I use two pans that seem to set one on top of the other. Bourbon sauce will not tolerate a lot of heat; if it simmers, it will curdle. I even lift the pan slightly away from the steam as I stir in the egg yolk. Mimi finds this unnecessary, but I have always conceded to her the possession of a more assured hand.

INGREDIENTS
1 C sugar
1 stick butter
1 C half-and-half
4 egg yolks, beaten lightly
1 pinch salt
1/2 C fine aged Kentucky bourbon whisky

DIRECTIONS
✔ In a double boiler, set the water to a light boil. Blend the butter and the sugar into the upper bowl, using a whisk.
✔ Add half-and-half and stir well until dissolved.
✔ Add the egg yolks and salt and stir until thickened.
✔ Add bourbon whisky.
✔ Served slightly warm.

Brown Sugar Bourbon Sauce

By the saints that grace the heavens, I declare that brown sugar bourbon sauce over homemade vanilla ice cream is Kentucky nectar. Brace yourself. Brown sugar bourbon sauce is not a food, it is an experience.

Homemade vanilla ice cream topped with brown sugar bourbon sauce stands pretty on its own. But be adventurous: place the vanilla ice cream and the brown sugar bourbon sauce in a blender, and it is an extraordinary eggnog; placed in a blender and spiked with additional fine aged Kentucky bourbon whisky and creme de cacao poured into a stemmed goblet, it is a wonderfully sweet after-dinner drink.

INGREDIENTS
1 C brown sugar
6 T butter
1/2 C whipping cream
2 T light corn syrup
2 T fine aged Kentucky bourbon whisky

DIRECTIONS
✔ Melt butter.
✔ Blend in sugar, then cream and syrup. Boil 1 minute.
✔ Remove from heat and add the bourbon.

Chocolate Sauce

Y'all listen to Colonel Michael on this recipe. A crowd favorite emanating from the Elmwood kitchen, chocolate sauce is really out of this world. Mimi brought out the chocolate sauce for every occasion. When victories and defeats would be shared within the family circle, chocolate sauce would appear to caress and comfort. The matriarch of Elmwood found chocolate sauce to be the most sought after recipe in her considerable repertory.

When I serve chocolate sauce, my guests, regardless of their age, go to the moon on the first taste of chocolate sauce over plain chocolate cake or vanilla ice cream.

Your friends will request chocolate sauce even if they have not been invited to dinner. However, it is useful to note that the lack of cake or ice cream will not inhibit passion for chocolate sauce. Your friends and family, if they know chocolate sauce is in the kitchen, will eat it with a fork, knife or spoon—be they doctor, lawyer, merchant or thief!

INGREDIENTS
3/4 C evaporated milk
1/2 stick of butter
3/4 C white powdered sugar
3 oz. bittersweet baking chocolate
1 t vanilla

DIRECTIONS
✔ In a pan, on a low heat, carefully blend together the milk and the butter.
✔ Add the powdered sugar and stir with the whisk until the sugar is thoroughly dissolved.
✔ Add the chocolate and stir until thoroughly blended. Lightly heat the sauce until very smooth, about 10 minutes. Continuously stir with a whisk, and do not let it simmer or it will stick.
✔ Turn off the heat and add the vanilla, gently stirring it in with the whisk.
✔ Refrigerate after it has cooled. Serve warm over plain chocolate cake or vanilla ice cream or anything else you can think of.

Elegant Banana Pudding

INGREDIENTS
2 C powdered sugar
1-1/2 C evaporated milk
1/2 C flour
1 stick butter
2 egg yolks, beaten
6 bananas
ladyfingers

DIRECTIONS
✔ In a double boiler on a medium heat, blend the sugar, milk, flour, butter and egg yolks. Allow to cool, then refrigerate for 2 hours to chill.
✔ When ready to serve, slice the banana lengthwise and place on a dessert plate with 2-3 ladyfingers. Spoon on the chilled banana pudding sauce.
Serves 6.

Bread Pudding

This recipe and others similar to it are desserts of old Kentucky. When we were children, we were completely enthralled with bread pudding. Every cook made it just a little differently, and we found ourselves sophisticated and worldly in articulating our personal preferences. Some used day-old bread crumbs, some fresh biscuits, others the latter half of a homemade bread loaf. Through the years, the fascination with bread pudding and a good "hard sauce," that we call bourbon sauce, has not diminished.

INGREDIENTS
6 C French bread, chunked
2 C half-and-half
2 C milk
3 T butter, melted in 9x13-inch baking pan, set aside
3 eggs, beaten
2 C sugar
1 C white raisins
1/2 C pecans, chopped
4 T fine aged Kentucky bourbon whisky
1 t cinnamon

bourbon sauce, by recipe

DIRECTIONS
✔ Slice the bread into 2-inch chunks. In a large mixing bowl, pour in the half-and-half and milk and soak for 1 hour.
✔ Mix in the remaining ingredients and pour into baking pan.
✔ Bake at 375 degrees for 1 hour.
✔ Serve on individual dessert plates with bourbon sauce.

Chocolate Charlotte

This is a lovely custard dessert. It can be presented in formal fashion or plainly. You will want to heat the custard for about 15 minutes, stirring constantly. I even lift the top pan from the steam every minute or so, so as not to overheat the custard. Just watch it closely and do not allow the contents of the double boiler to simmer. This dish can curdle or burn easily.

INGREDIENTS
12 oz. sweet chocolate chips
6 eggs, separated, yolks and whites reserved
2 T sugar
2 C heavy cream, whipped
1 T fine aged Kentucky bourbon whisky or
1 T brandy
2 packages. ladyfingers
sweet chocolate, shavings

DIRECTIONS
✔ Beat the egg yolks and set aside. Beat the egg whites until frothy, add the sugar, beat until stiff and set aside.
✔ Stirring constantly, melt chocolate in a double boiler.
✔ Add the egg yolks to the melted chocolate. Stir in half of the egg whites. Then, gently fold the remaining egg whites into the chocolate.
✔ Fold in the whipped cream gently, along with the bourbon or brandy.
✔ Line the bottom of a springform pan with ladyfingers. Pour in half the chocolate, line the pan again with ladyfingers and then pour on the remaining chocolate.
✔ Refrigerate at least 6 hours before serving.
Serves 6-8.

Baked Custard

Ichoose to give baked custard a place of honor in my cooking repertory, for baked custard is a timeless dessert classic. I have read
recipes for and annotations about baked custard as far back as the
Middle Ages in every European culture. That our forebears embraced
baked custard is understandable. The charm of baked custard is based
on its simplicity. A well-blended, perfectly baked custard, dark brown
around the custard cup, with the aroma of nutmeg permeating the
kitchen air is pleasing and requires no flavor enhancement. A chilled
baked custard is the way we use it.

If a flavor is desired, maple syrup, brown sugar or fruit jelly as a
substitute for the granular sugar in the recipe will present a wholly
different dessert.

INGREDIENTS
4 egg yolks, beaten
1/4 C sugar
1/4 t salt
1/4 t vanilla
2 C milk, scalded and cooled to room temperature
nutmeg

DIRECTIONS
✔ In a mixer at slow speed, blend the yolk, sugar, salt and vanilla.
Gradually add the milk.
✔ Pour into 5 glass custard cups. Sprinkle on nutmeg.
✔ Place custard cups into a pan with hot water that covers the
cups about three-quarters up the sides.
✔ Bake at 350 degrees for about 45 minutes. Serve warm or chilled.
Serves 5.

Strawberries Masters

When strawberries are in season, they are the foundation for many of the desserts we concoct. We are particularly fond of Strawberries Masters. For years I did not use chocolate sauce, but seeing my guests invariably liberate it from the refrigerator without so much as a word cast in my direction told me that this recipe was served with chocolate sauce. I think it is the appearance of whipped cream that simulates the brain synapse to the need for chocolate sauce.

Strawberries Masters is good served as a freestanding dessert. However, on request, we will ladle it over a bed of shortcake or ladyfingers. Vanilla ice cream has been known to make an appearance.

INGREDIENTS
2 quarts strawberries, hulled, cut in half lengthwise
1 quart cantaloupe, cut into quarter-size pieces
1 pint blueberries
1 pint raspberries
1 C powdered sugar
1 quart whipping cream
1/4 C fine aged Kentucky bourbon whisky or brandy
chocolate sauce, by recipe

DIRECTIONS
✔ In a large bowl combine the fruits and gently cover the fruit with the powdered sugar.
✔ In a mixing bowl at high speed, beat the whipping cream. Fold in the bourbon or the brandy. Pour onto the fruit and very gently toss the fruit so as to cover evenly but not bruise the fruit. Refrigerate for 2 hours before serving.
✔ Ladle the Strawberries Masters into a large dessert bowl. Heat the chocolate sauce just enough so it will pour and drizzle it over the dessert.
Serves 8-10.

Kentucky Flaming Peaches

A formal dinner for six seated at the table of McManus House on a cold blustery night in February requires flaming peaches for dessert. The peaches are served over vanilla ice cream accompanied by the warm blue blaze of the brandy.

Margaret Sue and her friends like chocolate sauce over the peaches. I have never thought the chocolate sauce necessary, as the Kentucky flaming peaches are so good by themselves. However, I have chosen to decline battle on this issue, as I have always deemed it wise to bow to the dessert preferences of women.

INGREDIENTS
3 C water
1-1/2 C sugar
2 t vanilla
1 lemon rind, grated
1 C strawberry jam
8 peaches, skinned, stoned and thinly sliced
1/4 C fine aged Kentucky bourbon whisky
vanilla ice cream
chocolate sauce, if you must
2/3 C brandy

DIRECTIONS
✔ The peaches are cut and the dessert mixture is made up in the pan it will cook in before the dinner. After dinner, bring the dessert mixture almost to a boil. Simmer for about a minute, stirring with a whisk.

✔ Add the peaches and the bourbon to the pan and stir in just before serving.

✔ Place the ice cream in large scoops into a silver or formal glass serving bowl and pour the peaches on top of the ice cream.

✔ If you are going to add chocolate sauce, this is the time to do it. Carry the bowl to the table along with a glass of brandy.

✔ Pour the brandy into a long-handled silver ladle, ignite the brandy and quickly pour the flaming brandy onto the peaches. Serve the dessert just as the flames disappear.

Lemon Squares

I love lemon, the more the better. This dessert fits the bill. It is very lemony, very rich and tremendously fattening. But if you can stand it, take a square. Your diet plan goes out the window. This dessert makes everyone feel a little foolish — as your guests will look for a second square to keep company with the lemon square they have just eaten, all the while protesting their indulgence. We serve lemon squares wherever and whenever.

INGREDIENTS
1-1/2 C flour
1/2 C powdered sugar
1-1/2 sticks butter
1/4 t baking powder
3 eggs, beaten
1-1/2 C sugar
4 T lemon juice, fresh squeezed
3 T flour
extra powdered sugar

DIRECTIONS
✔ Place the first four ingredients in a bowl and whisk briskly. Flour your hands and press into a dry baking dish. Bake at 350 degrees for 15 minutes. Set aside.
✔ In a mixing bowl, combine the eggs and the sugar and blend at a medium speed. Add the 3 T of flour and the lemon juice. Then pour the mixture into the crust you have just baked.
✔ Bake at 350 degrees for 25 minutes. Allow the lemon squares to cool, then cover with tin foil and refrigerate for use the next day.
✔ Before serving sprinkle powdered sugar across the top.

Vanilla Ice Cream

INGREDIENTS
3 C whipping cream
1 C milk, whole
1 C sugar
6 egg yolks, beaten
1 vanilla bean, sliced lengthwise
1/4 C fine aged Kentucky bourbon whisky
1/2-t nutmeg

DIRECTIONS
✔ In a double boiler over high heat and stirring constantly with a whisk, combine the cream and the milk and let it simmer for a minute.
✔ Lower the heat and add the sugar, stirring with a whisk until it dissolves. Add the egg yolks. Slice the vanilla bean lengthwise, scrape out the vanilla bean. Stir until thickened. Add the bourbon and nutmeg.
✔ Remove, strain, and refrigerate the vanilla ice cream custard for 2 hours. Then, after cooling, strain the vanilla ice cream custard and pour into an ice cream maker and make ice cream by the instructions.

Piecrust

I often buy a pie shell rather than make a piecrust pastry from scratch. When I am in a pie-making frame of mind, I make three or four pies at the same time, and purchasing the piecrust pastry eliminates a labor-intensive step. And unless I confess my crime of purchasing the piecrust, no one seems to care. The insouciance, I believe, derives from the fact that our guests are bereft of a proper comparison. Good pastry cooks in the home are becoming scarce.

But let me tell you, absolutely and unequivocally, that a homemade piecrust pastry is worth the fight. A made-from-scratch piecrust is flaky and light and emits that wonderful aroma of fresh-baked bread. I never, ever care if my piecrust is perfectly rolled out or that the rim of my pie is not picture-perfect. My guests, from adolescence to old age, love my pies made with my piecrust pastry. And for me, that is the bag limit.

Store your flour and shortening or oil used for baking in the back of the refrigerator. In making a piecrust, it is imperative that you keep the ingredients cold, thereby keeping the dough cool. Put the mixing bowl and the two pastry knives in the refrigerator an hour before use.

And by all means, handle the dough as little as possible and roll it out quickly from the middle out, taking care not to roll over the edges.

DIRECTIONS
✔ In a mixing bowl, sift together 3 C flour, 1/2 t baking powder and 1/2 t salt. Using the pastry knives scissors fashion, cut 1 C shortening into the flour until it is pebbly. Add 6 T ice water, a tablespoon at a time, and cut in with the pastry knives.

✔Using floured hands, remove the pastry from the bowl and place on a floured table. Separate the dough into two balls and roll from the center out to 1/4 inch. Each edge should be about 6 inches from the middle of the pastry.

✔ Fold the dough over north to south, then east to west, and transport it to a pie pan, leaving about a 1/2-inch overhang that you may trim or build up about the rim of the pan. The second pastry ball is rolled out in the same way and either placed atop the pie as a cover or cut into strips to crisscross the pie.

✔ In either case, press the top pastry edges into the pastry rim with thumb and forefinger. If you choose to cover the pie, cut several slits in the middle of the pie crust to vent the steam.

Graham Cracker Crust

INGREDIENTS
2 C graham crackers, ground fine
1 C brown sugar
1/4 C butter

DIRECTIONS
✔ With a rolling pin, grind graham crackers to a fine texture. Add the sugar and blend completely. Combine with the butter. Press into pie pan bottom.

Spirits

Wherever I have traveled in the world, and when I proclaim I am from Kentucky, people immediately tell me that our commonwealth is known for fast horses, bourbon whisky and beautiful women. I always heartily agree and add "for chivalrous men too!" They glaze over on that remark.

But when talking about a good drink, it is Kentucky bourbon whisky that captures my interest. There are many good bourbon whiskies distilled in Kentucky and a few great ones. It has a lot to do with individual tastes. I am enthusiastically partial to Breeder's Preference, my family's bourbon whisky, although it is a small-production bourbon whisky that is not for sale.

Even though I feel a great Kentucky kinship with bourbon whisky, I stock a variety of liquors and drinks for the enjoyment of our guests. A well-stocked bar for McManus House means that we will be prepared to mix about two dozen drinks typically called for in the commonwealth and across the South. Our bar offers bourbon, gin, scotch, dark rum, vodka, a sweet white wine, a burgundy wine, beer, soft drinks and iced tea.

We set up the bar with orange juice, cranberry juice, tonic, soda and bitters. Lemon and lime, fresh cut, are in their bowls. A jar each of maraschino cherries, cocktail onions and green olives are made available. A pitcher of water and a chest full of ice are at hand. We like to place out about double the amount of short and tall glasses as there are guests, for those either desiring a fresh glass or having misplaced the one they recently carried. Cocktail napkins are in good supply.

In formal dining, we will serve a wine that complements the entrée. After-dinner liqueurs are served in small snifters to reflect our notion that the evening is drawing to a close.

In every community, there are men and women whom you can employ to help in the task of tending the bar. Find a man or woman who enjoys mixing drinks; if you can find someone who has a great personality, all the better. A good bartender is a part of the social occasion, and I consider the man who comes when I call a friend. I always make certain that our bartenders receive generous plates of the foods we have prepared. They appreciate the courtesy; after all, they too are at the party.

Bourbon—Straight

Straight bourbon over ice is the drink of choice with our crowd. Bourbon is a uniquely Kentucky whisky, enjoyed throughout the world. It is a drink that finds itself in the company of our family and good friends.

Bourbon straight. It simply does not get any better.

Pack a short tumbler glass with cubed ice. Pour a jigger of fine aged Kentucky bourbon whisky into the glass. Allow the bourbon and the ice to get acquainted for about a minute. Raise the glass. Smell the bouquet. Sip fine aged Kentucky bourbon whisky.

Bourbon—Toddy

Pack crushed ice into an old-fashioned or tumbler glass. Add a teaspoon of sugar, a jigger of fine aged Kentucky bourbon whisky and a twist of lemon. Fill the glass with water. Stir briskly with a bar spoon. Put in a mint cherry.

Bourbon—Old-Fashioned

Make the toddy minus the mint cherry and add a maraschino cherry and a dash of Angostura bitters. Place a slice of lemon and orange on the rim of the glass.

Bourbon—Moon Glow

The Moon Glow is a potion I made up that finds favor with the gentlewomen. Watch this one; it will sneak up on you. It is so good that my friends press me to make them. Our bartender, who assists us in our home, is kept busy mixing the Moon Glow.

Pack a tall glass with crushed ice. Fill half the glass with equal parts cranberry and orange juice. Add 2 t maraschino cherry juice. Pour in a jigger of fine aged Kentucky bourbon whisky. Stir well with the bar spoon. Drop in 2 maraschino cherries. Place a straw in the drink.

Bourbon—Sour

Pack a cocktail shaker with cracked ice. Squeeze the juice of half a lemon onto the ice. Add 1/2 t sugar. Pour in a jigger of fine aged Kentucky bourbon whisky. Shake well. Uncover and add a spillage of club soda into the shaker. Using a strainer, pour the whisky sour into a tumbler glass. Drop in a maraschino cherry and place a slice of orange on the rim of the glass.

Bourbon—Mint Julep

The mint julep has long been associated with Kentucky in general and with the Kentucky Derby in particular. The Kentucky Derby is a truly international horse race that takes place at Churchill Downs in Louisville on the first Saturday in May of each year. The mint julep is a celebration of the springtime racing season in Kentucky.

Take your time in making the mint julep. Embodied in this drink is a taste of old Kentucky. The mint julep is a drink that we prepare throughout the summer, usually for out-of-town guests.

Use a silver julep cup when you can, as it frosts well and is part of the Kentucky tradition. Use a highball glass if you find yourself without a silver julep cup; it will not frost well, but it will do.

Take a sprig of mint and rub it around the inside of the julep cup, exerting a gentle pressure. Place this sprig of mint in a napkin and reverently dispose of it, for the mint has performed its service.

Place the crushed ice in the julep cup to the brim. Place the julep cup in the freezer for about an hour.

In a bowl place 1 T of sugar for each anticipated call for the mint julep. Pour in enough water to cover the sugar and stir until the sugar is dissolved. Collect about 6 sprigs of mint per julep, and with a firm pressure from a wooden pestle, crush the mint into the syrup mixture.

Retrieve the julep cup from the freezer with a napkin so as not to break the frost that has formed on it. Pour in a 1/2 T syrup, while holding back the crushed mint. Add 2 jiggers of fine aged Kentucky bourbon whisky. Mix gently with a bar spoon. Decorate the julep with two sprigs of mint and a dash of powdered sugar. Place a straw into the julep cup that is sized to peer just over the rim. Serve immediately.

And oh, by the way, please cleanse the bowl containing the syrup with a fresh napkin so as to capture the mint for disposal. There are two centuries of tradition in making the mint julep. We always try to act nobly toward our friends.

Scotch—Straight

I have a fondness for a good Scotch whisky in the same way I enjoy my old friends who reside in distant regions. In my opinion, there is only one way to enjoy Scotch whisky and that is straight, over ice, in a small tumbler glass. Some of my friends enjoy scotch in a tall glass with soda water.

Gin—Dry Martini

The classic dry martini is made by the silver pitcher packed with cracked ice and is 2/3 dry gin, 1/3 vermouth and 1 dash Angostura bitters for each jigger of dry gin. Stir with a bar spoon and, using a strainer, pour into the dry martini glass or a tumbler glass. I have always disliked seeing a good dry martini beaten to death by ice in a shaker and so gravitate toward the pitcher and the stir stick.

If making a single dry martini without the use of a strainer, pack a tumbler glass with cracked or crushed ice. Pour in a jigger of dry gin, 1/2 capful of vermouth and a dash of Angostura bitters. Stir.

Either way, add 2 green olives for the dry martini. Use 2 cocktail onions in place of the olives to create the Gibson martini.

Gin—Gin and Tonic

There is always a place for this popular warm-weather drink. Pack a tall glass with ice cubes. Pour a jigger of dry gin and fill the glass with tonic water. Squeeze a quarter of a lemon or lime into the drink and toss in the fruit. Delightful.

Gin—Tom Collins

This is my favorite gin drink with club soda. I do not see much call for it in this modern era, but it is excellent. Put 3 cubes of ice into a tall glass. Squeeze half a lime onto the ice. Add 1 t powdered sugar. Pour in a jigger of dry gin and fill the glass with club soda. Stir briskly with a bar spoon.

Gin—Screwdriver

This is a truly great summertime drink for the late afternoon. Pack a tall glass with ice cubes. Pour in a jigger of dry gin. Fill the glass with fresh-squeezed orange juice. Stir briskly. Squeeze a quarter of a lime into the drink and toss in the fruit but do not stir, just enjoy.

Gin—Gin Alexander

Margaret Sue and her friends love to drink this cocktail at the racetrack. The recipe I used for years called for cream, but I find that our crowd likes vanilla ice cream more, so that is the version I give you. I feel protective of Margaret Sue's well-being when she calls for a Gin Alexander. She never feels like she is partaking of a drink that sports alcohol. Mix a pitcher half full with 1/3 dry gin, 1/3 créme de cacao and 1/3 softened vanilla ice cream. Add crushed ice to within an inch of the pitcher rim. Shake well and strain the mixture into a cocktail glass. Brandy is a popular substitute for the gin.

Gin—Champagne Delight 1

This is a very flavorful drink for the ladies of the house who like a sweet drink with an attitude. Make the champagne punch in a glass pitcher with 2/3 dry gin, 1/3 lemon juice and 1 t powdered sugar for each glass of punch. Stir until you are certain the powdered sugar is dissolved. Fill a champagne glass with crushed ice. Fill the glass halfway with the punch and pour champagne to the rim.

Gin—Champagne Delight 2

Fill a champagne glass with crushed ice. Add a dash of dry gin, a dash of Angostura bitters, 1 t of sugar; stir and fill the glass with champagne. Add a piece of lemon peel for effect.

Vodka—Bloody Mary

The classic Bloody Mary mixture made from scratch is 2 jiggers tomato juice, 1/3 jigger lemon juice, 4 dashes of Worcestershire sauce, 1 dash of salt and 1 dash of pepper. The Bloody Mary pre-mix seems to be used more often, however. Either way, we moisten the rim of a tall glass, then upend it, pressing the rim into a small mound of salt. We pack the glass, with cubed ice, add a jigger of vodka and fill the glass with the Bloody Mary ingredients. The contents of the glass are stirred briskly. We then squeeze 1/4 of a lime into the glass and discard the fruit.

Vodka—Vodka Split

The Vodka Split is a drink that is a staple at McManus House and is a drink that the women in the Bluegrass invented, as far as I know. I veer around the Vodka Split as a matter of male pride, but in all honesty, it is a very good drink. Pack a tall glass with ice cubes. Pour in a jigger of vodka. Fill the glass halfway with cranberry juice, then fill the remainder of the glass with fresh-squeezed orange juice. Stir. Squeeze a quarter of a lemon on top, discard the fruit and place a fresh slice of lemon on the rim.

Vodka—Screwdriver and Dry Martini

Follow the recipes for a Gin Screwdriver and a Dry Martini, using vodka instead.

Vodka—Daiquiri

Pack a cocktail shaker with crushed ice. Place the juice of a whole lime into the shaker along with a heaping teaspoon of powdered sugar. Add 1 jigger of vodka. Shake well and strain the daiquiri into a cocktail glass.

Iced Tea

Iced tea is enjoyed at all of our warm-weather social functions. The way I make the iced tea is very popular. In a 2-quart saucepan, I bring 2 quarts of water to a furious boil. I put three times the normal ration of tea bags into the pan, cut off the heat and allow the tea to steep for 3 minutes and no more. I then pour the tea into my two quart pitcher, pressing the tea bags to extract the last of the tea essence.

This part is critical. I do not pack the pitcher with ice and pour the freshly steeped tea into the pitcher. I pour the tea from the pitcher into a tall glass packed with cubed ice. This allows each glass of tea poured to be treated equally by the ice.

The juice of a quarter of a lemon is squeezed into the glass and the fruit tossed in. Sugar or sweetener is added to taste. The tea then receives a few stirs. A sprig or two of mint is placed inside the rim of the glass, resulting in a refreshing cool drink.

When I can take the time, we place the tea in a covered gallon jar and place it on the rail of the porch to gather the sunlight for an hour. It is an old Southern custom to treat the tea this way, and I like it.

When I am ensconced at McManus House and when I repour a glass of iced tea, I use a fresh glass, replacing the ice and re-establishing the tea, lemon, mint and sugar or sweetener. I do not like to see my recently enjoyed glass of iced tea trying to keep up with a new batch of tea splashed down upon it, thereby, requiring additional flavoring. I never have been a fan of creating a lemon and mint compost heap that settles at the bottom of my glass.

Whisky Custard Cocktail

W hisky custard is delicious at any time of the year. The
Christmas holiday always gets whisky custard, but we like to
serve it throughout the winter months. Whisky custard tastes
best when it is extremely well chilled. Serve it in a pitcher that sets well
on a bed of ice. I use a 2-liter carafe nestled in an iced-down crystal
champagne bucket.

We serve whisky custard at a ratio of one ounce of bourbon to the
egg. For those desiring a more potent drink, we place a decanter of fine
aged Kentucky bourbon whisky on the sideboard as a neighbor to the
whisky custard.

Margaret Sue and her crowd put a scoop of vanilla ice cream in large
snifters and pour the whisky custard on top. They then sweeten the top
of this brew with crème de cacao and a spike more bourbon. The men
drive home when we see this one coming.

We make the whisky custard the morning of.

INGREDIENTS
6 eggs, separated
3/4 C sugar

2 C whole milk
2 C cream
2 C fine aged bourbon whisky
2 T grated nutmeg
1-t vanilla
1-t ginger, ground

DIRECTIONS
✔ Beat yolks and whites separately. Add the sugar to the whites
while beating. Then, combine the yolks and the whites.
✔Combine the egg mixture with the whole milk and cream. Add the
bourbon and the nutmeg.
Serve chilled.

INDEX

DESSERTS

SPIRITS

The Colonel's Cottage Inn

114 South Fourth Street, Bardstown, KY 40004
1-800-704-4917
www.kystyle.com

Shhh... Nobody needs to know!!

You deserve a romantic getaway. Escape to the wonderful privacy of the Colonel's Cottage Inn. You will have all six rooms in the cottage to yourself. Upon arrival we will greet you with fresh flowers from Colonel Masters, "The Host of Kentucky."

Dine upon the Old Kentucky Home Dinner Train, stay at the Colonel's Cottage Inn - both a little pricey but perfect!

The Colonel's Cottage Inn is located in the historic district of Bardstown, Kentucky, across from the beautiful Pioneer Park, one block from downtown shopping and dining.

I promise you, you will cherish your visit to the Colonel's Cottage Inn - it is that special. We offer *Hospitality — Kentucky Style.*

Very Truly Yours,

Col. Michael Masters
"The Host of Kentucky"

Hospitality – Kentucky Style

Kentucky Heritage Tour
Kentucky Fine Foods and Spirits
Kentucky Residents: $ 18.85 + 1.14 Tax + 3.00 S & H = $ 22.99
Non-Kentucky Residents: $ 18.85 + 3.00 S & H = $ 21.85
Wholesale Case Pricing Available

Kentucky Benediction

A Kentucky Prayer
Call for framed pricing.
See Page 19 of book

Kentucky Pecan Coffee and Colonel's Blend Coffee
Call for prices.

Equine Writer's Press
P.O. Box 1101   Bardstown, Kentucky 40004
www.kystyle.com   1-800-704-4917   masters@kystyle.com